Yellowstone Wildlife

YELLOWSTONE

WILDLIFE

ECOLOGY AND NATURAL HISTORY OF THE GREATER YELLOWSTONE ECOSYSTEM

Paul A. Johnsgard

Photographs by Thomas D. Mangelsen

UNIVERSITY PRESS OF COLORADO
Boulder

© 2013 by University Press of Colorado

Published by University Press of Colorado
5589 Arapahoe Avenue, Suite 206C
Boulder, Colorado 80303

 The University Press of Colorado is a proud member of
the Association of American University Presses.

The University Press of Colorado is a cooperative publishing enterprise supported, in part, by Adams State University, Colorado State University, Fort Lewis College, Metropolitan State University of Denver, Regis University, University of Colorado, University of Northern Colorado, Utah State University, and Western State Colorado University.

∞ This paper meets the requirements of the ANSI/NISO Z39.48-1992 (Permanence of Paper).

Library of Congress Cataloging-in-Publication Data

Johnsgard, Paul A.
  Yellowstone wildlife : ecology and natural history of the greater Yellowstone ecosystem / Paul A. Johnsgard ; photographs by Thomas D. Mangelsen.
    pages cm
  Includes bibliographical references and index.
  ISBN 978-1-60732-228-3 (pbk. : alk. paper) — ISBN 978-1-60732-229-0 (ebook)
  1. Natural history—Yellowstone National Park. 2. Animals—Yellowstone National Park—Pictorial works. 3. Plants—Yellowstone National Park—Pictorial works. I. Title.
  QH105.W8J64 2013
  508.787'52—dc23
                         2013007243

Design by Daniel Pratt

22   21   20   19   18   17   16   15   14   13   10   9   8   7   6   5   4   3   2   1

PREVIOUS PAGE. *A bull elk drinking at the edge of the Snake River before crossing with two cows from his harem, October, Grand Teton National Park, Wyoming.*

To Bert Raynes

and to the memory of Mardy and Olaus Murie

whose love of wilderness approached that of a religion;
one governed by only a single commandment: Preserve it!

Contents

Illustrations

Photographs

M Y CONCEPTION OF A BOOK on Teton natural history occurred in the summer of 1974, when I took a camping trip through the Rocky Mountains and spent about a week in Jackson Hole. It soon became apparent that the area around the Jackson Hole Biological Station would be ideal for making extended observations on sandhill cranes and trumpeter swans, two species of special interest to me. Dr. Oscar Paris, the station's director, later encouraged me to apply for research space there the following summer. As a result, I spent parts of the summers of 1975 and 1976 at the biological station and greatly appreciated the opportunities thus provided me by the station's sponsors, the University of Wyoming and the New York Zoological Society. Additionally, the great kindness shown me by Dr. Paris and all the other researchers occupying the station during those two years helped me enormously. I am especially grateful to Dr. Thomas Collins, Dr. Alita Pinter, and Dr. Margaret Altmann for their advice and help. "Locals" such as Franz Camenzind, Charles McCurdy, Morna MacLeod, Cindy Nielsen, and many others helped in diverse ways, while Tom Mangelsen and Paul Geraghty both made enthusiastic field companions.

The resulting book, *Teton Wildlife: Observations by a Naturalist,* was published in 1982 by the Colorado Associated University Press. In 2009 I had the book scanned and placed online through the University of Nebraska's DigitalCommons website (http:// digitalcommons.unl.edu/), and realized that it had "aged" appreciably. About that time I suggested to my ex-student and longtime friend Tom Mangelsen that we should collaborate on a book, using his wonderful photos and my text. He suggested that a book on the Greater Yellowstone Ecosystem would provide an attractive topic. I soon decided that, by updating the Teton-related text and adding materials on Yellowstone Park and nearby areas, I could provide an enlarged and updated text and some associated drawings, around which Tom could select an array of his color photographs. As in my earlier book, the resulting text is a mixture of my own observations and those of others; referring to the Bibliographic Notes and References will allow the reader to determine which is which. The drawings are my own.

I returned to the area again in the summer of 2010 to renew my memories of the Yellowstone-Teton region and especially to observe the effects of the massive fires of the late 1980s. While revisiting the Yellowstone region, fond memories of many now-departed friends such as Margaret (Mardy) Murie were stirred, and some new friendships were formed.

I had helpful conversations with many of these people, among the most valuable of them with Henry and Mary Ann Harlow, Terry McEneaney, Bert Raynes, and Benj Sinclair. I was also able to spend many wonderful days in the field with longtime friends and ex-students Linda Brown and Jackie Canterbury, as well as with Benj Sinclair. Benj provided me with many insights on current wildlife conditions in the Jackson Hole–Yellowstone region, Jackie was an ever-enthusiastic field companion, and Linda additionally helped in all stages of manuscript editing and book-related decisions. Bird-related materials were helpfully scrutinized by Bert Raynes, and the geological contents were critically reviewed by Scott Johnsgard and Robert B. Smith. Shalese Hill, photo editor at Mangelsen: Images of Nature, was a tremendous help in getting the photographs selected, properly placed, and reviewed.

Having decided to write essays covering the entire Greater Yellowstone Ecosystem, I realized it was important to define it. In 1983 the Greater Yellowstone Coalition was formed from many conservation groups such as the Audubon Society, Defenders of Wildlife, National Wildlife Federation, Northern Rockies Action Group, and Sierra Club. In 1985 the coalition estimated the ecosystem's total area at six million acres. Later increasingly larger definitions raised the total to eighteen million acres. As defined by the National Park Service and U.S. Forest Service, the Greater Yellowstone Area encompasses eighteen million acres (7.3 million hectares) in three states and includes two national parks, three wildlife refuges, parts of six national forests, Bureau of Land Management (BLM) lands, plus state and private landholdings. About six million acres of the total consist of national park and Forest Service wilderness areas, and another six million acres are represented by nonwilderness Forest Service lands (Keiter and Boyce, 1991).

To all the people just mentioned, and to the countless others who have maintained a watchful vigilance over two of our greatest national parks and adjoining areas during the thirty-five years since my two wonderful summers there, I offer my deepest gratitude. In many ways the Greater Yellowstone Ecosystem is the rarest and most precious jewel in the crown of America's Rocky Mountains. It is perhaps impossible to convey adequately the beauty and lure of the northern Rocky Mountains, the "Shining mountains" of Lewis and Clark, to anybody who has never been there, or to match the memories of those who have. I hope that in reading my descriptions of the lives of a few of the Yellowstone region's plants and wildlife, the reader may gain some sense of the beauty and complexity of their intertwined lives and thus better appreciate the need for preserving such areas and keeping them inviolate from destruction or "development." Perhaps the greatest obligation for one who visits a national park or national wildlife refuge is to recognize a debt of gratitude and to feel admiration for the foresighted people who had the courage to set aside these areas in perpetuity for their enjoyment by everyone and those who have since worked to keep that legacy alive.

PAUL A. JOHNSGARD
Lincoln, Nebraska

Yellowstone Wildlife

History of the Greater Yellowstone Ecoregion

THE WRINKLED SURFACE of northwestern Wyoming and adjacent Idaho is a complex myriad of mountainous uplifts and basins, of varied ages and origins. In a somewhat fanciful way it resembles the imprint of a raccoon's right forefoot that, having been pressed into sticky clay, was withdrawn to form a series of ridges and peaks that subsequently solidified into ranges of mountains extending southward from the northwestern corner of Wyoming.

In this imagined view, the Yellowstone Plateau of northwestern Wyoming represents a gigantic if somewhat fanciful paw print, which rises more than a thousand feet above the surrounding lowlands. The plateau has been pushed upward over long periods of time by pressures from the gigantic cauldron of molten magma that lies some fifty miles below and is the geological source for all of Yellowstone's thermal features and the cause of Yellowstone's frequent earthquake activity. From the Yellowstone Plateau the Bridger Plateau extends southeastwardly like a narrow forefinger as the Owl Creek and Bridger Mountains, which approach the "thumbprint" of the Bighorn Mountains. Between them the Bighorn River flows northward through the Bighorn Basin to join the Missouri River. To the south of the Owl Creek and Bridger Mountains is the Wind River Basin, where the Shoshone and Arapahoe Indians now live in relative obscurity and where the great Shoshone chief Washakie lies buried on the parched and shrub-covered hillsides.

The middle "finger" of the landscape's topography is made by the Wind River Range, the longest and highest of the Wyoming ranges. Along its crest runs the Continental Divide, and over such passes as Union Pass and South Pass came the earliest explorers, mountain men, and finally emigrants on their way west. At its western base is the Green River Basin, whose waters drain into the Colorado River and whose sedimentary rocks bear the fossil imprints of Eocene fish, reptiles, birds, and mammals interred there some fifty million years ago.

The fourth landscape "finger" is formed basally by the jagged upthrust of the Teton Range and farther south by the more gently folded overthrust ridges of the Wyoming and Salt River ranges, which nearly parallel the Wyoming-Idaho border.

Finally, protruding at nearly right angles westward from the Tetons and associated mountains is a small fifth "finger." This is the Centennial Range of the Idaho-Montana border, along which the Continental Divide continues westwardly.

Of all these mountain groups in the Yellowstone region, by far the most recent is the Teton Range, whose dramatic eastern face was exposed less than ten million years ago by a fault in the earth's crust, where the mountains were tilted upward and the adjoining valley floor of Jackson Hole dropped downward in a relatively rapid series of earthquake tremors. The Tetons are thus among the youngest and most spectacular of all the Rocky Mountain ranges, with their peaks and ridges having been subsequently eroded and sculpted by a variety of glacial processes, especially by ice. As the eastern escarpment of the Tetons rose and the floor of Jackson Hole dropped, rock strata that were deposited over long periods of geologic time came into view. Indeed, the slopes of the range thus exposed to view provide a sequence of rock layers representing more than half of the earth's geologic history. The most ancient of these strata are banded Precambrian layers more than 2.5 billion years old, some of the oldest exposed rocks on the North American continent. Above these archaic rocks are sedimentary deposits less than a billion years old, which formed from materials deposited along the margins of Paleozoic seas that then inundated the area. On the northern slopes of the Tetons and adjacent Gros Ventre Mountains the reddish sandstones, blue-gray limestones, gray dolomites, and black and green shales lie stacked on top of one another where layer after layer of deposits were added to older strata below, interring with them the remains of Paleozoic animals such as trilobites and brachiopods.

As the Paleozoic seas gave way to those of the Mesozoic era about 200 million years ago, soft reddish, iron-rich sediments as much as 1,000 feet thick were laid down and now may be seen on the northern flanks of the Gros Ventre Mountains. These more brightly colored rocks were subsequently covered by a much thicker layer of dull-hued silt, sand, and clay toward the end of the Mesozoic era, leaving a flat and featureless floodplain as the Mesozoic sea finally retreated eastwardly. At the very end of Mesozoic times, starting about sixty million years ago during the Eocene epoch, mountain-building in the area began as the Wind River Range was thrust upward and westward. During the last sixty-five million years, the Cenozoic era, massive mountain-building occurred in North America, and most of the modern groups of birds and mammals evolved. Uplifts in several areas of what is now Wyoming (the Laramide mountain-building period) produced the first of the Rocky Mountains, while erosion simultaneously began to bury the adjacent basins.

A new geologic element was added to the massive and generally widespread forces of mountain-building and basin-filling when volcanic eruptions from the Yellowstone and Absaroka region dropped enormous amounts of lava and other volcanic debris on the adjacent landscape. The present-day, relatively flat Yellowstone Plateau has been shaped by the thousands of feet of volcanic materials that were deposited on the land surface over the past several million years and lies over a veritable cauldron of molten magma located deep within the earth. This magma chamber, or "hotspot," has been the breeding grounds of the supervolcanoes that have exploded in the Yellowstone region at least three times over the past two million years and has a much longer volcanic history, going back nearly twenty million years.

The entire Pacific Northwest was affected by these volcanic eruptions, which have resulted from shifting tectonic plates far below the surface. Volcanoes associated with this magma chamber have periodically spread ash and volcanic debris over much of western North

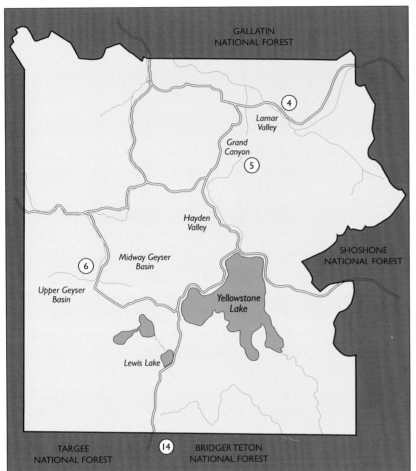

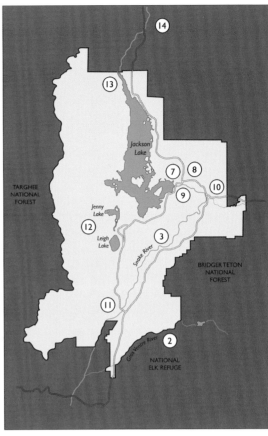

Map of the Greater Yellowstone Ecosystem. Numbers indicate chapters within the text.

America, beginning about eighteen million years ago in what is now northern Nevada. Since then a series of volcanic centers have seemingly moved northeastward, periodically erupting as one edge of one of the several tectonic plates that constitute the land mass of the North American plate moved southwest at about an inch per year above the plume, continuously feeding the volcanism of Yellowstone. As the edge of this plate has been forced under that of an adjoining massive plate, a series of supervolcanoes have erupted along a junction line roughly paralleling Idaho's upper Snake River Valley. Beginning in north-central Nevada (sixteen to eighteen million years ago), and as a result of the surface crust of western North America inching slowly southwestward, the hotspot marking the edges of the tectonic plates has correspondingly shifted northeastward across southern Idaho over a period of about twelve to fourteen million years before reaching the what is now the Yellowstone region. By about two million years ago this subterranean center of superheated magma was centered under what would become the present-day Yellowstone Plateau. The plateau was created by three giant supereruptions at 2, 1.2, and 0.63 million years ago. Since then it has risen more than a thousand feet and spread across a distance of about 125 miles, as a result of the pressures of the molten magma below, making it potentially the largest volcano in the world if it were to erupt again. The Yellowstone Plateau is the unique geologic product of the youthful Yellowstone hotspot and the buoyancy of the Yellowstone mantle plume. The Yellowstone

Plateau has two magma bodies, a deep mantle plume and a shallower crustal magma reservoir. The integrated plumbing of the magma from the plume into the crust has fueled the Greater Yellowstone region and produced its unique combination of volcanic elements, soil, and climate.

Major volcanic eruptions that occurred about 2.1 and 1.3 million years ago in what is now northwestern Wyoming and adjacent Idaho were violent precursors to one that occurred 600,000 years ago, or about the time that early humans (*Homo erectus*) were colonizing Eurasia. Then a caldera some 1,000 square miles in area literally blew the Yellowstone region apart. With a force perhaps a thousand times greater than the Mount St. Helens eruption of 1980, it sent ash over most of western North America and across the Great Plains. It cast deadly volcanic materials all the way to the Gulf of Mexico and deposited incalculable amounts of debris over the regional landscapes. The present-day geysers, hot springs, and other thermal phenomena in the Yellowstone region are modern evidence of the region's volcanic history, as are small but recurrent earthquakes, which are more frequent here than anywhere else in North America.

Since its major eruption the caldera has been relatively quiet, except for some smaller eruptions occurring as recently as 70,000 years ago. The now-inactive crater has gradually filled in through erosion and ash deposits. Lake Yellowstone now covers part of the southeastern edge of the crater's remains, which are some forty-five by thirty miles across. Its edges reach west from Lake Yellowstone nearly to the Idaho boundary and extend north to Mount Washburn. Much of the now-dormant crater is filled with a thick layer of rhyolite, a granite-like mineral commonly extruded from western volcanoes. The Yellowstone rhyolite bed covers much of the park and has fault zones forming subsurface channels that distribute and circulate hot water to the geyser basins and other parts of Yellowstone's vast thermal system.

After the eruption of 600,000 years ago, the area occupied by today's Grand Canyon of the Yellowstone River was also covered by rhyolite. Later heating chemically altered this material, making it brittle, relatively soft, and erodible. Much later, during one or more of the several glacial periods, the entire area was also covered by thick sheets of ice, probably leaving only the highest peaks of the Yellowstone region exposed. At the end of the last glacial period, 14,000 to 18,000 years ago, glacial melting formed Yellowstone Lake at the south end of the crater basin. It is believed that at the north outlet of that lake a huge ice dam may have formed. When that dam broke, immense volumes of water rushed out of the lake, cutting the V-shaped canyon that exists today. The yellow to russet colors of today's canyon walls are the result of oxidation of the iron compounds present in the thermally altered rhyolite, although the Yellowstone River is named for the similar color of riverside sandstones that are located far downstream.

Similar volcanic effects extended south into the Teton region. About eight to ten million years ago a large freshwater lake that had formed at the eastern base of the newly emerging Teton Range gradually began to dry up and be filled with volcanic sediments. Analysis of these lake sediments indicates that the area was inhabited by a variety of marsh and aquatic animals, such as snails, frogs, and beavers, and with adjacent forests of fir, spruce, pine, and associated plants.

FACING PAGE. *A common raven overlooks the Grand Canyon of the Yellowstone River, Yellowstone National Park, Wyoming*

OVERLEAF. *Bull elk crossing the Madison River, near a fire-killed stand of lodgepole pine, September, Yellowstone National Park, Wyoming*

Also about this time, movement along the Teton fault at the base of the mountains' eastern face initiated the tremendous uplift of the Tetons. Displacement of nearly 30,000 feet eventually occurred, lifting the eastern slope of the Tetons high over Jackson Hole and exposing their craggy surfaces to erosion by wind, water, and ice. At the same time, tens of thousands of large earthquakes of magnitude 7 or higher occurred. Later, Jackson Hole was covered twice by lakes for long periods of time. The first lake was eventually drained by additional warping and faulting of the earth's crust. The second lake persisted until less than a million years ago and perhaps almost until the initial glaciation that scoured the area and sculpted the Tetons into their present-day form.

The first and most widespread of these glaciations (the Buffalo Glaciation) probably occurred about two million years ago. Its ice centers were in the Beartooth Mountains northeast of Yellowstone National Park and in the adjacent Absaroka and Wind River Ranges. Ice sheets up to 3,000 feet deep streamed slowly southward over the Yellowstone Plateau, past the eastern face of the Tetons, over Jackson Hole and the canyon of the present-day Snake River. Their meltwaters ultimately drained into the Pacific Ocean via the Columbia River. A second and considerably smaller glaciation (the Bull Lake Glaciation) may have occurred about 160,000 to 120,000 years ago, when glaciers from the Tetons and the Absaroka Ranges merged and spread onto the floor of Jackson Hole. The third and smallest glacial event, the Pinedale Glaciation, extended from about 18,000 to 14,000 years ago and covered much of what is now Jackson Hole with ice. It produced terminal moraines at the base of the Tetons that resulted in the formation of Jackson, Jenny, Leigh, Bradley, Taggert, and Phelps Lakes (Knight 1994). As it receded, its meltwaters cut through its terminal moraine, allowing the Snake River to form and to cross the Potholes area, skirt Signal Mountain, and establish its present channel southward. Furthermore, pothole-like wetlands such as Cow Lake, Hedrick's Pond, and Christian Pond formed in the remains of ice-filled depressions in the moraines left by the receding glacier.

Similarly, during the Pinedale glacial period a thick ice sheet covered nearly all of what is now Yellowstone Park until only about 12,000 years ago. This frigid era began to change only grudgingly. A very gradual warming trend followed, but ended as recently as 4,500 years ago. In recent decades warming has resumed and accelerated at an alarming rate under the influence of human-caused global warming.

During the past 10,000 to 15,000 years the local Yellowstone forest vegetation has remained more or less intact, but with warming the extensive alpine tundra that probably covered much of the park was replaced by a whitebark pine forest less than 12,000 years ago. This plant community was later replaced by a lodgepole pine forest over much of the Yellowstone region, and still later by an open Douglas-fir community, at about 6,600 years ago. Since then the Douglas-fir forest has become denser, and the lodgepole pines have greatly increased, eventually becoming the most common trees in the Yellowstone region. Periodic fires not only have helped to increase the extent of lodgepole pines but also have favored grasslands in areas of fine-textured river- and lake-bottom sedimentary soils, at the expense of fire-sensitive shrubs such as sagebrush. Recurrent fires have also helped to maintain scattered stands of aspens, even in the presence of large browsing mammals, as they regrow rapidly from their roots following fires.

Until the recent suppression of forest fires in Yellowstone Park, relatively fire-tolerant trees such as ponderosa pines and Douglas-firs probably benefited from occasional relatively cool ground fires, which didn't penetrate the thick bark of older trees. However, the fire-sensitive lodgepole pines paradoxically benefit from major conflagrations. Some of the region's lodgepoles produce typical coniferous cones, which over time gradually open and drop their seeds. However, most lodgepoles produce resin-coated cones that strongly adhere to the branches and are resistant to opening by squirrels or other seed-eating animals. When these trees are burned, the cones are sufficiently scorched to burn away their glue-like resinous coats and release the abundant seed crop that may have been stored there for many years. The seedlings germinate rapidly in the ashy substrate, and the young trees may be able to begin producing a new crop of seeds in as little as ten years. By being able to mature rapidly and reproduce on the nutrient-poor volcanic-based soils that predominate across most of the southern half of the park, lodgepole pines now thrive there.

By about 9,000 years ago, the Yellowstone–Jackson Hole region was apparently already occupied by aborigines, and this region, which by then was rich in elk and other large grazing mammals, doubtless provided excellent hunting grounds. Evidence of prehistoric use of the Tetons by humans is still very limited, but an inundated campsite at the north end of Jackson Lake suggests that Paleo-Indians may have been using the area as early as 10,000 or 11,000 years ago and quite certainly were present by 5,000 to 7,000 BC. They were probably culturally related to the Plains Indians who depended on hunting a prehistoric species of bison. This bison eventually became extinct during a warm and dry period that persisted until about 2,500 BC. Thereafter, the modern species of bison appeared on the Great Plains. With it came a culture of Plains Indians that exploited these herds. By about AD 500 these Indians shifted from the spear to the bow and arrow as their primary weapon. This transition marks the start of the Late Prehistoric period. Traps for bison and pronghorns, probably used by Shoshone Indians, have been found south of the Tetons. The Shoshones apparently made regular visits to the Yellowstone region to obtain obsidian, a volcanic glass, for weapon points and tools.

The first white man to see the area was probably John Colter, who came through Union Pass in 1807 and explored the Yellowstone Plateau in 1808. His incredible stories of the area (often referred to as "Colter's Hell") stimulated the arrival of explorers, trappers, hunters, and finally settlers. Jackson Hole was originally called Jackson's Hole, meaning Jackson's Valley, and was named after David Jackson, an early trapper. French-speaking trappers call the high, central peaks Les Trois Tetons, or "the three breasts." This was, perhaps, a less apt name than that of the Shoshones, who had hunted there for generations and referred to them as Teewinot, or "many pinnacles."

Two

The Gros Ventre Valley

THE HIGHEST POINT IN THE WIND RIVER RANGE and indeed all of Wyoming is Gannett Peak, which towers nearly 14,000 feet above sea level. About twenty-five miles north is Three Waters Mountain, an enormous massif whose summits form several miles of the Continental Divide. Its eastern slopes drain into creeks that flow into such famous rivers as the Wind, the Bighorn, the Yellowstone, the Missouri, and the Mississippi. Water draining off its broad, inclined southwestern flanks forms the headwaters of the Green River, which merges with the Colorado and finally empties into the Gulf of California. Water from its northwestern slope flows to yet a third destination, the Gros Ventre River. This river eventually merges with the Snake River. The Snake, in turn, joins the Columbia River, and the Columbia River feeds the Pacific Ocean.

The treeless alpine zone of these mountains is snow-covered for all but a month or two in late summer, when a meadow-like carpet of grasses, sedges, and more colorful flowering plants suddenly emerges and provide summer food for bighorn sheep, elk, and yellow-bellied marmots. Here, amidst glinting talus slopes, pikas cut and cure supplies of grass during summer in preparation for winter, and black rosy finches nest in the rock crevices.

Timberline on the northwestern slope of Three Waters Mountain exceeds 10,000 feet in favored situations, where ancient whitebark pines form the uppermost battlements of the forest. Unless they are destroyed by fire or attacked by bark beetles, their stunted and twisted trunks may survive for at least five centuries, gaining only minimal sustenance during brief summers and standing resolute against winter winds. Here, too, snowmelt from the alpine tundra above forms small ponds in depressions, overflows, and drains into Fish Creek, then the Gros Ventre.

As the youthful Fish Creek dances down the mountainside, it passes the timberline stands of whitebark pines and soon enters the highest zone of coniferous forest, the Engelmann spruce–subalpine fir community. Although snow persists well into June at these high elevations, the cool forests attract elk and mule deer escaping summer's heat and flies, and they ring then with songs of hermit and Swainson's thrushes, mountain chickadees, western tanagers, and dark-eyed juncos. The less conspicuous high-pitched notes of golden- and ruby-crowned kinglets are also present, like vocal zephyrs in the needlelike foliage. There is also the junco-like chant of the yellow-rumped warbler, while Clark's nutcrackers periodically scream from the taller trees as they try to protect for themselves the increasingly meager seed crops of the whitebark pines. Mountain pine bark beetles have killed roughly half of the whiteback pines in Yellowstone Park during the past few years, and soon whiteback pines may be gone from the entire park, leaving the nutcrackers, grizzly bears, and many other birds and mammals without critically important food sources.

As Fish Creek flows to join the Gros Ventre, the spruces and subalpine firs gradually give way to Douglas-fir and, where there has been a history of fire, lodgepole pine. Wildlife use of Douglas-fir forests is much the same as for the higher spruce-fir zone; here snowshoe hares and red squirrels are common and are preyed upon by pine martens and lynx, while dusky grouse hoot every morning during late spring from the forest openings. The lodgepole pine forests are essentially even-aged stands of trees less than a century old, which were initiated by forest fires that stimulated seed-dropping. Their crowded and monotonously similar botanic structure supports but a limited variety of birds and mammals. Chipping sparrows and dark-eyed juncos forage on the forest floor, mountain chickadees search out insects in bark crevices, and yellow-rumped warblers feed on insects amid the canopy foliage. The most conspicuous avian residents are the gray jays, which together with pine siskins subsist mostly on seeds and other food gathered in the foliage and elsewhere.

As the river makes its way down the Gros Ventre Canyon, it is twice temporarily impounded in small lakes, Upper Slide Lake and Lower Slide Lake. Lower Slide Lake was produced by a massive landslide in 1925 that sent millions of tons of soil and rock down the mountainside, totally damming the river. Later the impounded waters burst through the slide debris and flooded the downstream village of Kelly, with the loss of eighty homes and six lives. As the Gros Ventre flows out of Lower Slide Lake and past the nearly deserted village of Kelly, it emerges onto the floor of Jackson Hole and leaves the coniferous forest behind.

The lower fringes of the coniferous forest are often marked by aspen groves, which grow on hillsides too dry to support coniferous forests, and on level sites adjacent to meadows and swamps. The aspen community is extremely important to wildlife; its buds and twigs are browsed by elk, moose, and deer and by ruffed grouse in winter. Its bark is the primary food of the beaver. Although the hillside stands of aspen are relatively low in both plant and bird diversity, flatland stands have a remarkably rich array of birds. Feeding on the ground are northern flickers, mountain bluebirds, American robins, Lincoln's sparrows, and white-crowned sparrows. Red-naped sapsuckers drill regularly spaced holes in aspen bark to draw sap, calliope hummingbirds seek out nectar-containing flowers on the forest floor, and a variety of insect-eating birds such as yellow and MacGillivray's warblers, black-headed grosbeaks, and house wrens harvest the abundant insects among the aspen leaves.

Soon the Gros Ventre begins to assume a new character; its streambed becomes broader and more wandering as it cuts new channels and shapes islands and oxbows in the soft glacial till of Jackson Hole. Stands of willows and cottonwoods grow along its banks, and willow and sedge thickets extend outward in the water-rich soils. Beyond the effects of the river, big

ABOVE. *Elk, adult male*

FACING PAGE. *Two western tanagers perching on a chokecherry tree branch, June, Jackson Hole, Wyoming*

OVERLEAF. *A western tanager, May, Wyoming*

sagebrush covers the low hills. The river's edge is the National Elk Refuge's northern boundary as well as the southern boundary of Grand Teton National Park.

The cottonwoods and willows along the Gros Ventre are the habitats of water shrews, mink, and meadow voles and support a dense summer population of yellow warblers, MacGillivray's warblers, common yellowthroats, and song sparrows. White-crowned sparrows sing from low shrubbery, and Wilson's snipes probe the moist soil. Lincoln's sparrows, fox sparrows, and American robins work through the underbrush, while western wood-pewees and willow flycatchers use the tallest willows and cottonwoods as convenient perches from which they fly out to hawk passing insects.

Where the soil becomes too dry to support a streamside forest, sagebrush dominates and lends tones of silvery green to the landscape of Jackson Hole. It is the winter habitat of elk and bison, and throughout the year coyotes and badgers are present. Greater sage-grouse, vesper sparrows, and Brewer's sparrows are characteristic breeding birds of the sagebrush community, and both red-tailed and Swainson's hawks glide above the sagebrush flats in search of such rodents as the ubiquitous Uinta ground squirrels. As the mountains become snow-free in spring, small herds of pronghorn move down the valley of the Gros Ventre River to forage on the sagebrush-dominated Antelope Flats.

The slopes and buttes of the National Elk Refuge are nearly devoid of trees, but runoff from the Gros Ventre Range to the south and from springs at the foot of the mountains spreads into marshes along Flat Creek. From the time that deep snow drives elk out of their high mountain meadows, usually in November or December, until late March or April, the National Elk Refuge is the traditional winter home of about 8,000 elk.

The elk of the Yellowstone and Grand Teton ecosystem consist of several herds. The largest two are a northern herd that summers through most of Yellowstone National Park and winters in the Yellowstone River Valley as well as a southern or Jackson Hole herd that summers in the highlands around Jackson Hole and the headwaters of the Snake River in southern Yellowstone Park and winters in Jackson Hole and southward. The National Elk Refuge was established in 1912 to protect and provide emergency winter food for these wintering animals, which, since settlement of Jackson Hole, had been increasingly dependent on foraging on private lands to survive. From its original size of less than 2,000 acres, the refuge gradually had grown to nearly 24,000 acres by 1935. Sharing the winter range with the elk is a flock of trumpeter swans, which forage in the relatively warm and unfrozen waters of Flat Creek. The swans are attracted there from both Yellowstone and Grand Teton parks.

By the time the elk arrive on their wintering grounds, the mating period is over, and the elk are in mixed-sex groups in which females strongly predominate. This partly reflects the tendency for adult males to winter on high, wind-swept ridges and partly the unbalanced sex ratio typical of polygamous mammals.

By mid-winter the elk are strongly concentrated on the refuge feeding grounds, and extensive supplementary feeding of alfalfa pellets is usually required to ensure their survival. Coyotes patrol the herds daily, waiting for crippled or sick elk to succumb and quickly devouring carcasses as they become available. February and March are the most critical months for elk not wintering on the refuge and other state-owned feeding grounds. Although the worst winter weather may be over, supplies of the more accessible and edible plants are gone, and the elk may turn to aspen bark, may be forced to dig through heavy snow to uncover sedges, willows, and rabbitbrush, or may even resort to eating pine and fir needles.

By mid-February deaths from a bacterial infection of the mouth may become numerous, and ravens, bald eagles, and coyotes briefly share the feast provided by dying elk. In late February males begin to lose their antlers. By mid-March they have nearly all been dropped and new ones have begun to grow. By then, too, females are six months pregnant or only two months from calving. The first thawing of snow cover in March thus comes none too soon and renews life for the elk.

As the snow cover begins to retreat up the hillsides of the Elk Refuge in late March and early April, the large concentrated herds of elk begin to break up into smaller groups, which move into side valleys and lower slopes. Slowly the first elk begin to leave the refuge. About half are mature, and 10 to 20 percent are bulls. Roughly three-fourths of the adult females are pregnant and will give birth by late May or early June.

Typically, the first elk to leave for the summer range are individual or small groups of old bulls. Next are groups of yearlings, two-year-old cows, and "dry" cows. Lastly come the pregnant cows, moving slowly and destined to give birth before they reach their summer range. The northward-moving elk are in groups of a few to as many as forty or fifty, typically led by an experienced mature female. She chooses the route and the time and place of crossing rivers, with the other elk following dutifully.

As the elk begin to leave the refuge, so too do most of the wintering trumpeter swans. They disperse in pairs and family groups to more northerly waters that are slowly becoming ice-free. Wintering Canada geese on Flat Creek also become restless, as do Barrow's goldeneyes and mallards. By late March some of the Canada geese will have moved up the Snake River toward Jackson Lake and northward into the river's headwaters near Yellowstone Park, while others arrive from more southerly wintering grounds. As they work their way up the Snake River, they fly over occasional groups of common mergansers fishing in the river and past a pair of bald eagles, which by late March are already renovating their last-year's nest to receive a new clutch of eggs.

By early April the Elk Refuge suddenly seems unusually full of potential; the swans and Canada geese are trumpeting their departure northward, the bull elk are milling about and beginning to drift off the refuge into the wooded hills, and the sounds of courting Barrow's goldeneyes enliven Flat Creek. Small flocks of green-winged teal, northern pintails, and American wigeon appear on Flat Creek, and male greater sage-grouse gather on snow-free ridges to begin their territorial strutting displays. Up the valley of the Snake River come the distant calls of sandhill crane pairs unison-calling as they settle into territories, and the sagebrush flats start to green up with the earliest of the spring grasses and flowers. And quite silently a pregnant female mountain lion settles into a rocky recess on a steep hillside overlooking the Elk Refuge to await the birth of her cubs.

ABOVE. *Mountain lion, adult head portrait*

OVERLEAF. *A female greater sage-grouse, February, Grand Teton National Park, Wyoming*

The Sagebrush Sea

LIKE A SILVERY GREEN SHEET, the sagebrush flats of Jackson Hole spread almost uninterrupted from the base of the Gros Ventre Mountains to the Teton Range, the slow-growing and long-lived sage providing unspoken testimony to the survival value of longevity and fortitude in a semiarid environment. The species of sagebrush dominating these flats is part of a vegetational type that evolved and spread widely throughout the Intermountain West during the uplift of the Rocky Mountains more than twenty million years ago. Only a few other species of shrubs, mainly rabbitbrush and a few other sagebrush species, manage to compete effectively with big sagebrush for the limited supply of water and associated nutrients on these flats. At their edges, however, the battle for vegetational dominance is constantly waged among sagebrush, aspen, and lodgepole pine. Where the land rises but a few hundred feet above the flats, stands of lodgepole pine form the primary shoreline of the sagebrush sea, while on arid hillsides occasional islands of aspens emerge out of the sagebrush flats like becalmed and abandoned ships in a windless ocean. But the sagebrush flats are anything but lifeless.

One early spring day a pair of coyotes began digging a den on a sage-scented hillside. The den was scarcely visible on the sun-warmed southern slope facing the Snake River Valley. The female began to dig it on a warm day in March, about a month after becoming pregnant. The entrance, well concealed by low sagebrush, was less than a foot wide and about two feet high. It extended back several feet to a widened area about three feet in diameter, above which an abandoned ground squirrel hole provided a built-in ventilation shaft to the surface. It was but one of several burrows that the pair of coyotes had throughout their extensive home range. Some they used for midday retreats on hot summer days. Several of these were merely abandoned badger diggings.

As the late April sun began to stir spring flowers to life, the female came to full term and lay in the den patiently awaiting birth of her litter. She had already removed the hair from her belly, exposing her milk-swollen nipples. Her mate remained nearby, only periodically leaving her to check the now mostly barren skeletons of winter-killed elk or to return with a meadow vole, a small rodent that is the bread-and-butter component of a coyote's diet in Jackson Hole. The two-year-old female, pregnant for the first time, had become progressively less tolerant of her mate's presence in the den during the past few days. Finally, as he

OVERLEAF. *Adult coyote, February, Lamar Valley, Yellowstone National Park, Wyoming*

returned from one of his mouse-hunting forays, he seemed surprised that, instead of being greeted by his mate's usual muzzle-grasping greeting, she lifted her ears, retracted her lips, and uttered a throaty growl. The confused male quickly retracted his ears and backed out of the den, unaware that the first of his six offspring was about to be born.

As the half-pound pups emerged, they were carefully cleaned by the mother with her tongue, exposing a dark, tawny brown fur, with slightly darker areas on their ears, faces, backs, and tails. Their eyes were shut tightly, their rounded ears lay flat against the head, and a short length of umbilical cord extended from their bodies. As the female cleaned each pup, she started by licking around the head, the first part of the pup to emerge. Aided by their mother's licking and muzzle movements, the newborn pups slowly worked their way along her belly and firmly attached themselves to her nipples. They formed a row of brown, furry objects, their heads gently resting on the mother's belly and their bodies in contact with one another for the entire length.

Life in the den for the next two weeks consisted of little more than alternating sleeping and nursing, with occasional excited squeaks from a pup when it lost physical contact with its mother or the other youngsters. After ten days, the pups' pink footpads had turned black, and their umbilical wounds had healed completely. Their teeth were nearly ready to break through the gums, and the inside corners of the pups' eyes were beginning to part. A few days later their eyes were fully open, and their ears were starting to become functional, making them aware for the first time that outside their den existed a world they would soon be eager to explore.

Within a few days of opening their eyes, the pups began to practice walking, and by the time they were three weeks old, all six were actively investigating the limits of their den. Throughout this vulnerable period the male remained very close to the den, sometimes approaching its entrance but usually remaining as inconspicuous as possible while guarding it. Whenever a pup began to stray too close to the den's entrance, a whine or squeak from the mother was enough to turn it back. At three weeks of age, the pups' canine teeth emerged, and when they approached the female to nurse, her behavior changed from acceptance to a low growl and avoidance. By then her belly and nipples were raw and sometimes bleeding from the nearly constant biting and scratching of her active litter. At times, she ran out of the den to avoid the hungry pups, and whenever they followed her the male gently picked them up by the head or body and carried them back to the safety of the den.

When the litter was some three weeks old, the female began to remain away from her den for an hour or more, leaving her mate to guard it against other coyotes while she searched the hillside for food. Soon she returned, uttering a whine that attracted the entire litter. As the pups pawed at her mouth and excitedly wagged their tails, she heaved convulsively and regurgitated several partially digested mice in front of the pups.

For the next two weeks the pattern remained much the same, with both parents bringing food and almost no nursing allowed by the female. Soon the young began to make short forays away from the den's entrance, spending their spare time in the roughhousing and play-fighting that establishes the dominance relationships so important to their later social life.

As the pups approached their fourth week of age near the end of May, they divided their time between feeding and fighting with their litter mates. Fights at this stage have little of the playfulness typical of older animals with established dominance positions. Instead their fights consisted of unrestrained biting and head-shaking movements, with the bites directed toward the face, neck scruff, or body. As each pup engaged in such fights, individual differences in strength and aggressiveness became apparent, and within a few days a dominance order began to emerge. Almost immediately the most and least dominant positions became established, but the other four pups took longer to establish their relationships with one another. When a clear hierarchy had been established, their serious fighting was gradually replaced with play-fighting. This usually started with an invitation-to-play posture by one pup, which crouched on its forelegs while keeping its hindquarters elevated or made approach and withdrawal movements. Jaw-wrestling, inhibited biting, and general body wrestling were interspersed with short chases. These bouts usually ended with the dominant pup standing victoriously above the subordinate one, which lay quietly and submissively underneath.

By the time the female completely weaned her young in May, they fed almost entirely on mice. This diet was soon supplemented by the much larger pocket gophers as these rodents became increasingly active above ground and as the snow cover that had provided their winter protection disappeared from the bottomlands. While snow cover was still patchy, the male coyote concentrated his hunting on the snowfields, where he stealthily prowled, listening for mouse activity below. As soon as he heard or scented one, he suddenly stopped and poised for a pounce, with his ears pointed forward and his tail irrepressibly wagging. Then he would suddenly spring almost vertically upward and crash through the snow cover with his forelegs, trapping the mouse in his paws. However, as the snow cover disappeared, the male spent much more time hunting for pocket gophers, since they could be easily caught by simply waiting at their tunnel entrance until they emerged.

After April had passed into memory and the snowline rose inexorably up the foothills to the east, a small herd of pronghorn began to move down from the Gros Ventre Valley after wintering in the Green River drainage. In Jackson Hole the snow cover is too deep for them to survive without danger of starvation. Thus each spring a small band migrates west into the upper Gros Ventre drainage between Bacon and Red Bluff Ridges. By April the bucks had mostly regrown the horny sheaths of their antlers, which they had shed the previous fall after the rut. Nearly all does in the herd at least two years old were pregnant, having carried their developing young through the winter. The pronghorns traveled in a single group for maximum safety from coyotes or other predators. So long as they could avoid crossing deep snow, their vulnerability to predation was minimal, but in soft snow they risked becoming bogged down and unable to escape the lighter and more agile coyotes. As the pronghorn

ABOVE. *Coyote, adult calling*

OVERLEAF. *Six-week-old coyote pups, June, above the Gibbon River, Yellowstone National Park, Wyoming*

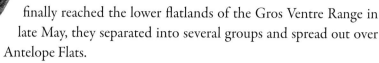

finally reached the lower flatlands of the Gros Ventre Range in late May, they separated into several groups and spread out over Antelope Flats.

The adult males immediately established territories. Those that had been territorial the previous year simply returned to the same areas, while newly maturing males tried to establish territories for the first time. Most of the immature males formed a separate herd that moved about the areas not defended by mature males, and a few bachelor males stayed to themselves. The last major group comprised the does, which wandered at will over the flats but were almost always accompanied by the resident buck through whose territory they passed.

As each adult buck returned to his old territory or attempted to establish a new one, his behavior was predictable. After attaining sexual maturity, each buck attempts to establish local social dominance every summer by marking various points about the area he selects for a territory. Periodically he would stop, paw the ground, urinate, defecate, and then move on to the next marking location. Wherever he encountered a large shrub or other unusually tall plant, he would sniff it, chew or bite off the tip of the plant, and rub his blackish cheek patch against it. Thus he transmitted his distinctive scent to the plant and established an olfactory "signpost" proclaiming ownership of the area. This marking was especially frequent wherever a possible visual or olfactory contact with another buck's territory might occur.

Whenever a male actually intruded into the territory of another, the response of the resident male was immediate and unmistakable. Snorting an alarm, he would then utter a series of wheezing notes descending in volume and pitch. Often these were sufficient to cause the intruder to flee, especially if it was a yearling. Otherwise the intruder was immediately approached and threatened. Walking deliberately toward him, the resident male lowered his head, compressed his mane and rump patch, and stared directly at the intruder. If this still failed to deter him, the resident male stood broadside about five or ten yards away, or the two males would walk parallel to each other at this distance, occasionally depositing territorial markers along the way. These displays, alone or collectively, were usually enough to cause the intruder to leave without contesting the issue further.

By the middle of May the does approached the end of their pregnancies, and the female herd began to break up. Each pregnant female, sometimes accompanied by her yearling fawn, sought out a suitable place to give birth, usually a place where the sagebrush was at least twenty inches high and thus tall enough to hide a newborn fawn.

Such a site was selected by a two-year-old female one day in late May. Lying down in the heavy sage, she began to lick her udder and belly, occasionally standing up and walking about for short distances. Her two fawns were born less than thirty minutes apart. As soon as each was free of the mother, she licked it, thus removing the fetal membranes and perhaps also stimulating it to breathe. Almost as soon as it had been cleaned, the fawn struggled to rise and within thirty minutes of being born was on its feet and attempting to walk. On finding its mother, each fawn sought out her udder. She responded by standing still and arching her back to allow sucking. When but a few hours old, the well-nursed fawns began

ABOVE. *Pronghorn, adult male portrait*

to make short forays away from the mother and soon bedded down nearly twenty yards away from her. Amazingly, except for the relatively short time spent nursing, essentially all of the newborn's time was spent out of physical contact with its mother while lying motionless on the ground. Probably this represents an antipredator adaptation, but the young fawns are easy prey for coyotes.

By the time that they were two weeks old, the fawns began to form groups, producing a nucleus of nursery herds made up of newborns and their mothers. Although fawns in these groups attempted to nurse from females other than their mothers, they were quickly rejected by being gently butted away. In these nursery groups the fawns associated almost entirely with others fawns, since their mothers left them unattended except for short periods of nursing and grooming. By late August male fawns started to perform pairing behavior toward their mothers, and the weaning process was well under way. Nursing gradually diminished as the fall rut approached, and adult males began intensively courting the mature females.

As summer ended, the territorial males spent an increasing amount of their time trying to herd females toward the centers of their respective territories. Likewise, the mature but nonterritorial males, which previously moved about the area in groups or alone, now spent increasingly more time trying to intrude into the territories of established males. Fighting resulting from these encounters sharply increased, and by the end of September many males were limping or showing patches of missing hair where they had been badly bitten.

Four

The Lamar Valley

THE LAMAR RIVER HAS ITS ORIGINS high in the Absaroka Range east of Yellowstone Lake, where it dances down mountain slopes until it encounters Soda Butte Creek. Joining forces, their waters turn west to flow through a broad and mostly unforested valley, the Lamar Valley. During late glacial times this valley was scoured and shaped by a sudden immense surge of water when an upstream ice dam broke, bringing a mix of water, rocks, and mud into the valley. After merging with the Yellowstone River and a few other tributary streams, the now considerably enlarged river finally leaves the northern boundary of the park. This large area of the Yellowstone River Valley constitutes the park's northern range, which consists of about 250,000 acres of largely unforested land.

Unlike most of Yellowstone Park, the Lamar and Yellowstone River Valleys are relatively dry, and their vegetation mostly consists of perennial grasses, mainly Idaho fescue–bluebunch wheatgrass, interspersed with open stands of big sagebrush. These grass-dominated habitat types represent the most important winter foods for the park's largest grazing mammals, especially elk and bison. Its moderately level terrain and open country vistas also provide a perfect hunting habitat for wolves while capturing large prey by prolonged and cooperative chases.

Conifers in the Lamar Valley occur as single trees, in linear groves along drainages, and as larger stands at higher elevations and on north-facing mountain slopes. The conifers largely consist of Douglas-fir and, at progressively higher elevations, lodgepole pine, Engelmann spruce, and whitebark pine. The volcanic soils supporting these spruce-fir forests are derived from andesite rather than rhyolite and have considerably higher nutrient levels and water-holding abilities than do the rhyolite-based volcanic soils that predominate over most of the park.

In some areas of the Lamar Valley there are single-species stands of lodgepole pines. Bark beetles often attack and kill lodgepole pines, producing areas of mostly dead timber that are highly vulnerable to fire. However, the lodgepole pine is a kind of phoenix-like tree, able to rise quickly from the seeds that are released during burning and then germinate among the ashes. Not only can lodgepole pines thrive in Yellowstone's poor soils, but they also grow remarkably fast and may begin producing viable seeds within five to ten years, whereas most other conifers may require fifty to seventy years.

Willows and cottonwoods historically grew in dense thickets along the river floodplain, and, where soil moisture conditions allowed, aspens were abundant on lower and moist upland slopes. During the long period of large elk populations in the park, few aspens have been able to grow to maturity. Both willows and aspens are favored foods for elk, and any plants within reach have been avidly browsed. As a result, most of the aspens on the northern range are now very old trees, since any new root sprouts that emerge are quickly eaten by elk or other herbivores as soon as they are discovered. Because of this intense degree of browsing, young aspens rarely grow large enough to exceed the heights that elk can reach. Yet some of the surviving trees may reach a century or more of age, and when individual stems die they are rapidly replaced by suckering from the roots.

Aboveground parts of aspen are easily killed by fires, but their roots quickly produce new sprouts, and after the 1988 fires there was also a rare and widespread appearance of aspen seedlings in the blackened soil, newly fertilized with the nutrients released by the charred forest. Many of these seedlings appeared within two years of the fire, some of them magically growing as far away as nine miles from any seed source.

Because of its vegetation and topography, the northern range is the heart of the summer, and to varying degrees winter, range for elk, bison, pronghorn, and mule deer. It is also the home of many predators, such as coyotes, cougars, and grizzly and black bears, but the National Park Service killed the last of Yellowstone's wolves in 1926, the last one shot in the Lamar Valley.

The question of whether to reintroduce wolves into Yellowstone Park has been extensively researched and debated ever since they were eliminated from it. During that period the elk population was actively controlled by human management in the absence of wolf predation pressures. During the 1920s the park's winter elk populations ranged from 10,000 to 15,000, but from 1930 to 1970 their numbers slowly declined to about 4,000 under the combined influence of legal sport hunting outside the park and the park removal policy of trapping and exporting elk to other locations. In 1969 the Park Service decided to stop its removal policy. Winter elk numbers then slowly recovered and had reached about 10,000 by 1980.

To the delight of tourists and the disgust of most ranchers, in 1995 and 1996 wild wolves returned to Yellowstone Park. The reintroduction of wolves into Yellowstone Park after an absence of seventy-five years occurred only after many years of planning and intense battling between environmentalists and ranchers. By 1996 packs within Yellowstone Park had formed at Rose Creek (three animals) and Crystal Creek (six animals), both in the Lamar Valley, and a pack of four animals had settled in the northwestern corner of the park.

By 1997 three more packs had become established in central and southeastern Yellowstone Park. A fourth group, the Druid Peak pack, was formed by five wolves from British Columbia that were released in April of 1996, consisting of an adult pair and three yearling females. Within a month they attacked and expelled the Crystal Creek pack, forcing them southward, and became firmly established along Soda Butte Creek and the lower Lamar Valley.

The Druid's alpha male was illegally shot when the pack left the park and ventured into Wyoming during November of 1997. By early December the surviving Druids consisted of only two females and five pups. Yet a few days later a male from the adjacent Rose Creek pack managed to become accepted by the two adult females and very soon had taken on the role of the new alpha male. The Druids have since become one of Yellowstone's most dominant packs as well as the most famous of America's wolves. By the end of the 2000 pup season their number had increased to twenty-six animals, and as they expanded westward they captured the area previously controlled by the Rose Creek pack as well as the area once controlled by the Crystal Creek pack. By 2001 the powerful Druids numbered no fewer than thirty-seven members, a phenomenally large number for any wolf pack. By 2002 their vast domain included much of northeastern Yellowstone Park, east to the vicinity of Cooke City, and west to the Blacktail Deer Plateau.

From the founder population of 31 wolves introduced into Yellowstone Park in 1995 and 1996, the park's wolf population steadily grew. The three packs released in 1995 (Rose Creek, Crystal Creek, and Soda Butte) grew to six packs totaling 34 wolves in 1996, with the addition of the Druid Peak, Chief Joseph, and Nez Perce packs. The wolf population reached 50 in 1997, 82 in 1998, and 111 in 1999. Two new packs had formed by 1997, followed by three more in 1998, two in 1999, five in 2000, two in 2001, and four in 2002. By 1999 the Yellowstone wolves had expanded their range south into Grand Teton National Park and the National Elk Refuge, and by 2002 they had extended southeast at least as far as the Pinedale region. By 2003 there were about 175 wolves in the park, and a total of more than 300 were roaming through the Greater Yellowstone region.

By 2004 wolves had occupied nearly all of Yellowstone Park and included more than a dozen packs. They were mostly concentrated in the northern half of the park, the area of densest elk concentrations. During the period 1995 through 2003 nearly 2,350 prey animals were documented as wolf kills, of which 88 percent were elk and 4 percent were bison. The remainder consisted of moose, deer, pronghorn, and other or unknown prey. With the elk winter numbers now about half of what they were before the wolf reintroduction, aspen browsing has been much reduced, and new groves have formed where they were absent before. Willows and cottonwoods have begun to stabilize stream banks and have helped to restore natural water flows. Beaver populations have increased, producing new dams and ponds. Streamside bird populations have thus probably benefited from the resulting improved riparian habitats. Coyotes, magpies, ravens, and eagles have probably benefited from the increased amount of carrion provided by wolf kills. Coyote numbers initially declined under competition pressures and direct attacks from wolves but have slowly recovered. In contrast, pronghorn numbers have increased; coyotes are serious predators on pronghorn fawns.

After their initial population spurt, wolf numbers in Yellowstone declined from a peak population of 175 in 2003 to 118 in 2005. They rebounded to 171 in 2004 but dropped again to 116 in 2009 and to 85 in 2010. The alpha female of the Druid pack died in the fall of 2009, and the alpha male disappeared soon thereafter. By early 2010 three of the remaining Druids had been killed by other wolves while scavenging, The last surviving member, a starving two-year-old female, was killed while attacking a cow near Butte, Montana, over 150 miles north of the pack's home base.

The death of female 690F spelled the end of the fourteen-year reign of the Druid pack, the largest, most fully documented, and most photographed of all North American wolves. They had been seen by an estimated 100,000 park visitors and watched by millions

OVERLEAF. *The Druid Peak wolf pack running the Lamar Valley in search of prey, February, Yellowstone National Park, Wyoming*

on television documentaries, resulting in a new public appreciation for wild wolves and their roles in natural ecosytems. Since then, new wolves have moved into the Lamar Valley; one group designated as the Silver pack settled in the eastern part of the valley, and one named the Lamar Canyon pack moved into the area that had once been occupied by the Slough Creek pack. In the winter of 2011–2012 the Lamar Valley was invaded by a powerful pack of nearly twenty wolves, Mollie's pack, which had moved in from Pelican Valley.

The recent declines of Yellowstone wolves have been attributed in part to infections from canine distemper and to other diseases such as parvovirus and especially mange. Mange results in increased chances of bacterial infection, bodily weakness, and hair loss, thereby increasing the probabilities of winter deaths through frostbite and starvation. Winter elk numbers in the park have also declined since the wolf introductions, from about 17,000 to 6,800 in 2009, with about twice as many present during summer as in winter. During their extended contacts with wolves, the elk herd has also become more fit by the removal of its weaker animals and by the elks' increasing wariness and abilities in avoiding capture.

By 2008 there were nearly 1,650 wolves in the northern Rocky Mountain region of Idaho, Montana, and Wyoming. They were distributed in 217 packs, with about 1,500 of them living outside national parks. However, at least 50 of the packs were centered within the Greater Yellowstone Ecosystem. During 2008 there were also 529 confirmed wolf-caused deaths of cattle and sheep in the three-state region as well as the loss of 268 wolves that were killed for attacking livestock. Wolves were accused of causing 1,300 sheep losses in Idaho that year, out of a total of 125,000 sheep deaths. By comparison, 28,500 of the deaths were attributed to weather effects, and 31,600 were said by sheep men to be coyote kills. Blaming coyotes for such massive sheep mortality may be a convenient explanation for ranchers, but almost certainly is also an erroneous one, for mice and other small rodents are the primary prey of coyotes.

In the spring of 2009 the Interior Department adopted the Bush administration's decision to remove the wolf from its Endangered Species Act protection, opening the way for state-authorized wolf hunting in the Rocky Mountain region. Idaho established a quota of 220 wolves that might be killed during its long 2009–2010 season, which extended into March 2010. Montana set a killing quota of 75 for the same season. In addition to such mortality, about 150 wolves die each year from illegal killing, legal control, and natural causes. By mid-winter of 2009–2010 more than 180 wolves had been killed in the two states. At least 8 were killed just outside the northern border of Yellowstone National Park, and at least 4 of those were from the park's Cottonwood pack, including the pack's alpha female. Idaho has set a goal of reducing its wolf population from about 1,000 to 518 animals, "by whatever means possible."

ABOVE. *Wolf, adult head portrait*

PREVIOUS PAGE. *Common ravens taunting wolves near their kill, National Elk Refuge, Jackson Hole, Wyoming*

In 2009 thirteen conservation groups challenged Interior's decision to delist the gray wolf, pointing out scientific deficiencies in the department's proposed management plan. In 2011, with the West's wolf population at more than 1,700 animals, the Center for Biological Diversity filed a notice that it would sue the US Fish and Wildlife Service if it failed to create a new nationwide wolf recovery plan and to establish new wolf populations in regions where they have long been extirpated. In contrast, the Montana governor declared a wolf hunt in defiance of their national protection, and the Idaho legislature urged its governor to declare a state of emergency relative to its wolf population. Perhaps in response to increasing political pressures, the Fish and Wildlife Service indicated that it intended to propose that the wolf be delisted from the protections given it under the Endangered Species Act's provisions by the end of 2011.

As of January 2011 there were 400 to 450 wolves in the Greater Yellowstone region, with around 120 individuals in the park. In September 2012 the US Fish and Wildlife Service announced that wolves could be shot in about 90 percent of the state's area (the Greater Yellowstone region excluded), which supports an estimated population of 270 wolves. Wyoming's wildlife agency decided to offer unlimited hunting licenses for the fall of 2012. The plan would halt the season after 52 wolves had been killed, with a long-term goal of reducing Wyoming's wolf population outside the national parks to about 100, or ten breeding pairs.

~ ~

The male western jumping mouse had gone into hibernation in a spacious nest chamber at the base of a twenty-inch hole that he had dug in the deep soil in the floodplain of the Lamar River during the previous summer. The hole was deep enough below ground so that the temperature of the hibernation chamber remained fairly uniform, at about ten degrees above freezing, over much of the tiny mammal's nine-month hibernation period. The mouse had luckily been able to add enough body fat to increase his total weight by nearly a third before entering hibernation and over the winter period had slowly used up just enough energy to keep him from freezing or starving to death. Prior to becoming dormant he had plugged the opening to the burrow with soil and prepared a latrine area to use during the rare times that he would awaken over the next nine months. Finally, he curled himself up into a nearly perfect sphere, to reduce the loss of body heat to a minimum, and fell into a deep sleep, nearly shutting down most of his bodily functions. Now, in early June, he was awake and very hungry. He would have to eat ravenously during the bare three-month summer period to again replenish his fat stores before the onset of its next hibernation in early September.

As the mouse clawed away the soil plugging his burrow, he peered outside. He saw that since he had gone underground the Lamar Valley had been transformed into a verdant green. An abundance of small insects and other arthropods were present in the

ABOVE. *Western jumping mouse*

grasses and would serve well as a nutritious food supply until grass seeds again became available.

The jumping mouse was not the only hungry animal about that morning. A coyote had spent the night hiding and resting from a nearly fatal attack by wolves, which had occurred when she tried to snatch a food morsel from the carcass of a dead elk that the wolves had killed the previous evening. She had escaped only by dashing into a tangle of tree roots that were exposed along the eroding riverbank. The wolves had been unable to penetrate easily and, rather than waste any more time, were content to let the thoroughly frightened and cowering coyote escape with her life.

As the morning sun appeared over Druid Peak, the coyote cautiously emerged from the root tangle refuge, and her keen nose caught the scent of mouse lingering in the dewy grasses. The jumping mouse had just passed by, busily seeking insects, until he was suddenly aware that he was being stalked. Realizing that it was too late to return to his burrow, the mouse startled the coyote by suddenly making four quick zigzag leaps, each covering a full three feet in distance, which carried him back nearly to the river's edge and safely into the same dense tangle of tree roots that had ironically saved the coyote's life only a few hours before.

The morning sun now increasingly illuminated nearly a dozen members of the Druid Peak wolf pack, which were still relaxing and digesting the meals that the elk had provided. They were mostly offspring of the alpha pair, plus a few unrelated immigrants that had been accepted into the pack. The alpha male and female were both nearly a half-mile away, the female tending to her new litter. The month-old pups were well hidden in an excavated den that had been picked because of its remote location as well as its proximity to both water and shade and that had been used successfully the year before. The alpha female had stayed with her pups for most of the early nursing period, with the alpha male and other pack members hunting for her and bringing food to both her and the pups. The pups' eyes had opened two weeks previously, and their new teeth had erupted sufficiently that they were just beginning to chew on solid food. In another month they would move to another location, where the youngsters would be able to play and romp about over a large area and where play-fighting would be important in later survival and establishment of their social position in the pack.

The relaxing wolves were lying not far from the remains of the elk kill, which had attracted more than a dozen ravens and a few black-billed magpies. These birds posed no problems for the wolves, which were content to watch them fight over the scraps of meat scattered about the kill site. Some had just returned from carrying food to the alpha female, which would soon be able to rejoin the pack and increasingly participate in their social interactions. But for now she was content to watch over her four youngsters and enjoy the pleasures of motherhood and of being regularly tended by all the others.

More serious than the presence of the ravens and magpies was the appearance of an adult female grizzly bear. She had been roaming through the greening meadows in search of early plants such as springbeauty, clover, and other green forbs as well as a variety of underground roots and tubers that she dug up by her persistent grazing and digging activities. She was in the process of swallowing the unlucky jumping mouse that her powerful forelegs and long claws had suddenly exposed when she caught smell of the elk carcass. Her long-distance vision was poor, but by standing up she could see the carcass and wolves.

The elk carcass was a welcome discovery for the grizzly. Now nearly three years old, she had emerged from her long five-month period of hibernation in early April. During that time she had lost nearly all of the fat that she had built up the previous fall, mostly by eating the nutlike seeds of whitebark pine and countless army cutworm moths that she unearthed among rocks in boulder fields at a elevation of nearly 10,000 feet. Weighing nearly 300 pounds prior to winter, she was now slightly over 200 pounds and was almost constantly hungry. Since her spring emergence, she had been feeding on a diverse mixture of green plants and the sometimes rotting remains of elk, pronghorn, and bison that she occasionally stumbled upon. She had remained close to the wolf pack, scavenging their kills, but hadn't managed to get close enough to their pups to make a meal of them. The wolves, in turn, never hesitated to try attack the bear whenever they had a distinct numerical advantage.

By early June both the wolves and the grizzly would have moved upward to higher meadows to search for newborn elk, but for now the recently dead elk was a true windfall. The grizzly had emerged from her den in late March and had still not recovered all of the weight that she had lost during her four-and-a-half-month denning period. Freshly thawed carcasses of elk had gotten her through her first postdenning month, but she had increasingly relied on succulent green plants growing along the Lamar River for providing easy access to regular and delicious meals. Bounding toward the dead elk, the grizzly flushed the ravens and magpies, but they quickly returned, keeping a safe distance between them and the bear. The still-hungry coyote also soon arrived and, being much more agile than the bear, was able to creep close enough to occasionally tear off small pieces of meat.

The female grizzly was part of a population of about 600 that were roaming widely over the Greater Yellowstone region by early in the twenty-first century. From the 1970s to 1980s about 200 to 300 grizzlies had occupied the park and its surrounding Greater Yellowstone region; from 1972 to 1984 an average of about 12 females (range 9–17) produced cubs, typically about 2 per female (range 1.7–2.2). By the end of the twentieth century the Greater Yellowstone population had increased substantially, and in 2007 the population was removed from the list of federally threatened species. Only two years later it was returned to the threatened list, where, as of 2011, it remained. In 2009, 14 Yellowstone females produced 33 cubs, a much better-than-average reproductive rate of 2.4 cubs per female. Given the increasing bear populations in the Greater Yellowstone region, trigger-happy hunters could barely wait for the day when they could again get the crosshairs of their scopes focused on what they regard as the greatest of all American trophy heads to hang on their game-room wall.

ABOVE. *Grizzly bear, adult head portrait*

OVERLEAF. *Famous grizzly 399 after nursing her triplets, May, Grand Teton National Park, Wyoming*

Five

The Canyon

THE RAVEN'S FAVORITE PERCH looked out over a canyon that is nearly a half mile wide and some 1,000 feet deep, with tall conifers growing right up to the brink of the steep cliff. From that vantage point, the raven had an uninterrupted view for a mile or more in each direction. At its back was a large parking lot, where tourists would emerge from vehicles, with cameras or binoculars in hand, and sometimes also with candy or various other edible items. It was a warm summer day in mid-July, and the raven preferred to perch in the shade to avoid overheating and flew out into the sun-drenched parking lot only when the potential food reward made it seem worthwhile. Life for the raven was easy in July; most of the nesting songbirds had easily accessible young still in the nest, or their fledglings were barely able to fly and escape the raven's agile maneuvers. In addition, there was an abundance of half-grown and easily caught least chipmunks, golden-mantled ground squirrels, and Uinta ground squirrels. The young yellow-bellied marmots that occupied the crevices and talus piles along the canyon's walls were already too large for the raven to consider attacking, but they provided easy prey for a golden eagle that regularly patrolled the area.

The adult marmots also apparently enjoyed the view, at least when they could stop foraging long enough to sun themselves on the steep west-facing slopes that caught the afternoon sunlight for a few hours. One of them was a female that, unlike most others in the local population, had a completely black pelage rather than the usual reddish-yellow underparts and dark brown upperparts of her nearby neighbors. She had just finished weaning her four offspring and had also recently molted into a lustrous shorter and cooler summer coat. She was part of a small colony of marmots living on a broad, nearly level canyon ledge. The group consisted of a single adult male, several female mates, and a few immatures. All of them stayed well within earshot of the others, on the alert for any warning calls from the others, and with the male guarding the group's territory against possible intrusion by other male marmots.

Like the chipmunks and squirrels in the Yellowstone region, female marmots give birth to only a single litter per year. The short growing season and the need to store enough body fat to see the animals through their long hibernation preclude spending any more energy on the young than is absolutely needed. If too little fat is present when hibernation begins, the marmot will simply starve to death in its sleep. The black-pelaged female had already lost

OVERLEAF. *Yellow-bellied marmots sunning themselves outside their burrow, July, Grand Teton National Park, Wyoming*

nearly half of her six-pound body weight while hibernating, and since emerging in April she had been fully occupied with mating, pregnancy, and nursing her ever-hungry litter. She was now finally sufficiently free of her maternal activities to spend much of the day feeding and regaining her store of body fat in preparation for the next long stretch of hibernation.

Lying in the mid-afternoon sun, the black color of the female's fur quickly absorbed the sunlight and helped warm her body. She was soon lulled into a drowsy state and gradually fell asleep. It was a fatal mistake. Her conspicuous black color had attracted the attention of a female golden eagle soaring 500 feet above. The eagle quickly partially retracted her huge wings and began a controlled, forty-five-degree dive that approached eighty miles per hour. Coming down in line with the sun, the eagle was nearly invisible in the sun's glare, and the only sound she produced was caused by the vibration of her outer flight feathers and longest scapular feathers. The rustling sounds of her feathers were not enough to rouse the marmot, which was suddenly impaled by the eagle's two long rear talons and a nearly simultaneous piercing of her rib cavity by the six, almost equally long front talons. Even before she died, she was being carried out over the immense canyon by the eagle, which was struggling to carry nearly a quarter of her own weight. Slowly losing altitude, the eagle landed on a rock pinnacle and began to tear apart and consume the now-dead marmot.

The eagle's nest was situated on a narrow rock platform high on Mount Washburn, almost five miles away and about 2,000 feet higher in elevation. After eating part of the carcass and resting for a time, the eagle clutched the heavy marmot carcass and began the long flight back to her nest, where her three half-grown eaglets were impatiently waiting to be fed.

Another onlooker to the golden eagle and marmot drama was an adult female great gray owl, tending her brood on an abandoned goshawk nest that had been built among the branches of a tall Douglas-fir. Her gray coloration blended well with her shaded surroundings, and her offspring were also a dull gray color. She had just received the gift of a still-warm golden-mantled ground squirrel from her mate, which had already left to find more food for her and their quickly growing brood. Of the four eggs that had hatched, only the three oldest still survived, the youngest having hatched almost a week later than its oldest sibling and proving unable to compete with its larger and stronger nest mates for food. However, the surviving owlets were growing at a remarkable rate, each doubling its hatching weight by the time it was five days old and weighing slightly over a pound when only two weeks old. With such appetites the male not only hunted during the darkest hours of night, when his favorite prey, voles and pocket gophers, were most active, but also during daylight hours, when chipmunks and ground squirrels were most likely to be active.

In spite of the owl's huge size, by virtue of his soft-fringed flight feathers he could fly in total silence, while his huge facial disks served at perfect stereophonic receptors. Even when his prey was totally hidden in a runway under the soil or moving about below deep snow in winter, the owl was able to accurately judge its location by the faintest sounds it produced. Then he would hover briefly and drop vertically downward, striking the substrate with all of his weight and trapping any unlucky rodent within the broad perimeter of his long and widely spread talons.

During daylight hours the male owl preferred to hunt well away from the deep woods and instead would perch unseen in a tall Douglas-fir at the edge of the conifers a few hun-

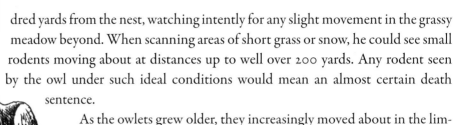

dred yards from the nest, watching intently for any slight movement in the grassy meadow beyond. When scanning areas of short grass or snow, he could see small rodents moving about at distances up to well over 200 yards. Any rodent seen by the owl under such ideal conditions would mean an almost certain death sentence.

As the owlets grew older, they increasingly moved about in the limited space the snag provided, and by the time they were slightly more than three weeks old they were leaving the nest and clambering about the tree's branches. Occasionally one would lose its grip and fall partly or all the way to the ground but was always able to climb back up to the security of the nest before dark. During the rare occasions when the male owl was not actively hunting, he would return to the nest and affectionately preen the female's head feathers or carefully comb her breast feathers with his talons.

As the owlets grew older and more independent, they increasingly ran the risk of being taken by a predator, and even after they were able to fly when nearly two months old, they remained close to the nest and under the watchful eyes of their mother. During the daylight hours northern goshawks were a constant threat, and from twilight to dawn the equally dangerous great horned owls were on the prowl.

Near the owl's nesting tree was a mature but scorched and partially dead Douglas-fir, with a broken-off crown and several woodpecker holes neatly drilled on the south-facing side. One of the actively used holes had been drilled and was being used by a Williamson's sapsucker while a lower nesting cavity had been excavated by a pair of Lewis's woodpeckers.

The Williamson's sapsuckers were relatively rare in this region and far less common than red-naped sapsuckers, which were mostly associated with aspen groves and riparian thickets of willows and cottonwoods. Both species of sapsuckers have tongues that are shorter and less extendible than those of other woodpeckers, but sapsucker tongues are also unique in having stiff hairs that allow tree sap to adhere. By drilling a series of regularly spaced holes in a horizontal row across an aspen trunk, sapsuckers would not only consume the flowing sap but also a variety of insects attracted to the sap. The sapsuckers thus divided their time in sap-drinking, aerial fly-catching, and gleaning insects from nearby vegetation.

As compared with the red-naped, the Williamson's sapsuckers preferred to forage among conifers and snags, especially in pines and Douglas-firs. Their usual foraging technique throughout the year was drilling for sap in Douglas-firs and ponderosa pines, supplemented by insect-gleaning from tree surfaces. At times the birds would tear away pieces of bark to facilitate sap flow or to get access to the nutrient-rich phloem layer of wood just below the bark. Ants were their primary food, and at times the birds would also forage for ants on the ground.

For both sapsucker species, drumming on wood and uttering distinctive call-notes were very important forms of mate attraction and territorial advertisement. The two sapsucker species had very similar drumming patterns, but the Williamson's was slower, more regu-

ABOVE. *Great gray owl, adult, threat posture*

lar, and with longer beats. The drumming display of the Williamson's sapsucker consisted of a steady drumroll of taps, followed by a single or as many as four single loud taps given at irregular intervals. Drumming was performed mostly by the males, and most often during early-morning hours. After pair bonds had been formed, drumming was confined to late-afternoon hours. The males each had several favorite drumming sites, usually dead tree limbs, that perhaps had been selected on the basis of their locations or relative sound-producing qualities.

The Lewis's woodpecker pair sharing the Douglas-fir trunk had only recently returned from southern Colorado, where they had wintered among ponderosa pines and oak groves. There they had fed mostly on acorns, which they cracked open and the nut-meats of which they stored in the rough bark of oaks or other crevices. Returning to Yellowstone, where there are no oaks, the birds shifted to a diet of berries and, as the weather improved, live insects. To a greater degree than any other woodpeckers in the Yellowstone region, the Lewis's captured their insects during prolonged aerial chases. Sometimes the birds would join flocks of foraging swallows, but more often they would catch a singe large insect such as a grasshopper and then return to a nearby perch to eat it.

The open woodlands of the partly burned forest around Canyon Village provided excellent hunting habitat for the Lewis's pair. Soon after he had returned to Yellowstone in April, the male established a territory that including the nesting tree he had used the year previously and a large surrounding area for foraging. His past-year's mate had wintered separately but had returned to their old nesting area, and their pair bonds were soon renewed. At times the male would display by raising his wings partly above his body, exposing the pink feathers of his abdomen and flanks while fluffing out the feathers of his throat and breast and lowering his head. At other times he launched out into a circular display flight, gliding with his wings partly raised above the horizontal and finally landing next to his mate.

After reestablishing their pair bonds, the pair returned to the nest site of the previous year and investigated it. The presence of new neighbors in the form of the Williamson's sapsuckers in the same tree was unexpected but tolerable, given the very different foraging behaviors of the two species. Furthermore, two extra pairs of eyes provided an additional warning system against such serious threats as goshawks and Cooper's hawks.

ABOVE. *Lewis's woodpecker, adult pair*

Six

The Geyser Basin

THE STILL-BLACKENED SNAG HAD two decades previously been a mature lodgepole pine, and its gaunt skeleton was still standing amid the debris of other pines strewn about on the ground like giant toothpicks. It was a stark reminder and relic of a massive wildfire that had enveloped the area in 1988, when more than a third of Yellowstone Park, nearly 800,000 acres, had been consumed by rampaging fires. The most heavily burned areas mainly consisted of ancient lodgepole pines, some up to 200–250 years old, resulting from seeds that had germinated after fires had swept through the region perhaps as long ago as the late 1700s or early 1800s.

The snag was at the edge of a cluster of charred lodgepole pines close to Old Faithful geyser, where in late August of 1988 one of the largest of Yellowstone's eight major fires was approaching Old Faithful from the west. On September 7, strong winds allowed this fire to grow suddenly by 50,000 additional acres, surrounding Old Faithful and nearly setting the roof of the famous and venerable Old Faithful Inn ablaze. The height of the battle against the multiple fires occurred during the first ten days of September, when 9,500 firefighters and 117 aircraft were all engaged in desperately trying to control them. A mixture of rain and snow on September 11 helped turn the tide, and heavy snows in November put a final end to the fire's remnants. In spite of the visual devastation presented by the forest, the carcasses of only 345 elk, 36 mule deer, 12 moose, 9 bison, 6 black bears, and 1 grizzly bear were later found throughout the entire fire-ravaged region. These mortality figures are relatively small considering Yellowstone's enormous mammal population, which probably then totaled 20,000–30,000 individuals of these six species. They are also small when compared with the starvation or freezing deaths of about 5,000 elk during the following harsh winter, which represented about a quarter of the park's total winter elk population at that time.

Within two years after the fire, tiny lodgepole seedlings had appeared among the fire-blackened trees and ashes, along with a profusion of quickly responding wildflowers such as fireweed, which thrived and flowered profusely in the suddenly sunny environment. It hadn't taken even that long for woodpeckers to exploit the sudden food bonanza. The trees had hardly cooled before several kinds of woodpeckers descended on the charred trunks. The earliest of these to arrive were American three-toed and black-backed woodpeckers, both of which have predominantly black plumages that closely match the charred snags. Hairy

OVERLEAF. *A male northern flicker perching near its nestling at the nest hole, June, Grand Teton National Park, Wyoming.*

woodpeckers arrived soon afterward and, like the black-backed, relied on drilling holes into the bark to extract the larvae of wood-boring beetles. The American three-toed woodpecker uses a different foraging technique, of flaking the surface bark away, exposing the bark beetle larvae underneath. This flaking activity not only provided immediate food for the wood-peckers but also exposed the beetles to attack by wasps and other insects that parasitized or preyed on the beetles. In both of these three-toed woodpeckers the loss of the innermost toes somewhat reduces their clinging abilities, but a shortening of their legs and changes in the head skeletal and muscle structure maximizes the striking power of their beaks.

The three-toed and black-backed woodpeckers began selecting trees for their nest sites in mid-May, the back-backs preferring completely dead lodgepole snags, especially smaller dead trees with higher amounts of the softer sapwood, or still-living lodgepoles with exten-sive heartrot. The three-toed woodpeckers likewise preferred living or dead lodgepoles hav-ing extensive heartrot. By mid-May one of the three-toed woodpecker pairs had selected a slightly leaning lodgepole snag with extensive heartrot for its nest site. Both members of the pair worked on excavating the nest for nearly two weeks, selecting the underside of the trunk for their hole, which would help keep rain out. It required nearly two weeks for the cavity to be completed, with a nearly perfectly round entrance and a pear-shaped interior.

The black-backed woodpeckers breeding in the same location also chose to make most of their similar cavities on the undersides of slightly leaning snags, with the cavity entrance beveled on the lower side so that the hole slanted slightly upward. By the end of May the nests of both species were finished, and most egg-laying had been completed. Both sexes began to incubate as soon as their clutches of three or four eggs had been completed, the females doing most of the daytime incubating and their mates tending to the eggs through the night.

Dark-eyed juncos also arrived soon after the fires were out and began feeding on seeds scattered about on the ash-covered forest floor. By the following April a few chipping spar-rows and American robins had also appeared. By June the floor was garlanded with the deep pink blossoms of fireweed, the small, parachute-like seeds of which had blown in, inter-spersed and contrasting with the rich golden hues of heartleaf arnica.

The woodpecker population increased rapidly during the first five years after the fire, with an influx of northern flickers being added to the species mix by the third year. The flickers foraged mostly on the ground, especially on ants. All four of the woodpecker species excavated nesting and roosting cavities in the dead pine snags and the few surviving conifers, most of which were abandoned after they had been used for a single nesting season. By the third postfire year, mountain bluebirds, tree swallows, and house wrens were claiming many of the recently vacated apartments. Some noncavity-nesters had also appeared by the third year following the fire, including western wood-pewees, which found countless perching sites from which to sally out and catch flying insects. The wood-pewees built their saddlelike nests on high, horizontal branches, lining them with the downy, silken seed tufts of fireweed and binding them to the tree branches with spider webbing.

By the fifth year after the fires, a few Cassin's finches had also appeared as well as the first Clark's nutcrackers. The finches concentrated on eating a variety of seeds and berries produced by the now-recovering ground vegetation, while the Clark's nutcrackers adaptively

OVERLEAF. *An adult Clark's nutcracker, January, Shoshone National Forest, Wyoming*

altered their usual diet of pine seeds and dug beetle grubs out of the bark by hammering on the trunk in a woodpecker-like manner. The nutcrackers also remained vigilant for any food scraps discarded by the countless summer visitors to Old Faithful, sometimes fighting for them with a few gray jays, common ravens, and black-billed magpies that somehow magically appeared whenever any food was anywhere in the vicinity. Of these, only the ravens and magpies nested nearby, the gray jays placing their well-hidden nests near the tops of a few fortuitously unscathed lodgepole trees several hundred yards away. The magpie pair built an untidy nest of sticks that they plastered inside with bison dung to help waterproof it and lastly provided with an inner lining of grass stems, bison hair, and rootlets. It was constructed in one of the tall, dense shrubs that had been planted decades earlier near Old Faithful Lodge. The ravens built a similar but larger nest on top a dead lodgepole pine, the upper quarter of which had been badly charred and had broken off not long after the fire.

Meantime, the nesting Clark's nutcracker pair was collecting long-hidden pine seeds, which they had foresightedly deposited by the thousands in many different hiding places during the previous autumn. Flying as far as fifteen miles, the birds would pick up and stuff as many as 150 pine seeds in their expanded throat pouches, then look for new places to hide them. They preferred to use hiding locations that were free of most vegetation and distinctive enough to be easily remembered. In these caches the birds had stored up enough food to sustain themselves and their next brood throughout the winter and much of the following year. With their phenomenal place-memories adult nutcrackers can recall where many of their cached seeds have been placed, based on the presence of nearby landmarks, such as rocks or bushes. Over a thousand seeds had been recovered by the birds over the course of the winter and spring, leaving thousands more unfound, with the potential of germinating and establishing a new generation of pines.

The nutcracker pair began nesting in late February, while snow still was deep on the ground, weeks ahead of any other Yellowstone birds, so food-finding in the snow and keeping their eggs warm during late winter weather represented serious challenges. During the entire spring nesting season and while feeding their young, pine seeds were the nutcrackers' primary foods. Their nestlings were initially fed macerated pine seeds; insect foods were not added until the young were about seventeen days old, or just a few days prior to their leaving the nest. The parents continued to feed their fledglings seeds until July, when they were nearly four months old and were otherwise essentially independent.

Not only did the nutcrackers sometimes forget where they had hidden their seeds, but the ever-vigilant magpie pair often watched from a nearby hiding place and would dig up the stash as soon as the nutcracker had flown off to find another load. The magpies were compulsive cache-makers too; they would often remove ticks from moose, elk, and deer and bury them alive on open ground to feast on at some later time, and at times would even cache coyote scat. The few gray jays living in the area were likewise occasional recipients of the nutcrackers' diligence in providing free food. The gray jays have an advantage over the magpies in their abilities to carry and store food. These birds secrete a sticky saliva from salivary glands with which they can impregnate a mouthful of seeds. This produces a single mucilaginous mass that gradually hardens on exposure to air. They attached these to forks in trees, jammed them into crevices, or hid them in exposed locations by attaching pieces of bark to them. The jays varied both the directions and distances when they cached their food stores, thereby reducing the chances of the food being easily found by other scavengers.

BELOW. *Bison, adult male head portrait*

OVERLEAF. *A male mountain bluebird perching at his nest hole, Yellowstone Natonal Park, Wyoming*

By the seventh year after the fire old woodpecker holes were abundant in the charred forest, and the most common summer birds in the regenerating community were cavity-nesting tree swallows and mountain bluebirds as well as thriving populations of dark-eyed juncos, American robins, and Clark's nutcrackers. By then, as the supply of available beetles gradually diminished, the black-backed and American three-toed woodpeckers had nearly disappeared, and both the hairy woodpecker and northern flicker were becoming scarce. As the woodpecker population declined and the decaying snags increasingly began to topple over, the availability of already-furnished nesting cavities also began to vanish, and the tree swallow and mountain bluebird populations similarly began to slowly disappear.

After ten years the new generation of quickly growing lodgepole pines had grown to the height of an adult moose, and some of the young trees were already starting to produce cones. By the summer of 2008, twenty years after the fire, chipping sparrows were nesting in the pines, as were a few yellow-rumped warblers and gray jays. A few pine grosbeaks, mountain chickadees, and pine siskins were also appearing and attempting to nest, providing early indications that the area was destined to eventually become a mature coniferous forest again. It would still take a century or two for the slow-growing and shade-tolerant conifers such as Douglas-firs to begin to gradually replace the densely crowded and increasingly senescent lodgepole pines. Then forest-dependent birds such as the Swainson's thrush, red-breasted nuthatch, and golden-crowned kinglet would also begin to appear and complete the ecological cast of this long-running if glacially slow forest drama.

The twenty-six-year-old bull bison ambled slowly through the meadows just west of Old Faithful, having wandered south during the course of the prior winter from the Lower Geyser Basin, past the Midway Basin and Biscuit Basin. He was old enough to remember the fires of 1988 and had outlived the majority of animals in his herd. Most of that herd had wintered farther east, in the sedge-rich meadows of Pelican Valley and Hayden Valley. With the slow coming of spring during late May, the herd was gradually moving from these lower traditional wintering valleys into higher summer ranges as they became snow-free and grazing areas were progressively exposed.

Together with other male bison, the old bull had remained in a favorite wintering area along the Firehole River. The warm thermal areas along the geyser basins of the Firehole Valley had resulted in reduced snow cover there, making it easy for him and other bulls to reach green vegetation, especially the sedge bottomlands, pond borders, and the edge of the Firehole River. The Firehole Valley offered many other attractions to the older bison, such as easy access to sedge meadows, warm bottomlands associated with the presence of several thermal sites, and nearby thermally warmed, ice-free streams. Over 90 percent of the foods consumed by the bison were sedges, with grasses comprising much of the remainder. Only very small amounts of shrubs, forbs, or other vegetation were eaten.

During May the mixed herd of adult females, their newborn calves, and juveniles up to nearly two years of age had crossed the Firehole and moved westward toward summer grazing ranges. These areas included montane meadows of Hayden Valley, Pelican Valley, and the Madison Plateau near the western edge of the park. Their calves had been born in early May but within days were able to keep up with their mothers on the long trek to summering grounds along the crest of the Continental Divide.

Many of the younger and stronger bulls had wintered well away from the Firehole's thermal features and were content to cope with deeper snow, pushing aside the deep drifts with their head and powerful neck muscles. All of the males at least three years old were sexually mature, as were many of the two-year-olds. These males closely followed the herd of departing adult females and remained as close as possible to them, for the rutting season would begin by August. Soon

BELOW. *Bison, rutting adult male*

OVERLEAF. *An adult gray jay, January, Shoshone National Forest, Wyoming*

these males would begin to investigate each female in the herd to test her state of estrus. The more dominant males would then begin to form tending-bonds with the most promising females. Bulls rarely moved very far from any prospective mating partners and challenged any other males that ventured too close to them. Through head-to-head pushing contests and fights, the next few months would test each male's strength and virility and would determine the future genetic structure of the local bison herd. Although a few three-year-old bulls managed briefly to keep cows under their control, those from six to eight years old had the best combination of strength and experience to control most of the breeding activity.

FACING PAGE. *Bison pair amid summer wildflowers, July, Grand Teton National Park, Wyoming*

OVERLEAF. *Bison at thermal pools, October, Yellowstone National Park, Wyoming*

Seven

The Willow Flats

AS A SMALL FLOCK OF greater sandhill cranes flew north out of the National Elk Refuge in late April, they gradually broke up into the four lifelong pairs that had been formed several years before. Two pairs remained on the Elk Refuge to establish territories along Flat Creek, another settled into a beaver pond on a small creek below Teton Point overlook in Grand Teton National Park, and a third pair headed for a beaver pond on the lower Buffalo Fork River. The remaining pair continued north to the willow flats just below Jackson Lake dam.

This table-flat area of willow thickets and boggy grasslands is impenetrable to nearly all large mammals except moose, is rich in succulent green plants, and has adjoining areas of sagebrush where the cranes can easily forage on the roots and shoots of sprouting spring herbs. Even coyotes, which regularly hunted mice on the sagebrush flats, tended to avoid the heavy vegetation of the wet willows in favor of easier hunting grounds. But moose reveled in the combination of willow cover and shallow ponds. For several months a small group had been wintering here, eating almost nothing but willow twigs and often cropping the branches down to the snow line. The cow moose with their nearly year-old calves wandered through the area, avoiding contact with other moose, while the antlerless males often mingled in little groups of twos or threes.

The cranes, finding their last year's nesting territory still under a foot of snow, flew daily to the sage-covered hillsides, where south-facing slopes provided snow-free ground and an abundance of spring plants. With their chisel-like bills, they dug up the enlarged roots of springbeauties, keeping a watchful eye for coyotes and periodically announcing their ownership of the entire area with their duet-like unison calling.

Their appetites temporarily quieted, the pair flew to the edge of a marshy creek, where they waded and dug up mud and decaying vegetation of the previous year. Then they methodically spread these materials over their almost uniformly gray winter plumage, slowly staining it rusty brown except for their heads and upper necks, which they could not reach. Gradually the birds came to resemble more closely the dead-plant background where their nest would soon be located.

As the pair claimed their fifty-acre territory on the flats, they spent part of each day standing close together and calling simultaneously, with their bills pointed skyward, their wings slightly drooped, and their elongated inner wing feathers slightly raised. The male tilted his beak back nearly to the vertical with each call, uttering a rapid series of loud single notes, while the female held her beak diagonally upward, uttering double-noted calls in near-synchrony with the male's. This unison calling served both as a territorial proclamation and to strengthen their pair bonds.

Sometimes when they had finished calling, one would reach down to the ground, pick up a bit of vegetation, and throw it high above its head. Then, on stiffened legs, the pair would bound into the air, spreading and thrusting their wings downward with each leap and raising them again as they landed. With each bound they lowered their heads and necks in a kind of bowing posture as they faced each other. Often, as they leapt into the air, they would turn slightly, landing at a somewhat different angle. The dance stopped as unexpectedly as it began, and the birds soon began preening sedately, as if nothing had happened.

This was the second year this pair of cranes had attempted to nest. Each was approaching five years of age. The male had been hatched near Grays Lake in eastern Idaho, and the female was one of the few cranes that had been hatched and raised in the grassy meadows of the National Elk Refuge near Jackson. The pair had met and formed a pair bond on their wintering grounds of central New Mexico two winters before, and the female had led her mate northeastward from their spring staging area near Bear Lake. They had established their first nesting territory around a small beaver pond in willows that moose had clipped nearly to the surface. But their first nesting effort had met with disaster; a raven had watched the entire nest-building proceedings and patiently awaited its opportunity. The close guarding of the nest by both parents had effectively forced the raven to keep a safe distance away until well into the incubation period, when one day a cow moose nearly stepped on the incubating bird. With a frightened scream the crane flew from the nest. Before her mate could drive the moose away with its flailing wings and beak, the raven had quickly flown in and neatly pierced both eggs. Whether out of inexperience or otherwise, the cranes simply abandoned their territory and spent the rest of the summer in a remote meadow, where they molted and underwent their flightless period.

This spring the cranes had selected a nesting site close to their previous year's nest, but on a beaver lodge surrounded by water. This provided a commanding view of the adjacent flats and was unlikely to be trodden upon by a foraging moose. At the same time, the brown-colored birds blended well with the lodge. When the incubating crane lowered its head and neck as far as possible, it resembled nothing more than an unusually large log on top of the lodge.

During the second week of May the pair had attained undisputed ownership of the willow flats; the only other cranes in the vicinity were nesting more than a mile away on a small island at Oxbow Bend, where a U-shaped stretch of the Snake River has been nearly cut off and isolated from the river's main course. Another pair was using the sedge meadow at the northern end of Christian Pond. The three pairs were in daily vocal contact, hurling territorial threats at one another, but sometimes two of the pairs occupied neutral ground together while foraging on the sagebrush hillsides.

As the female made the few adjustments to the top of the lodge needed to make it a suitable nest, the male closely patrolled the area for signs of coyotes and moose. Every coyote seen was closely watched and followed discreetly. If one happened to approach the nest

FACING PAGE. *Bull moose feeding among willows, September, Moose, Wyoming*

THE WILLOW FLATS

too closely, it could be readily lured away with a "broken-wing act." The few pregnant cow moose that ambled through the area soon learned to avoid the vicinity of the beaver lodge after being fiercely attacked and pecked on its sensitive nose by the fearless male crane.

Occasionally the male would visit the nest and help with its construction. The week prior to egg-laying the pair mated almost daily, often between foraging sessions. Circling the female from behind, the male approached cautiously as the female tilted her head upward at a forty-five-degree angle while lowering and partially spreading her wings. He mounted her by placing his toes over the leading edges of her wings, lowering his feet so they rested on her wings, and grasped her nape with his bill. Slowly flexing his wings to maintain balance, the male quickly completed mating, then jumped forward to stand beside his mate in an arched-neck posture. Later, after the pair had preened at length, the female returned to her nest.

The female laid her first egg, a study in earth tones of brown, buff, and black, on May 13; the second on May 15. By then, not only was the lodge snow-free, but the pond was entirely thawed and snow was mostly limited to the interiors of the willow clumps that lined the pond. During the time between the laying of the two eggs, the female never left the nest. As soon as the second egg was laid, the male approached the nest, moved a few twigs around with his bill, and eased the female off the nest. Thereafter the two birds took turns incubating, often for sessions of several hours, with the female taking over in late afternoon to remain on the nest through the night, while the male stood guard nearby.

Within the crane's territory were a pair of nesting Wilson's snipes, one nest each of green-winged teal and mallards, and several pairs of yellow warblers and common yellowthroats. Each of these species was as closely tied to the willows as the moose and beaver. The snipes and ducks nested at the base of willow clumps, and the warblers nested in the crotches of branches. The male warblers persistently advertised their territories with singing, but the male ducks had already abandoned their mates and were gathering with others in small groups along the shore of Christian Pond. Every morning and evening was marked by the distinctive sound of winnowing snipe. High above the marsh the male performed an undulating territorial flight consisting of climbs alternating with shallow dives, while simultaneously spreading his outer tail feathers as far as possible. These narrow feathers were set into noisy vibration, which was regularly interrupted as his moving wings intercepted the airflow. After several minutes of circling the beaver pond, the snipe suddenly raised his wings nearly vertically and dropped quickly back into the marsh near the crane nest.

With the laying of her second egg, the female crane or her mate remained constantly on the nest, inconspicuously observing activities around the pond and periodically turning their heads sideways to watch a pair of red-tailed hawks wheeling in the sky, seemingly sweeping it clean with their orderly convolutions.

On Blacktail Butte to the south, the old dirty snow was gradually replaced with the pink tones of springbeauty blossoms. Nearby a male bald eagle kept his daily heraldic vigil near the top of a dead cottonwood, patiently staring at the rushing water below him, as if trying to extract some hidden meaning (other than a fish meal) from the swirling currents.

ABOVE. *Sandhill crane, adult calling*

By early June the lifeless brown willow flats had been transformed into a brilliant green, and the rich, brown-stained plumage of the nesting cranes had become increasingly conspicuous to the ravens that made periodic inspection flights over the beaver pond. The morning din of warblers, snipes, and chorus frogs began progressively earlier, and the eastern face of Mount Moran became ever more pink with alpenglow each morning as the sun neared the northern end of its seasonal circuit.

In mid-June, thirty days after the cranes began incubating, one of the two eggs began to click and vibrate as a tiny excavation appeared at its larger end. The female sat even more closely, only occasionally standing up to look at the pipping egg and sometimes to move it gently with her bill. Then she would settle back down, aligning the eggs so they rested on either side of her breastbone parallel to each other. After twenty-four hours of pipping, the first chick finally kicked free of its shell and lay cold and wet in the nest. Its golden brown down soon dried, and the chick was quickly transformed into an enchanting fluff of newly minted gold, with a pale-tipped pink bill and sprawling, pinkish-blue legs and feet that seemed three times too large for its body. The female reached down and slowly nudged the chick with her bill until it moved to the warm pocket of safety between her flanks and her folded wings, and then settled back down to await the hatching of her second egg, which was just starting to pip.

Within a few hours the chick peeked out from the bend of its mother's wing and tried to climb up onto her back. By then the mother had crushed the remains of the hatched egg. After eating most of it herself, she held tiny fragments before the chick's bill. Perhaps responding to its whiteness, the chick opened its bill and began to nibble at the bits of shell. Soon it was scrambling actively over the mother's back, and as the male climbed back onto the nest to take over tending the remaining egg, the chick followed its mother as she slowly moved away from the nest. Floating lightly on the water, the chick quickly paddled behind its wading mother, occasionally stopping to peck at a bit of floating debris or a swimming insect. Soon it tired and moved back to the nest where it snuggled close against its father's underwing. When its mother finished foraging, she returned to the nest and pushed her mate aside. Through the night the female tended her chick and the still-pipping egg, but by the following dawn the second chick was also free of its shell and drying in the nest beside its older sibling.

By noon the second chick was dry and actively wriggling around in the nest with its mother. The other chick tagged closely behind the adult male, which ever more impatiently

ABOVE. *Sandhill crane, chick and hatching egg*

OVERLEAF. *A female greater sandhill crane on its nest protecting young from a June snowfall as its mate stands guard, Yellowstone National Park, Wyoming*

began to stray farther from the nest toward heavier cover provided by aspens and cotton-woods. Soon the female, in response to the repeated soft calls of her mate, stood up in the nest, nudged the chick with her bill, and called softly. Responding with a peeping note, the youngster stood on its gangling legs and followed her as she gradually moved toward her mate. Then, with the male in the lead, the older chick at his heels, the female next in line, and the young chick beside her, the family slowly moved away from the nest for the last time. In its cup the crumpled remains of the second eggshell were the only evidence of the drama that had so recently unfolded.

By the time they were only a week old, the two crane chicks had grown remarkably and could realistically be called colts. The color of golden palominos, the chicks were also becoming much stronger. They were easily able to stride through tall grasses where only a few days before they would have stumbled or become entangled in foliage. Insects abounded in the grasses. While their parents searched for succulent herbs growing in moist pockets, the colts specialized in insect-chasing. Each was tended by one parent, who kept them well separated. This prevented the slightly older and larger colt from chasing and fighting with its younger sibling and competing for food. Only at night, when the female bedded down in heavy grass cover to brood them both, did the two colts come into close physical contact. One chick snuggled under each of their mother's slightly raised and folded wings. The female thus slept with her bill tucked back into her shoulder feathers. In this relaxed posture her bare crown skin was retracted into a small area above and in front of the eyes, contrasting strongly with its greatly expanded area when she was alert or frightened.

After the colts were a month old they had increased almost tenfold in weight, from five ounces to nearly three pounds, and stood nearly two feet tall. Two weeks later their flight feathers began to break out of their sheaths. By the time they were two months old they were attempting their first short flights. Weighing almost six pounds and nearly as tall as their parents, their cinnamon downy coats had been worn away except for a few frayed wisps at the back of the head, on the back, and on the wings. The newly developing feathers looked much like those of the adults, but had tawny to rust-colored tips. Unlike their bare-crowned parents, the colts had entirely feathered crowns. When called by their parents, they quickly responded with peeping calls, but with each passing day their call seemed to acquire more of a rolling character and began to sound like *peee-r-r-r-r*. Soon they began to take short daily flights with their parents, moving from the wooded bottomlands to the sage-covered flats near the river. There they fed while their parents spent many hours preening away their shabby and brown-stained breeding plumage to expose the incoming, smoke-gray winter plumage. Both adults had molted their flight feathers in late June, shortly after their chicks had hatched. By the time the colts fledged in late August, the parents were also back in perfect flying condition.

As the increasingly cooler days of August passed, the colts became stronger flyers and progressively safer from unexpected attacks by coyotes. Thus, the birds spent ever more time foraging in the open sagebrush flats, where the youngsters ineffectively but excitedly chased grasshoppers and the adults methodically probed the gravelly soil for fleshy bulblets and roots. Now and then a family of foraging Canada geese shared the same area, but the Canada geese were increasingly gathering into flocks and moving toward small lakes. Each night the cranes rested in the cover of the aspens and awakened in the morning to find thin ice covering their previously invulnerable beaver-pond refuge, thus increasing the possibility of a nocturnal stalk by coyotes. Around them the aspens were turning golden yellow and starting to drop their summer-worn leaves into the pond's dark waters.

Eight

The Pond

ONLY A FEW HUNDRED YARDS EAST OF AN ELE-
gant hotel overlooking Jackson Lake lies a small, shallow pond in a depression in the glacial moraine. It is
annually recharged by snow meltwater, and its outlet
into Christian Creek has long been efficiently dammed by beavers.
At its deeper southern end an extensive bed of bulrushes fringes the
shoreline. The central portion is fairly deep, open water, and the
northern end merges into a succession of communities dominated by
emergent rushes, low grasses and sedges, and willow thickets. Thus, in
a very small area a remarkably diverse and highly productive aquatic
ecosystem has developed. Its architects and resident landlords are beavers, which provide rent-free space from ice breakup in mid-May until
freeze-up in late October. Its prime tenants are a pair of trumpeter
swans.

As the pond became progressively ice-free in early May, the waterfowl and shorebirds that had been using Jackson Lake and the Snake River flocked to the food-rich waters of Christian Pond. Mallards, pintails, American wigeons, buffleheads, Barrow's goldeneyes, and ring-necked ducks were suddenly everywhere and were quickly followed by coots and yellow-headed blackbirds. White-crowned sparrows took up territories in the peripheral sage-covered hillsides, while yellow warblers and common yellowthroats claimed the willow thickets. Yellow-rumped warblers sang from the small cluster of conifers at the north end of the pond, and cliff swallows swarmed over the pond by the hundreds. When not feeding, they collected mud along Christian Creek to construct their nests on the underside of the bridge that crosses the creek.

The trumpeter swans, which spent most of the winter near Oxbow Bend of the Snake River only a mile south, moved onto the pond as soon as it started to become ice-free around the lip of the beaver dam. They immediately began investigating the dense stand of bulrushes at the southern end of the pond. Every year for more than two decades the swans had nested on the pond, usually on a mat of bulrushes from the previous year. They had raised dozens of young, which often remained in the same general area and sometimes tried to visit their parents' nesting pond. Although the pair freely mixed with their offspring on the wintering ponds, they would not tolerate them on their nesting territory and greeted their recognition calls with threats or even chases. Even less tolerated were "stranger" swans that sometimes flew overhead or attempted to land on the pond. Immediately the male would utter a challenge

and take flight by running at full speed over the water toward the intruders. This was usually enough to force the birds into full flight, whereupon the male would circle back and land with a skidding stop beside its waiting mate. Facing one another in the water, they would trumpet loudly and wave their wings excitedly in a mutual triumph ceremony. By these displays the pair had managed to maintain a close bond that would last throughout their lives.

As the female, or pen, began nest construction, she trampled the bulrushes into a well-packed mound. From this platform she reached out as far as her long neck would allow to gather additional bulrushes and add them to the mound. Soon she established a nearly bulrush-free moat around the nest as she added to its height, making it more conspicuous while providing 360-degree visibility. The male, or cob, assisted in a rather desultory way, generally swimming around the nest, gathering bulrushes from beyond where the pen on the nest could reach, and dropping them over his shoulder in the general vicinity of the nest. The pen then added them to the nest.

Within a week the nest was essentially complete, just as the pond was becoming completely ice-free. Each morning the pair spent an hour or two foraging. They also usually mated sometime during that period. Indeed, to the average observer the mating preliminaries looked no different from foraging behavior, as the swans swam side by side and repeatedly immersed their heads and necks in the water. However, their behavior gradually became more and more synchronized and increasingly began to resemble bathing movements. Soon the female lowered herself in the water and the male moved on top of her, grasping her nape in his bill and lowering his tail to meet her uplifted one. As mating terminated, the pair rose strongly in the water, trumpeted loudly while spreading their wings, and then gradually settled back into normal swimming positions.

The pen laid her first egg on May 10 and four more on alternate days thereafter. By May 20, the nest cup was filled with five white eggs. As egg-laying neared completion, the pen spent progressively less time away from the nest and began to add to it a sparse mixture of white down and breast feathers. Finally, after laying her last egg she settled down comfortably over the clutch and began her thirty-four-day incubation period. At the same time the male selected a mat of bulrushes about twenty yards away as a resting and waiting station, where he could watch the nest and have an unobstructed view of the marsh and surrounding hills.

There was little danger of predation from land mammals, since disturbance of the deep water around the nest would likely deter the hungriest coyote by announcing its presence. To be sure, a watchful raven frequented the lodgepole pines at the far end of the marsh. One morning during the pen's foraging break it apparently decided to test its chances. Taking off from the trees, the raven skirted the shoreline at a height of about thirty yards, tilting its head down slightly as it passed the nest, but continuing on without veering until it reached the far end of the pond. Then, it abruptly reversed its course and, when directly above the nest again, it suddenly spiraled down toward the down-covered clutch of eggs. At that moment

ABOVE. *Trumpeter swan, adult wing-flapping*

the cob, feeding about fifty yards away, gave a loud alarm call and began running over the water in a frantic attempt to reach the nest before any of the eggs were destroyed. Just as the raven was starting to peck at the first egg, the cob arrived at the nest. Jumping into the air, the raven eluded the swan's charge and flew quickly to a high perch in the lodgepole pines. From there it watched as the swans performed a prolonged and noisy triumph ceremony at the nest, and the female again settled down on the undamaged clutch.

As the pen continued incubating, the marsh became a remarkably noisy place. Wilson's snipes that had taken up territories at the meadow-like northern end of the marsh performed their daily winnowing displays. The deeper end of the pond was being fully occupied by dozens of coots and yellow-headed blackbirds. Both of these species require emergent vegetation for nesting as well as open water for foraging. The coots were especially aggressive in staking out territories, often engaging in spirited battles over the choicest stands of bulrushes, with wing-beating, biting, and foot-scratching. Ultimately one combatant would get the worst of the battle and turn tail, skulking off through the reeds with its tail raised and the two white undertail patches looking like little beacons against a black background. The most aggressive males continued to cruise over their territories with the persistence of coast guard patrols, swimming to and fro, heads low over the water and wings lifted, challenging all comers.

The yellow-headed blackbirds likewise lost very little time initiating their breeding activities. Unlike the Brewer's blackbirds nesting in the sedge and willow flats to the north, or the redwings simultaneously taking up territories around a small, lily-covered pond to the west, the yellow-headed blackbird makes tall bulrush stands the center of its world. Some males were soon spread over the stand of rushes, each announcing his territorial occupancy by perching on one of the tallest rushes, spreading his tail and partially opening his wings, then bending forward, craning his neck, and uttering a hoarse, rasping call. Within a few days, females and immature males also began arriving, causing the males to rise to ever greater levels of display. Each male attempted to attract more than one female into his territory if possible, but in contrast to the red-winged blackbird, many yellow-heads remained monogamous. This is probably because, unlike the red-wings, yellow-headed blackbird males regularly help gather food for the young and particularly help feed their initial mate's brood. Thus, while red-winged blackbird males sometimes have as many as six females nesting within their territory, yellow-heads rarely have more than two.

Some late arrivals to the pond were two pairs of pied-billed grebes and a small flock of ruddy ducks. Arriving in May, the inconspicuous pied-billed grebes soon divided the pond roughly in half, one pair occupying the bulrush-filled end and the other retreating into the shallower area, from which their calls emanated every day; but they rarely appeared in open water. By contrast, the ruddy ducks remained in a small flock through May and well into June. The sienna-red males occasionally initiated a brief burst of display by chasing one another or jockeying for position in front of one of the unattentive females. Once in position, the males would cock their long tails, inflate an air sac in the neck, and begin a long series of rapid tapping movements of their bills against their necks. With each stroke, the tail was more strongly cocked and air forced from beneath the breast feathers, forming a ring of bubbles around the displaying bird's breast. As the series of strokes ended, the bird pushed his cobalt-blue bill forward, opened it, and burped. The females remained magnificently indifferent to these incredible proceedings, not only rejecting the opportunity to follow the drakes but even gaping at them if they approached too closely.

The sage-covered hills were equally alive with newly resident birds. White-crowned sparrows were especially noisy as they sang from sagebrush or low aspens only a few feet above the belt of willows lining the pond. Each white-crowned sparrow territory contained three basic elements: grass, bare ground, and shrubs. Most also included part of the shoreline of Christian Pond and often encompassed some of the taller aspens growing on the hilltop above it. The amount of grass and bare ground was always adequate to provide foraging opportunities but not so great that the birds were unnecessarily exposed to danger. Sturdy sagebrush and other shrubs likewise provided nesting cover but were not so dense as to separate the birds too far from their favored ground-foraging areas.

As the male white-crowned sparrows sang their plaintive whistling song repeatedly from the tops of the sagebrush, the females began fluttering their wings and uttering low, metallic trills. A male would respond by chasing the female with beak-jabbing and by following her about persistently, singing loudly until mating occurred. A few days prior to mating, the female began to pick up twigs and grasses and even started constructing a nest in a low sagebrush bush. Within a week the nest was completed, and the first of three eggs was laid in mid-June. With completion of her clutch the female began incubating, while the male even more strongly advertised his territorial boundaries.

As June matured, the hillsides beside Christian Pond flushed golden with balsamroot, willows along its shore cast out clouds of yellow pollen, and new growth of bulrushes gradually began to hide the incubating pen swan, which had rarely left her nest for more than a few minutes since incubation had begun. She would occasionally lower her long neck to drink, but in contrast to the male, she never took long daily foraging trips to the middle of the pond where coots, ring-necked ducks, and lesser scaups foraged by the dozens. Around the margins of the pond surface-feeding ducks such as wigeon, mallards, and teal milled about. On the deepest parts, a few male Barrow's goldeneyes and buffleheads were always loafing away the days while their mates incubated clutches in hollow trees in the adjacent woods.

The pen seemed unusually restless the morning of June 24. She repeatedly stood up, lowered her bill beneath her belly, and readjusted the eggs as if to make herself more comfortable. From each egg came soft clicking sounds; the cygnets inside had broken through their air sacs and were slowly chipping away at the inner surface of the shells with their egg teeth. As the pen rose to stretch, she dropped her wings slightly, as if to shield the hatching eggs from the sun. The cob, noticing the pen's slight change in posture, positioned himself closer to the nest.

By evening only three of the five eggs had hatched. One was infertile, and the remaining unhatched egg had been only partially pipped before the cygnet within exhausted its energy and died. Two of the hatched cygnets were covered with a slightly gray-toned whitish down, which graded to pure white on the front of the head and extended out on the top of the pinkish bill to a narrow point. Their large and ungainly feet were pink. The third cygnet was of the much rarer white phase and lacked the gray tones of its broodmates. All through the evening the female sat tightly on the nest, preventing the squirming mass of cygnets below her from peeking out from beneath. Even in late June the nights of Jackson Hole are

FACING PAGE. *Incubating trumpeter swan, June, Lamar Valley, Yellowstone National Park , Wyoming*

sometimes very cold, and chilling or other weather-related factors seem to be serious sources of mortality in cygnets during their first few weeks of life.

The following morning dawned clear and calm. As the morning mists slowly burned off Christian Pond, the cygnets began to peek from under the sides and rump feathers of their mother, trying to see the world about them. Early that morning the cob moved in beside the pen and soon began to energetically clear bulrushes from around the nest. Ripping and pulling out the new growth, he piled it onto the nest, at times almost covering the cygnets. All morning he continued clearing until by noon the nest was six inches higher and the surrounding area was again barren of emergent plants.

The cygnets weren't the only brood to appear on the pond that day. A female Barrow's goldeneye suddenly materialized with an entourage of nine black-and-white ducklings, having brought them to the pond from their nest in a nearby hollow aspen, where they had hatched the previous day. As their mother led them out on the pond, they followed in a cluster immediately behind her while she cleared the route of coots and ruddy ducks by threats and attacks. In her zealous efforts to attack all waterfowl in sight, she at times totally neglected her own brood, which began to scatter and lose sight of their mother. As they swam past the swan nest, plaintively peeping, both swans ignored them, and several soon became lost in the maze of bulrushes.

Near noon, the cob finally stopped his nest-building and swam away to feed, followed closely by the three cygnets. The pen remained on the nest, still covering her two unhatched eggs. Toward mid-afternoon, after carefully covering the eggs with down, she too left the nest and joined the family foraging in the middle of the pond. As the cygnets picked small invertebrates from the water surface, she and her mate reached to the bottom of the pond, pulling up pondweeds. The cygnets swam closely behind their parents, quickly consuming plant fragments and small insects brought to the surface in their parents' wake. Often one of the adults stopped to make vertical foot-paddling movements. This created strong turbulence that carried additional organisms from the bottom of the pond to the top. Small beetles, crustaceans, and insect larvae were caught by the youngsters as soon as they appeared, and the cygnets swam repeatedly from one parent to the other as they tried to satisfy their vast appetites.

As the swan brood foraged, the coots followed behind as closely as possible, picking up vegetation torn from the bottom by the swans. Wigeons and gadwalls followed slightly farther behind, always staying well out of pecking distance of the adult swans. By then, many of the coots were incubating full clutches in the bulrushes, and most of the male ducks were beginning to molt their colorful breeding plumage. The foraging coots were mostly pairs that had been incubating eggs since the first week in June, and the three-week incubation period was nearly over. Although the males had done most of the incubation, the females took on these duties during hatching. Since incubation began before the clutches were complete, the coot eggs hatched at different times. Within a day or two, several nests contained three or four active chicks. Then the females often called their mates to care for the remaining unhatched eggs and left with the early hatchlings. Tagging closely behind her, the striking golden-red and blackish chicks with scraggly down on their heads clustered tightly about their mother as she immersed her head in the water and pulled up plants. After patiently tending the

remaining eggs until
most had hatched,
the males too left
the nest, leaving
any unhatched eggs
to be eaten by sharp-eyed ravens
or magpies that happened to find them.

By this time, the begging sounds of young
yellow-headed blackbirds in their deeply cupped
and semidomed nests produced a nearly constant
background noise, interrupted by the frequent chattering of coots.
Ruddy duck males in full breeding plumage patrolled their bulrush-lined
territories vigilantly searching for intruders, while their mates closely huddled over clutches
of chalky-white eggs that seemed far too large to have been laid by them.

Every morning for the next few weeks the swan family swam from its brooding place on
an old beaver lodge to the middle of the pond, with the cob in the lead, the cygnets in the
middle, and the pen behind. Each day the pond's surface seemed to be increasingly occupied
by new waterfowl broods and littered with feathers from molting adults. Two weeks after
the cygnets had hatched, the pen began to lose her flight feathers. The male had become
flightless almost three weeks earlier and was ending his molt and flightless period of about a
month at the time that the female became flightless.

As July passed, the cygnets grew rapidly. From their hatching weight of seven ounces,
they increased nearly tenfold their first month. By the end of August they weighed nearly
sixteen pounds, a thirtyfold increase in about two and a half months. By then the cygnets
had attained their full juvenile plumages. Two were normal brownish-gray, but the one
that had been pure white when hatched had developed into an immaculately white juvenile
that was nearly indistinguishable from its parents. The calls of the cygnets also gradually
changed from flutelike piping notes to more wavering calls sounding like toy trumpets, but
they still lacked the volume and resonance of the adults' calls. Their bills slowly changed
from pinkish to olive black, and their legs and feet became more grayish and ultimately,
black.

By early August the yellow-headed blackbirds were all fledged, the earliest of the duck
broods had left the pond, and the last broods were appearing. Two female ruddy ducks
emerged from their nests in dense bulrush clumps with broods of four and five young, which
were miniatures of their mothers. Little heeding their mothers, the precocious ducklings
soon strayed. One joined the brood of a lesser scaup, another was pecked to death when it
approached too closely an adult coot feeding its young, and a third became lost and froze to
death the following night.

Thin ice was forming periodically along the shore of the pond, and aspens were starting
to sprinkle the slopes of Lozier Hill with golden flecks. The cygnets were still a month from
fledging but were large enough to be safe from freezing or predators. Not until the end of
September would they finally fledge, more than three months after hatching. Remarkably,
all three survived the long fledging period, a better rate of success than that of most years.

ABOVE. *Ruddy duck, male in
courtship display*

OVERLEAF. *A trumpeter
swan pair taking off, Flat
Creek, National Elk Refuge,
Wyoming*

NINE

The Oxbow Bend

FROM HIS PERCH IN THE TALL COTTONWOOD edging the Snake River, the male bald eagle scanned the river downstream toward Oxbow Bend. A half mile away a pair of ospreys was diligently fishing where the river encircles a wooded island and the main channel turns sharply southward along the base of Signal Mountain. Twelve feet below him his mate had just laid her first egg in a gigantic nest of twigs and branches. Both birds were nearly five years old and in full adult plumage. They had selected this nesting site the year before, spent months constructing the nest, and gone through all the motions of breeding, but the female had not laid any eggs. After spending a month in the area, they had gradually abandoned the nest and moved to a more secluded part of the river.

It was early April, and although the river was ice-free, the land still lay under several feet of snow. The ospreys were still a month away from the start of their nesting, although last year's nest still perched conspicuously on the top of a tall lodgepole pine, only a few dozen feet from a group of equally large and also uninhabited great blue heron nests. Few of the herons had returned to the area, and none had yet attempted to establish territorial rights. Thus, the eagles and the ospreys maintained almost exclusive fishing rights to this stretch of river. To be sure, a few common mergansers sometimes patrolled its edges, and a frolicking family of otters occasionally passed downstream, but there was more than enough fish for all.

The bald eagle nest was a ponderous structure, about sixty feet up in an old, slowly dying cottonwood, which was being gradually undercut by the swift river. In March both eagles began adding to and refurbishing their nest. They collected broken branches on the ground, or more frequently flew full force against dead branches of standing trees, breaking them off with their feet and carrying them to the nest. The largest branches, as much as three feet long and two inches in diameter, were held by the talons, while smaller ones were carried in the beak. After establishing the new nest platform, the eagles added dead grass, weeds, and clods of earth that were incidentally attached to roots. Flying over the nest with a bundle of grass in his claws, the male would drop it into the nest while the larger female would work it into the interstices of the branches and twigs.

Within a few days they had completed a mattress-like layer of grass and straw around the raised margin of the nest surface, and by the beginning of April the nest was finally ready to receive its first eggs. Each morning during that week the female perched for a time

OVERLEAF. *Three bald eagles share a tree on neighboring perches above the Lamar River, Yellowstone National Park, Wyoming*

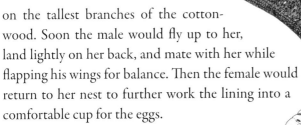

on the tallest branches of the cottonwood. Soon the male would fly up to her,
land lightly on her back, and mate with her while
flapping his wings for balance. Then the female would
return to her nest to further work the lining into a
comfortable cup for the eggs.

She laid her first egg April 4 and two more
at intervals of three days each, so that on April
10 a full clutch of three dull white eggs were being
warmed beneath her. After laying the first egg the female remained on the nest nearly constantly. Whenever she left it for any period, the male would harass and dive at her, driving her back to the nest. Soon, however, he began to help with incubation. Changeovers in
nest-tending were achieved by attracting the mate to the nest with a simple chittering call.

For more than a month the two eagles guarded the nest assiduously. The first egg
hatched on May 9, thirty-five days after being laid. The second hatched two days later, but
the third embryo had died during development. As the two eaglets dried, their smoky gray
body down contrasted with whitish down on the head, chin, and underparts. Weighing only
three ounces at hatching, the chicks opened their eyes a few hours later and almost immediately begged for food. When the first egg hatched, the male began to bring in food, primarily
suckers and other rough fish. After dropping it into the nest both parents tore the fish into
tiny bits and gently passed them to the hungry chicks.

Within a week, both eaglets had grown substantially and had even begun to wave their
stubby, down-clad wings. There was plenty of food for both eaglets, but the earlier-hatched
bird, a female, was always fed first and soon was substantially larger than her broodmate. For
the first few weeks after hatching, the female closely brooded her offspring each night, rak-
ing up the dead grass and leaves around her huddled body as the sun dropped behind Mount
Moran. Her mate spent the night about twenty feet away on a higher branch of the same
tree, his white head catching the last rays of the setting sun and the feathers tinted reddish
in the evening afterglow.

During the day each adult alternately foraged and tended the nest. By the end of May
both eaglets were large enough to peer over the rim of the nest and watch for the arrival of
their parents. As one appeared in the distance, the eaglets peeped excitedly, anticipating the
feeding soon to follow. When the young were five weeks old, they weighed over four pounds
and were starting to replace their down with juvenile feathers. By then they could tear up
their own food when it was dropped in front of them, but they could still barely rise on
their toes and take a few halting steps. Most of their waking hours were spent preening and
manipulating their rapidly growing primaries, which were already about half of their ultimate length. Fluffs of down from the tops of their incoming juvenile feathers lodged in the
edges of the nest or were carried away by the wind until caught in vegetation or were snapped
up by tree swallows for lining their own nests.

By their sixth week, the eaglets were fully into their brown juvenile plumages, sleek and
shiny, and with their flight feathers approaching full length. Now the eaglets watched and
waited even more impatiently as their parents constantly flew back to the nest with fish, and

ABOVE. *Bald eagle,
adult in flight*

began screaming with excitement whenever they came into sight. Even the sight of a flying osprey carrying a fish excited them, since the adult eagles frequently dove on the ospreys until they were forced to drop their newly caught prey.

The ospreys too had been busy the past few weeks. A lightning-rent snag in a group of tall lodgepole pines on the Oxbow held a nest that the ospreys had used for several years. From it the territorial pair could not only fish about a mile of the river and the adjoining backwaters of the Oxbow but also fly the short distance to Emma Matilda Lake and scan its clear water whenever the Snake River became too turbid for easy fishing.

In early April most of the great blue herons had returned either to a rookery in a stream-side grove of cottonwoods immediately upstream from the village of Moose or to Oxbow Bend, where another rookery was in lodgepole pines. Over the years, heron wastes had increasingly fouled the trees and begun to kill some of them, so the remnants of the previous year's nests protruded conspicuously above the tree line. Adults of both sexes were arriving at the same time. Males that were at least three years old tried to reclaim their old nest sites, leaving the two-year-olds to try to establish territories at the edges of the colony. Gaining possession of an old nest gave a male a great advantage, since it provided the primary location from which mating displays could be performed.

One of the first males to return to the colony established his territory on the highest of the old nests and immediately began displaying. The most conspicuous of his displays was a slow, smooth lifting of his head and bill toward the vertical, stretching his neck to the utmost and uttering a low moan. This display informed passing females of his availability for mating and would later be used as a greeting between mates during nest-building and nest-relief ceremonies. In another display he moved his head forward while erecting the plumes of the neck, breast, and body. When the neck was nearly straight, he would clack his mandibles together and bend his legs. This display also informed females of his availability and probably also warded off other males. Sometimes the male would take off and fly in a rather large circle while beating his wings slowly and noisily and with his neck fully extended rather than retracted on his shoulders.

After a few days of these activities, the male finally attracted a female to his nest platform. Erecting all his plumes and standing as tall as he could, he suddenly made a bill-stabbing lunge toward the female's head, with his bill closed and his wings extended. Easily avoiding the thrust, the female simply stood her ground with open bill and awaited the next lunge. This time she simply caught the male's bill in her own and held tightly, producing a kiss-like clinch that the birds held for several seconds. After a few such exchanges the male began to tolerate his nest partner, and the female avoided most confrontations whenever the male approached too closely by keeping her eyes averted, her head low, and her crest depressed and by industriously poking at twigs in the nest.

Soon both of them, but especially the male, were gathering sticks to bring to the nest, usually simply stealing them from nearby nests. As the male returned with a stick and passed it to his new mate, she shoved it with a trembling movement into the nest platform. No lining was added to the nest. The first egg was simply deposited on the flattened platform a few days after the female had joined and been accepted by the male. Like most other pairs in the colony, this female eventually produced three eggs, each at two-day intervals. During egg-laying the pair spent much of their time on the nest, mating frequently and often gathering additional twigs. After every mating the male flew off to get a twig to present to his mate for addition to the nest. However, after the clutch was completed and incubation began, only the incubating bird tended the nest while the other fished or stood some distance away.

The pair regularly took turns incubating. When one descended to the nest to replace its mate on the eggs, it would extend its neck, erect its crest, and call repeatedly. The sitting bird would respond with a neck-stretching display and then fly away, leaving the eggs to be tended by the newly landed mate. Often before the bird settled on the clutch, it would readjust the twigs on the platform by shoving some of their ends a bit farther into the nest or roll the eggs about with its bill.

From the start of incubation until the young were nearly three weeks old, the nest was almost never untended, for the colony was constantly watched by ravens. So long as the ospreys were close by, there was little danger of raven attacks, but occasionally the entire colony would be put to flight by passing canoeists. Then the herons would race to get back to the nests first.

The osprey pair began nesting about the same time as the herons. The male arrived before the female and immediately began to make display flights above the nesting area and add materials to the nest. Like the eagles, he sometimes broke small branches from trees while flying but also often picked up materials from the ground. When his mate returned, she too gathered nest materials but concentrated on smaller twigs and on moss and bark for nest lining. By the first week in May they had renovated their treetop nest.

From the time the female arrived, she spent nearly all of her time tending the nest, while the male alternately gathered nest materials and fished. The birds mated frequently during this period, often on the nest but sometimes while perched in a nearby tree. The pair initially roosted some distance from the nest at night, but the night before she laid her first egg the female remained on the nest and deposited her first egg the next morning. Two additional eggs were laid the next several days, but from the laying of the first egg the birds never left the nest uncovered. From the first day, the male participated in incubation, but the female always spent the night on the nest and also tended it for much of the day.

Thus, the male was kept busy fishing for both adults. When he returned to the nest to take over incubation, he usually brought a fish for her. As he settled over the eggs, she flew to a nearby perch to consume her food. In the third week of June, thirty-seven days after incubation began and about ten days after the heron eggs were hatching, the osprey eggs also hatched. They hatched in the same sequence and at the same intervals as they had been laid; thus the oldest appeared nearly a week before the youngest. With the hatching of the first egg the male stopped nest-tending and fished full time. He brought fish to the nest and passed them to the female; she tore them into tiny pieces and carefully fed them bill-to-bill to each of the young.

BELOW. *Osprey, adult landing at nest*

As the young birds grew, they were brooded progressively less by the female, but during rain or hailstorms she huddled over them and sat out the storm. During one storm the youngest and weakest chick was fatally chilled, but even with one less offspring in the nest the two remaining soon nearly filled it. After they were nearly a month old they required little parental attention. They spent much of their time viewing the heron colony activities and flapping their rapidly growing wings, attentively watched by their parents from a nearby tree.

By early August, when the eldest of the young herons were starting to take tentative flights from their nests, the osprey family was growing apace. Finally, by the middle of the month, as the young ospreys approached eight weeks old, the older one boldly climbed to an outer branch and launched itself into the air. Within a few days its younger sibling was also fledged, and thereafter the birds spent their days practicing flying skills and trying to catch fish for themselves. Often they returned to the nest to consume their prey, but as August passed, less and less time was spent in the nesting area.

Finally, by the end of August, both the osprey eyrie and the heron colony were deserted. Only the deteriorating remains of a few baby herons that had fallen from their nests and died testified that the colony had bustled with life but a few weeks earlier.

Ten

The Aspen Island

LIKE RANDOMLY SHAPED PIECES in a gigantic ecological jigsaw puzzle, the aspen groves of Jackson Hole form a series of golden-green islands of various sizes in a matrix of silvery green sage. Sometimes they form a narrow belt between the sagebrush flats and the darker green conifers on the mountain slopes, often growing on low moraine hills shaped by the last glacier about 14,000 years ago. Each aspen grove is virtually an island unto itself, often made up of genetically identical descendants that sprout and spread from the roots of a single seedling. Sometimes a "fairy ring" of young aspens forms around an older tree or group of trees, with the ring gradually expanding at its perimeter but with the older dying aspen at the center being replaced with grass and other nonwoody vegetation. More often, however, the new sprouts are avidly browsed by elk, moose, and other mammals, which pull down any branches they can reach and even gnaw the bark during winter. Beavers also preferentially cut aspens for food whenever the trees are near enough to water. The older aspens are often destroyed faster than new sprouts can proliferate. Thus, many aspen islands, instead of growing and encroaching on the sagebrush flats, die out from continued browsing, and the sagebrush sea eventually covers the dead aspens.

One aspen island on a north-facing hillside overlooking the Buffalo Fork River east of Moran was the year-round home of a pair of ravens. From leaf fall in October until the first opening of leaves and flower buds in May, the aspens stand gaunt and white against the sky, offering little cover for the ravens. Occasionally a ruffed grouse will fly up into the branches and nip off the developing buds, but the ravens depend on the vagaries of fate to provide a supply of road-killed mule deer, or they may resort to picking over the remains of elk that were killed during the hunting season or later died during the winter months.

In late February and early March the three-year-old ravens began serious work on their first nest in one of the oldest and tallest aspens at the edge of the grove, which provided unobstructed visibility of the surrounding valley. Carrying branches and sticks up to two feet long, the ravens gradually produced a bulky nest in a crotch near the center of the tree. This was lined with elk and moose hair, dried grasses, and mosses. During the warming days of March the ravens alternated between nest-building and performing courtship flights. Soaring on updrafts high above the valley, the male stayed slightly above his mate, with their wingtips nearly touching. Then they would dive nearly vertically for several hundred feet,

OVERLEAF. *A common raven, October, Yellowstone Lake, Yellowstone National Park, Wyoming*

the two birds tumbling over and over in the manner of tumbling pigeons, until nearly reaching the earth.

Each day, the ravens ranged widely over the territory, looking over the skeletons of long-dead elk slowly being exposed by the melting snow or picking through garbage dumps. Often they watched coyotes dig through a snowpack to expose a carcass; then they would fly to a nearby perch and wait patiently. Sometimes they had to wait until the coyote had eaten its fill, but more often they would try to sidle up to the carcass while the coyote was engrossed in its feeding. Snatching quick bites, they would fly back to the nearest perch, often just out of the frustrated coyote's reach. Soon magpies would join the party, goading the coyote into endless unsuccessful efforts to keep the birds from its hard-earned meal.

Their appetites temporarily stilled, the ravens often spent time at the garbage dump in Moran, tearing up bits of paper, playing king-of-the-mountain by pushing other ravens from the tops of gravel piles, or having free-for-all chases, with the leader carrying off small articles in its bill, to be passed from bird to bird as the chase progressed.

By the middle of April their nest was nearly completed, with its cup lined with aspen bark, moose hair, and grasses. By then the pair had stopped associating with the yearling and two-year-old nonbreeder flock. The male proclaimed his territory daily from the tallest trees in the aspen island, while constantly watching for intruders and noting every activity within his view. Yet the breeding ravens were surprisingly tolerant of the nonbreeders. When a flock of these noisy and playful ravens invaded their territory, the nesting pair simply watched them in resigned silence from near their nest. But a single raven or a small group was quickly chased from the hillside. No other raven nest was within a half mile of theirs, and they quickly claimed any road-killed rodent or other food that could be readily carried away.

Within a week after the nest lining was added, the first egg was laid. Thereafter the female laid an egg each day until she had completed a clutch of six. At least one raven remained at the nest from the laying of the first egg, and the female began incubating almost immediately. Her mate spent most of the day in a convenient lookout perch on a high aspen, but a few times each day the pair would fly off together to feed on a moose carcass nearby, never remaining more than about half an hour before returning to the nest.

Just three weeks after being laid, the first egg hatched, followed by four of the remaining ones on successive days. Thus, toward the end of May the nest was filled with five nearly naked young of various sizes. The remaining unhatched egg and the shells of those that had hatched were quickly removed by the female and dropped several hundred yards away, probably to reduce the chances of the nest being located by predators. Within a week of hatching, however, the nest became fouled with droppings from the youngsters and the uneaten remains of food brought to them. These included road-killed rodents and the eggs and nestlings of many bird species, particularly of great blue herons from the Oxbow colony. This area, only four miles away from the hillside nest, was a source of food for the ravens throughout May and June. Sitting on a nearby lodgepole pine, the male raven simply waited patiently until something startled the incubating herons. Frequently it was a bald eagle flying low past their nesting colony or a canoeist passing below. In any event, the slightest panic of the heron sent the raven into action. Flying full speed toward the nearest nest, it would land on its rim about the time the heron realized what was happening and uttered its croak of alarm.

Quickly piercing an egg or grabbing a nestling by the neck, the raven would drop out of sight into the trees and head back to its nest.

With such an abundance of fresh food, the young ravens grew fast and were well feathered by a month of age. At that age they often moved onto the edge of the nest where they would precariously perch and practice wing-flapping. The oldest sometimes ventured to the adjoining branches. One day in late June, just eight weeks after the first egg was laid, the nest was abandoned. The adults flew to a nearby tree and coaxed their unequally developed young to follow them. Although the older ones managed the flight without trouble, the youngest misjudged its landing badly and fell with a thud to the ground. Dazed but unhurt, it managed to reach a lower branch where the rest of the family joined it.

The frightened screams of the falling young raven wakened a calf elk that had been sleeping in low brush nearby and caused its mother to look about in mild alarm. The female elk had reached this area in early June. Accompanied by her yearling offspring, she had simply separated from the herd of other pregnant females and their young of the past year and sought a sunny slope rich in greening grasses. There, early on one crisp June morning, she lay down, licked her side and genitals carefully, and within twenty minutes gave birth to her calf. Then she thoroughly cleaned it with her long tongue. Within minutes the delicately spotted calf struggled to its feet on wobbling legs and nursed. The yearling moved closer to investigate this new competitor, but the cow laid her ears back and raised one front foot and her head, an unmistakable threat that caused the confused youngster to retreat and watch from a safer distance.

After the calf nursed, it dropped back down into the lush grass and slept. Its mother began grazing and moved slightly away from the resting calf. Frightened that it would be left behind, the calf tried to get up and follow, only to be pushed back down with the cow's foreleg. There it remained nearly motionless, moving only its ears to keep insects away and letting its bright brown eyes rove as far as possible without moving its head. Every few hours the cow returned to nurse the calf, but otherwise it was left alone. There was no real danger from coyotes by this limited abandonment, since very young calves have little scent. Coyotes often would walk within a hundred yards or less of the hidden and motionless calf, unaware of its presence. However, bears more methodically search the grasslands for calves and are a much more serious threat to newborn elk and pronghorns.

After it was about two weeks old, the calf began to move about and joined a "pool" of several calves. One or two adult cows guarded the calves while the other mothers grazed. This particular pool spent most of its time at the edge of the aspen grove, where the youngsters could lie in the morning sun yet quickly retire to heavy cover if necessary. By the time they were three weeks old the calves left the pool and moved about with their mothers. The yearlings, which learned from repeated threats or beatings to avoid associating with the mothers, formed a loose group of their own.

With the increased mobility of their young, the cows became restless. Soon the entire group moved out of the aspen grove and concentrated along Buffalo Fork River before migrating toward higher summer range in the Teton Wilderness Area. There on the river bank the cows familiarized their calves with water by playing splashing games and encouraging them to run through the water. In the middle of such a game, a wandering coyote

OVERLEAF. *Cow elk and calves gather in a nursery, July, Grand Teton National Park, Wyoming*

materialized close to one of the frolicking calves. Its mother quickly attacked the coyote, striking it with its front hooves. Fleeing as rapidly as possible, the coyote retreated into the safety of a mound of large rocks. Carefully sniffing the area, the cow finally discovered the hiding coyote and kicked him. The coyote then fled to a second hiding place, only to be sought out and flushed again. This time the coyote ran until it was out of sight; nevertheless the cow patrolled the area for several hours.

Finally the calves gained sufficient strength and self-confidence to allow the herd to continue its migration. Early one morning the cows led their month-old calves to the river, followed by those persistent yearlings still showing attachment to their mothers. Encouraging the calves to enter the water, the cows crossed immediately behind and downstream from their calves, where they could readily prevent them from being swept away if they fell into deep or swift water.

As the elk crossed the river they flushed a male green-winged teal. His mate had been incubating a clutch of eggs in a willow clump near the water until they had been found and eaten by a mink. By then the male had already abandoned his mate. He spent his time on small gravelly islands in the river, loafing and preening free the bright feathers of his nuptial plumage, which were gradually replaced by the duller and female-like tones of his eclipse plumage. Though still functional, his flight feathers were being pushed out by the buds of the new primaries. As the teal flew downstream, his labored flight was noted by a male prairie falcon circling high above. His eyrie, which overlooked a flat, sagebrush-covered valley, was in a rocky recess on the south-facing slope of the same hill that supported the aspen grove. The prairie falcon had been searching for his usual food, the abundant young Uinta ground squirrels just emerging from their burrows, but the obviously troubled flight of the teal caused the falcon to veer off course and fly parallel with the teal.

Normally, the swift and agile teal would be nearly on even terms with the falcon, but now the teal was at a distinct disadvantage and unaware of the falcon. When he was nearly abreast of the teal, which was flying only about fifty feet above the water, the falcon partially closed his wings and dived nearly vertically, the tips of his primaries vibrating in the more than 100-mile-per-hour wind. The teal, hearing the sound, tilted his head to look upward the instant before his back was raked by the falcon's talons with such force that the teal's neck was broken. The teal tumbled over and over to the ground beside the river, while the falcon turned quickly and followed the trail of floating feathers downward. Landing beside the dying teal, the falcon quickly bit through the bird's neck, then covered the carcass with outstretched wings as he rested before carrying the heavy prey back to his eyrie.

The prairie falcons had nested on this hillside for many years. The shady aspen-covered northern slopes provided abundant small birds for prey, and the sharply eroded and arid

ABOVE. *Prairie falcon, adult with green-winged teal*

southern slopes became snow-free early in March, thus exposing a nearly vertical rock face with innumerable crevices for hiding a nest. In past years the falcons had sometimes moved their nest, usually alternating between two sites, each with sheer rock faces above, a sheltered and nearly level ledge, and enough gravel for a nest scrape, and recessed enough to keep out most rain. The two falcons wintered separately in the Green River basin, feeding mostly on horned larks, and returned to Jackson Hole in March. They immediately examined their old nest sites and renovated one of them simply by removing some debris blown in during the previous autumn. Then they began a month of courtship and territorial flights, culminating in the laying of the first egg on May 4, followed by four more at daily intervals. From the laying of the first egg the female ceased to hunt. The smaller male hunted for them both. Several times a day he brought small prey to feed her, frequently mating with her during the same visit. But when the clutch neared completion and she started incubating, the male visited only occasionally, spending most of his time watching from a rocky outlook well above and about 100 yards away from the nest. Whenever he brought in fresh food for her, he took over incubation while she hungrily devoured the prey.

Hunting here was superb: red-winged blackbirds were nesting along the small creek that drained the valley, the aspen grove on the other side of the hill was teeming with juncos, tree swallows, and other songbirds, and Uinta ground squirrels swarmed over the valley floor. The clumsy and dull-witted ground squirrels were much easier prey than songbirds but required different hunting tactics. Instead of power diving, the falcon coursed swiftly along the ground nearly at shrub height, much like a goshawk, and knocked the rodents off their feet with a powerful blow of the talons.

About a month after incubation began, the falcon eggs hatched over a period of three days, the last on June 12. By then, many young ground squirrels were available, and the male easily provided adequate food for his larger mate and their brood.

One day the resident raven from across the hill ventured too close to the nest. The small male quickly took to the air, repeatedly uttering a hoarse alarm. Instantly the female flew from the nest in pursuit, gaining quickly on the slow-flying raven, which suddenly found itself defenseless and far from protective tree cover. As the female swooped, the raven closed both of its wings and plummeted to the ground like a rock, barely breaking its fall before hitting the rocky slope. Frantically escaping into a crevice, the raven huddled quietly as the female hawk repeatedly swooped past the opening, screaming in rage. Not until well after dark did the raven emerge and retreat quickly to its nest in the aspens.

ABOVE. *Prairie falcon, adult stooping*

ELEVEN

The Spruce Forest

THE RUFFED GROUSE MOVED BEFORE DAWN from his favorite roost in the aspen grove to his primary drumming log in a dense stand of tall spruce trees. Lying on the moist and still partially snow-covered soil were variably rotted logs of generations past. A carpet of soggy needles cushioned the grouse's footsteps as he approached the log in the half-light of the mid-May dawn. He lightly jumped onto the smaller end of the log and walked slowly toward its larger portion. A few feet from the end he stopped, turned his body at right angles to the log, placed his tail flush against its surface, and dug his claws tightly into the slightly decayed wood. Then, slowly at first but with increasing speed, he thrust his open wings forward and upward, stopping them abruptly before they struck each other, and quickly returned them for the next stroke. The dull, throbbing *brum-brum-brum-br-br-brrrrrrrrrrr* was the only sound in the hushed woods. Stopping between drumming sequences and listening intently, the male heard no challenge to his territorial proclamation. The only grouse whose territory was close to his had been killed by a northern goshawk only a few mornings previously. He had drummed too late in the morning to be safe. Hitting hard from behind, the goshawk knocked the grouse off his drumming log in mid-display. Only a few feathers remained scattered about the display log, which ruffed grouse had used for many years.

The spruce forest that was home and haven for the grouse and goshawk was on the Snake River floodplain near the village of Moose. The river with its cottonwood fringe comprised one boundary, while the steep slope rising to rock-strewn benches formed by earlier and higher river channels represented the other. Between them a few small creeks flowed slowly toward the river, interrupted repeatedly by beaver dams. A few of these dams created ponds sufficiently large and deep to drown the shoreline spruces and allow water lilies to grow. One such pond, Sawmill Pond, was the undisputed territory of a pair of trumpeter swans. The Colorado blue spruce forest behind it was the unassailable domain of a family of pine martens.

The martens' den was under an old deserted log cabin that in earlier days had been part of a dude ranch. The martens' home range extended from the cabin in all directions to include nearly a square mile. Within this dense spruce forest red squirrels were extremely abundant, and none were safe during the martens' daily excursions. Since the female had whelped in mid-April, she had remained in the den almost continuously, caring for the three pups. For their first month of life they nursed and slept but did little else. At the age of five weeks they opened their eyes. The female marten, slightly smaller than her mate and with a brighter yellow chest, had depended on the male to provide food for them both.

Each night the male silently left the den to search for prey, and while the female was actively nursing, he was forced to make several daytime excursions as well. Making a roughly circular trip through the forest, walking whenever possible on the upper surfaces of downed trees, he would frequently pause to stand on his hind legs to survey the landscape better. The daytime trips were largely frustrating; as soon as any red squirrel saw the marten, it retreated to the highest and most secure location and uttered a piercing chattering alarm. Having thus lost its cover, the marten moved quickly along its regular train, pausing only briefly to scan the thawing surface of Sawmill Pond.

The Sawmill Pond trumpeters had nested there for many years. Lacking the dense bulrush beds of Christian Pond, Sawmill Pond nevertheless provided abundant spatterdock water lilies and pondweeds for food. As the pond became ice-free in early May, the trumpeters claimed it all for their territory. They renovated their old nest on a pile of soil and beaver-gnawed branches at the base of four flooded spruces and a living alder clustered about twenty yards from one shore. The site was ideal. The spruce trunks and alder branches nearly hid the pen while she sat on the nest; yet she needed to move only a foot or so from the nest to be in water of swimming depth where food was abundant. Along the shore of the pond, Colorado blue spruce, lodgepole pine, and narrow-leaf cottonwoods grew thick and tall. A great gray owl pair had a nest in one of the tallest spruces, and two pairs of ring-necked ducks had been allowed to share the pond with the swans. A hen mallard was nesting under a willow clump not far from the pond, and a female Barrow's goldeneye nested in a hollow cottonwood. Farther away toward the Snake River, a pair of sandhill cranes occasionally trumpeted.

Only twenty yards from the swan's nest was a large beaver lodge. It was the home of two adult beavers, male and female, two two-year-old males, two young of the previous year, and a litter of three small kits born early in May. They had depleted their stored larder of willow and cottonwood branches during the long, unusually cold winter, but with the April thaw the male had been able to break through the thin ice near the lip of the dam and replenish their food supply. He also reestablished scent marks along the downstream edge of his territory where it abutted that of another colony. Every few yards along the shore he methodically spread a mixture of mud and vegetation out on the ground and deposited a few drops of oil from his castoreum gland.

After replenishing the scent marks, he began searching for food. Finding a young cottonwood about thirty yards from the dam, he stood up on his hind legs and braced himself with his tail. Then, reaching as high as possible, he cut a large bite from the side of the tree by chiseling with his two long lower incisors, with the smaller upper ones serving as a brace against which pressure could be exerted. Next he made another cut several inches lower and wrenched out the wood between the two cuts. Then he shifted slightly to one side and repeated the process. Soon he had completely girdled the tree, and not long afterward it fell fortuitously toward the pond. The beaver then cut away the bigger branches and hauled them to his food cache near the lodge. Hearing the tree fall, the yearling beavers soon appeared to help, and before the evening was over, all that remained was the largest part of the trunk, which would soon be stripped of bark and abandoned.

Also momentarily disturbed by the falling tree was a pregnant cow moose, which had been foraging with her yearling in the beaver pond. She was eight years old and unlikely to survive another year. The previous winter had ended none too soon, for she had lost much weight, and her badly worn teeth made browsing on willow shoots arduous. Her new spring pelage had finally covered all the scars left from a heavy tick infestation the previous winter and spring, but she moved ponderously through the beaver pond, as if every step were painful. The pond was the favorite part of her home range, which was only about a mile in diameter. Although many of the male moose using the same wintering area along the Snake River had moved as far as twenty miles toward higher mountain summer ranges, the female had scarcely shifted her daily pattern of activity. But she was in little danger in spite of her reduced mobility. Grizzly bears only occasionally appear in Grand Teton National Park, and wolves are still uncommon. Barring an accident, the cow would likely survive until winter starvation or disease finally took its toll. Almost miraculously, she had become pregnant the previous November. The pregnancy had caused additional physiological stress. Now she spent most of her time standing in the shallow pond pulling up water crowfoot and submerged pondweeds and retiring during the hottest part of the day in the shaded spruce forest, where she could leisurely browse thimbleberry and rusty-leaf menziesia shrubs.

The male pine marten largely ignored the beaver and the moose; neither was a threat nor a potential source of food. What the marten needed was a quick, easy kill to carry back to the den. As he climbed a spruce for a better view, his attention was drawn to a movement in a clearing near some old buildings. It was the location of a colony of Uinta ground squirrels. These common large rodents had emerged from hibernation in early April and begun breeding behavior almost immediately. Two months later, in early June, the young were emerging from their holes and beginning to explore their surroundings. Gaining confidence, they

ABOVE. *Marten, adult standing*

OVERLEAF. *Adult pine marten, January, Shoshone National Forest, Wyoming*

ranged well away from the security of their burrows. Other than perhaps chirping in alarm, the adults largely ignored their offspring once they began their aboveground life. On this occasion a young squirrel had wandered off into tall weeds. Unable to see above the vegetation, it had no warning of the marten. In a flash the marten pounced, crushed the ground squirrel's skull instantly, and, carrying its still-twitching body high above the ground, quickly returned to its den. The female marten greeted her mate with an excited note, and the nearly weaned litter eagerly fought over the prize. Again the male left the den to hunt but soon returned, this time with a junco he had chanced upon while it was incubating its nest at the base of a low shrub growing next to a lodgepole pine.

Scarcely five feet above the unfortunate junco, a female calliope hummingbird sat resolutely on her tiny nest of willow down, spider webs, bark and cone fragments, and lichens. The nest was beside two lodgepole pine cones and incredibly well hidden, looking just like another cone in the cluster. But the artistry did not end there. Besides its beautiful camouflage, a large, horizontal branch directly above the nest also hid it from above and helped to shield the incubating bird from rain. The nest tree was at the eastern edge of the forest where the earliest morning sunlight warmed the incubating female after a long and chilly night, during which her body temperature had dropped several degrees.

The female began her nest in early July when the aspens and willows were casting out great clouds of cottony seeds. The location was the same as the year before, so she merely had to renovate the old nest by raising its rim with a mixture of bark fragments and a binding of spider webs, which she wound around the nest while in flight. Next she firmly packed in a thick layer of willow down. As the nest grew to its eventual height of nearly an inch, she gathered bits of lichen from the bark of the nearby trees and neatly pasted them around its exterior with spider webbing until the whitish lining was completely obscured and the nest blended perfectly with its surroundings.

Although the female calliope mated with the same male as the previous year, this was purely by chance, since hummingbirds don't establish the monogamous pair bonds common to many other birds. The female, in seeking out her old nesting tree, had simply entered the territory of the same male that had defended the forest edge the previous year. Indeed, the male even perched in his usual position on top of a moose-browsed willow where the tiny creature had a commanding view of the clearing. Periodically he drove away any intruding male hummingbirds, including the larger black-chinned species, which sometimes flew into the meadow to feed on the abundant Indian paintbrush flowers just blossoming. Frequently, too, he sallied out to capture a passing insect. Sometimes even a robin would be persecuted by the diminutive bird, with the male towering high in the air before diving down on the confused intruder, which simply chose to disappear into the heavy forest rather than try to defend itself.

Whenever not occupied with such activities, the male calliope watched closely for any female hummingbirds attracted to the Indian paintbrushes and scarlet gilias. With the first arrival of a female, the male instantly flew off, gained altitude, and hovered almost seventy-five feet above her, orienting himself so the sun reflected from his iridescent throat patch toward the foraging female. Suddenly the tiny, inconspicuous object in the sky was transformed into a beam of ruby light. Then, shooting downward at full speed in a broad arc, he passed only a few feet above the female. Pulling out of his dive and soaring up again, he completed the arc, again hovering and flashing his gorget toward the female. After three such performances, the male landed on a nearby perch and continued to expose his magnificent coloration to her view. This female had not yet begun to nest and therefore was receptive to his attentions. Thus, within a few days, two females were nesting within his territory; yet he continued to look for more.

The female calliope incubating the first nest tended its two eggs almost without interruption for fifteen days. Taking short breaks to feed only during the warmest part of each day, she was showing signs of exhaustion. Only the night before she had sat tight on the nest throughout a violent wind, hail, and rainstorm, with her needlelike bill pointed directly upward and her wings spread over the nest cup to form a tiny cone off which the raindrops flowed. Amazingly, she and her eggs had survived the storm. Indeed, the eggs soon hatched. After they had finally kicked themselves free of their shells, the babies lay motionless on the floor of the nest, no larger than peas, virtually naked, and totally blind. Their tiny yellow bills were short instead of needlelike; yet they could gape, and when they did, the female carefully inserted her long tongue into their throats and regurgitated a mixture of nectar and tiny insects.

As the days passed, the babies slowly assumed a more recognizable form, and within ten days they were finding the tiny nest cup too small. By then, they were impossible to brood, even at night. As they grew, the combined bulk and weight of female and her young started to flatten the nest. By the time the babies were two weeks old they could remain on it only by standing side by side. The female was constantly busy bringing them nectar and insects, sometimes temporarily storing the insects in her throat but often carrying them in her bill and passing them directly to the youngsters.

As the young hummingbirds reached the end of their third week of life, they could hardly be distinguished from their mother. Now they spent much of their time flexing and tentatively vibrating their wings, and carefully venturing out on the branch beside their fully flattened nest. As one of the young thus exercised, it "raced" its wings more strongly than usual and briefly rose a few inches above its perch. Momentarily frightened, it settled back on the branch. But a few minutes later it tried again, and this time, rather than simply rising vertically like a helicopter, it shifted into forward gear and sped to a nearby branch. There it landed and rested while the other youngster watched. Later that day the other young hummingbird took off for the first time, and by the following day the nest was abandoned.

Twelve

The Cirque

THE LITTLE LAKE REMAINED TIGHTLY ICEBOUND in the spring sunshine, even though patches of green were appearing around its edges and white calthas and yellow avalanche lilies were poking their perennially optimistic blossoms through the quickly melting snow. Around the snow-hidden circular lake, named Solitude by some unknown explorer, a spectacular amphitheater rises sharply for nearly 1,000 feet. It closely clasps the lake in its rocky grasp except to the southeast, where the walls open to provide a stunning vista of a triumvirate of massive pinnacles, the Grand Teton, Mount Owen, and Teewinot Mountain. Melting snow and ice from the slopes of the glacial-carved cirque feeds the lake and, in turn, a tiny creek that flows steeply down Cascade Canyon to spill into Jenny Lake five miles away and more than 2,000 feet lower. Along the way, the stream tumbles through a magnificent forest-edged canyon, gaining strength from innumerable rivulets leaping down the mountainsides. A massive glacier once bulldozed down the same canyon, crudely gouging it into a broad, U-shaped valley. Now, however, the stream is only a few feet across in many places and choked with boulders and fallen trees. Small waterfalls commonly toss the stream into spray and foam.

One of these is a free fall of about ten feet where a rocky outcrop slowed the cutting edge of the creek. A small gray bird occasionally burst out from behind the streaming water like a shot from a hidden cannon or just as surprisingly flew full force into the misty spray from downstream. The pair of dippers that had built their nest behind the falls ranged up and down a half mile of Cascade Creek, strenuously defending their territory from other pairs upstream and downstream from them. They were intimately familiar with every twist and turn of their part of the creek, but virtually everything beyond it was terra incognita. The dippers invariably followed the winding stream when flying up or down it and rarely flew more than a few feet above the swirling waters.

During winter the dippers moved downstream toward Jenny Lake, but in spring they returned to their previous territory. Even before returning, the male began singing exuberantly. Indeed, both members of the pair sang loudly from January on, usually while perched on a rock in the middle of a stream, but the male was especially vocal while in the presence of his mate. At times they engaged in spirited chases, the male singing loudly while flying closely behind the female, which twisted and turned as if trying to escape, but which goaded the male to chase her whenever he seemed to tire of the game. Sometimes they collided in midair and tumbled together into the water, but mating occurred on a sandbar after the pair alighted there normally.

Their nest had been in the same location for several years. The dippers simply repaired it each year by adding grass and moss. It was a simple globular structure about the size of a football, with a downward-pointing entrance hole that opened toward the falling water. In fact, the outside of the nest was constantly moistened by the spray. But within this soggy structure was a cup of coarse, water-resistant grasses and a dry inner lining of leaves. Within a few days of replacing the inner lining, which the pair had removed the previous summer as soon as the young had fledged, egg-laying began. One egg was laid on each of four successive days.

Throughout this time, both dippers spent most of their time foraging in the rushing stream by flying headlong into the icy waters. As they entered the water they threw their wings out and back slightly and swam quickly to the stream bottom. They worked their way upstream by walking and using their wings, picking among the rocks for stonefly and mayfly larvae and occasionally also taking small fishes. When they had trouble finding food, they sometimes remained submerged for fifteen to twenty seconds but often popped back up to the surface after only five or ten seconds.

After completing her clutch, the female abandoned her food searches and incubated full time. The male was forced to work ever harder to obtain enough food for himself and his mate, since he fed her on the nest while she incubated. With the hatching of the young after some sixteen days of incubation, the situation changed. The female gradually assumed the initiative in food-getting, although she also brooded a good deal of the time the first week after hatching. With room for only one adult on the nest, the female would rise on her legs far enough to let the young poke their heads out from beneath her to receive their food when the male appeared at the nest opening. Frequently he carried a fecal sac away from the nest, but within a week after hatching the young birds began to extrude their capsules directly out the nest opening into the water below.

By then the young were extremely vocal, calling for food so loudly that they could be heard over the roar of the waterfall. Their dark, beady eyes watched every movement through the peephole in their nest. They had been in the nest for three weeks and had become so crowded that they could hardly move by the time they were twenty-four days old and finally ready to leave the nest. As their parents watched and called from below, the young birds fluttered down from the nest one by one. Although their wings were well grown, their tails were still fairly stubby. They moved awkwardly about the edge of the pool at the waterfall's base, testing the water with their toes, poking their heads underwater, and bathing in the shallows. But most of the time they explored the rocks around them, falling into crevices, climbing steep banks, and generally testing their coordination.

Beside the cirque-enclosed lake, where the sound of the distant waterfall was barely audible, the silence was occasionally broken by the groaning of heaving ice and by a plaintive bleating from near a boulder at the foot of a talus slope, where the rubble of uncounted millennia of erosion had come to rest in an uncertain truce with gravity. The face of the boulder jutted out toward the top, forming a parapet below that was somewhat sheltered from the wind and rain. Peering out occasionally from this refuge was a rodent-like animal with stubby ears, an almost nonexistent tail, and short legs that looked as if they had been designed for an animal half its size. It was a pika, a distant relative of rabbits, that lived under the boulder. Its den was at the bottom of the rock slide. An indistinct pathway led from the boulder field to a meadow about forty feet away. Scattered near the den were the remains of several piles of hay that had been gathered the previous summer and fall for consumption over the long winter.

Most of the haystacks, which were relatively exposed rather than hidden under boulders, were composed of grasses, herbs, and even a few sprigs of Douglas-fir and aspen. Scattered on the tops of some stacks were the dried scats of yellow-bellied marmots, which the pika had apparently also gathered to consume with the nutritious grasses and herbs. The owner of this particular haystack eyed his diminishing pile of food and made a tentative survey trip toward the meadow. The soggy ground was still mostly snow-covered, and it would be at least another month until the new growth of grasses and sedges would be high enough to warrant gathering. Until then, the male had to simply defend his territory of about a tenth of an acre from other pikas, primarily by advertising his claim with repeated *lank* calls.

Below the rocky outlook and several feet back from its opening lay a female pika with a litter of three. They had been born early in the spring, and by early June they were virtually weaned and showing signs of independence. Within a month they would be expelled from their comfortable burrow and forced into trying to establish their own territories and gather enough hay to carry them through the long winter. But for now, at least, they basked in the comfort and warmth of their mother's body, scarcely aware of the persistent territorial calling of their father. The male, between calling bursts, sunned himself from the top of his favorite boulder, which had become extensively white-stained with dried urine and littered with tiny round droppings at its base. Suddenly rocks clattered above, and the startled pika jumped back into the safety of his rocky refugium. Peering carefully out, he saw a bighorn sheep clambering up the rocky slope 500 feet above, kicking small rocks loose to tumble noisily downward until coming to rest on the talus slope. The ram was part of a small group that had wandered east over the crest of the Teton Range from their usual home on its western slopes.

They had spent the late winter on the steepest south-facing slopes of the cirque, where snow couldn't accumulate to great depths and where the weak winter sun tended to melt it sooner than on the more sheltered northern or western slopes of the cirque. As spring slowly came to the alpine zone, the retreating snow line erratically moved up the slope and around to these protected exposures, but the first greenery was to

BELOW. *Pika, adult with vegetation*

OVERLEAF. *American pika, October, Bridger Teton National Forest, Wyoming*

be found on the steep southern ledges. The females had wintered separately from the rams and left the wintering areas about a month earlier to return to their traditional lambing areas several miles away. Most had become pregnant during the fall rut, and by late winter they had begun to ignore their own lambs of the previous year. A few of these allowed themselves to be "adopted" by lambless females. Others associated with the rams, but all were tolerated by the older sheep.

Several older rams bore splintered horns and scars from the terrible fighting of the past rutting season, which began in November and peaked in December. Then the mountains fairly rang with the crashing head charges of rams fighting to establish dominance. Much of the fighting occurred shortly after the rams moved to their rutting grounds, but occasionally even in late spring dominance fights developed whenever two strange rams happened to meet. Facing each other on the steep slope, two rams would approach with head low and neck stretched forward until they were close enough to kick forward and upward with one of their forelegs, striking each other on the chest or belly. Then, slowly moving past each other with their heads held low and noses almost go touching the ground, they would pace off several steps, suddenly whirl, rise on their hind legs, and bring all of their weight and strength downward and forward in a skull-jolting clash. Time and again they would strike each other until one accepted defeat by behaving submissively like a female, quietly accepting the kicks, threats, and sometimes even the sexual advances of the other ram. These dominance battles were not engaged in to acquire a harem but to allow uncontested access to females during their very limited period of sexual receptivity.

As the pregnant ewes left their wintering areas for their lambing grounds, they remained together until about two weeks prior to giving birth. Then they separated to seek sheltered sites in extremely steep, rough terrain. This reduced the probability of predation on the ewes and their newborn lambs during this vulnerable period. But the lambs were very alert and active almost from the moment of birth. As the ewes licked their lambs dry, they learned their special scent that thereafter enabled each ewe to recognize her lamb. From that time on, no other lamb would be accepted for nursing. Likewise, within a few days after birth each lamb learned to recognize its own mother by visual rather than scent characteristics.

About a week after giving birth, the ewes led their lambs back to the group of lambless ewes and juvenile sheep. The lambs soon formed nursery groups and spent much of their time playing, fighting, and frolicking about the mountain slopes. During the first month or so of their lives, the lambs remained together in their nursery herd, roaming about with the ewes. All returned periodically to their mothers to nurse but were otherwise left largely to themselves without special attention from their mothers or other ewes. By late summer the lambs' baby coats began to be replaced by darker, adult-like pelage, and they were also gradually being weaned. From then on, the ewes showed little interest in their own offspring. Nevertheless, when the herd moved toward their late summer foraging areas, each lamb followed dutifully behind its mother and would continue to do so until the following spring.

As the lambs charged and clashed with one another on a rock-strewn alpine meadow, they scarcely heard the excited calls of a male black rosy-finch calling to attract his mate. The pair had reached the area in May when the cirque was still mostly covered with ice and snow. They soon began courtship activities in spite of their bleak surroundings. Holding his tail

almost perpendicularly over his back, the male extended and vibrated his wings while lowering his head and pointing his bill skyward. As the male chirped almost continuously in this extreme posture and held a bit of grass in his bill, the female adopted a very similar posture and was almost immediately mounted by the male.

Soon the pair sought out a nesting territory. They concentrated their searches on a deep, thirty-foot crevice in the mountain that provided protection from wind, snow, and rain. Selecting a site about halfway up the crevice, the female carried grasses to a tiny ledge about five inches back from the opening. Within a few days she fashioned a deeply cupped nest of grass on a mossy base and added a soft lining of mountain sheep hair. On the first day of summer the nest had a full complement of five white eggs, all laid within a week.

During most of this time the male had been kept busy defending the female from the attentions of unmated males, for there was a considerable excess of males. However, once incubation started he had little to do except when the female interrupted her nest-tending to forage. Then he would once again drive other males away from their foraging grounds. Early in the summer the birds had eaten seeds remaining from the past year, but as June gradually passed, more and more insects appeared. Many were carried upward by the wind and deposited numb and helpless on the snow. When the young hatched in early July, there was an abundance of insect food to be gathered for them. Initially the female did all the feeding as well as all the brooding of the young. However, about a week after hatching the male also began feeding the demanding babies. They did not try to venture from their nest until they were nearly three weeks old. By then they had acquired a gray, buffy plumage that matched the surrounding rocks so well that the young could hardly be seen when they were immobile. By late August all the animals in the cirque were basking in the life-giving sunshine of the all-too-brief alpine summer.

Thirteen

The End of Summer

AUGUST IS THE TIME OF WARM DAYS and easy living for animals in the Yellowstone region. Mosquitoes that had plagued the birds and large mammals during June and early July disappear, and an abundance of food makes foraging almost a spare-time activity rather than the central preoccupation of life.

The young pine martens were almost grown and soon began to hunt with their parents. Usually the family was up by dawn, with the young eager to be out. The youngsters delighted in racing up and down an old cottonwood near their den, playing games of tag. At times they jumped from the lower branches to the ground or they would hang on to them with only their forelegs or hind legs. Or they would roll about on the ground in mock fighting, snarling and growling ferociously, but never really hurting each other. When they had nothing more exciting to do, they stalked grasshoppers and ate them with apparent delight. But by and large they still depended on food caught for them by the adults, which ranged from ground squirrels, flying squirrels, and chipmunks to occasional animals as large as marmots and snowshoe hares. During the middle of the day, when their prey was mostly under cover, the family sometimes returned to the coolness of their den or any other shade. Then the young martens would take a short nap curled up beside each other, with their tails wrapped around their noses.

By the middle of August the female marten was again coming into heat. She soon began to utter clucks that tended to attract the male, and to make scent markings by urinating or rubbing her belly on various objects near their den. She also became much more aggressive toward her mate, at times treating his approaches with tail-twitching and wrestling, although she was only about two-thirds as large as he. But the male was equally rough with her, often dragging her about before mating with her, with the skin of her neck in his mouth. Afterward they would peacefully associate, as if unmindful of their intense struggling and fighting only a few minutes previously.

Nearby, the beaver lodge was also the scene of summer ease. During most of the day the beavers were sound asleep or resting. Toward the end of the day they would awaken, leave the lodge, and spend the night repairing the dam, feeding, and loafing, returning to their lodge about sunrise. The baby beavers were more reluctant than the adults to retire for the day, and they often whined in protest before falling off to sleep. They were also the last to wake up and begin their evening activities. As each beaver awoke, it would stand up, often bumping its head on the roof of the tiny lodge chamber, and step out almost noiselessly through the exit hole into the water. Swimming out about twenty feet, it would turn around, return to the nest chamber, and shake itself free of water. After it thus freshened itself, it would again leave the lodge and begin foraging for an hour or more. August was still too soon for the beavers to begin storing food for the winter, and so these foraging trips had no sense of urgency. Frequently, in fact, the beavers would simply sit for a time on top of the lodge before going out to feed, or perhaps swim for a while in aimless circles as if enjoying the exercise. All the beavers knew the location of every aspen tree within several hundred yards of the pond, and they would often bypass stands of willows and alders to enjoy this delicacy. A beaver might spend an hour or more feeding on an aspen tree before going elsewhere. If one beaver started cutting down a tree, the other lodge members never helped until the tree had been felled. Then the others would quickly appear to help cut it up. Soon the larger branches would be dragged to the water. The bark and leaves would provide food for several days. Next the smaller part of the trunk would be cut into pieces and pulled to the water, but the largest parts of the trunk would eventually be abandoned.

When the kits were still young, they typically stayed in the lodge all night while their mother towed in leaf-laden branches for them to eat inside. As they grew older, their mother delayed more and more this delivery of their food. Soon they began to venture out on their own, and by mid-August the mother rarely brought food to them. The first kit initially ventured out with its mother when it was almost two months old. As it cautiously swam toward the shoreline, its mother followed closely behind with her chin resting on the end of the kit's tail. At times the kit hesitated and would turn back to its mother to touch its chin against her head. Then, gaining confidence, it tentatively dived. As soon as it emerged, the mother caught up with it, and they once again continued their exploration of the pond.

The youngster soon tired and repeatedly turned back toward its mother and tried to climb on her back. After enduring this for a few minutes, the mother simply dived and left the kit to swim on its own. As the two animals reached the shoreline, the mother left the water to gather leafy vegetation for her kit. It remained in the shallow water, whining with discontent until she appeared with a leafy aspen branch. Then it avidly grabbed the branch with its forepaws and stuffed the succulent leaves in its mouth, almost ignoring the larger twigs and branches. Little attention was paid to the kits by their father and the immature beavers. They seemed to go their various ways when foraging and repairing the dam or lodge. None ever overtly helped another in these tasks, but each seemed to recognize that these duties had to be done if their limited world was to remain intact.

Mule deer, adult male in fall

As summer passed, the two two-year-old males became increasingly restless and were tolerated progressively less by the adult male. He frequently chased them from favored food supplies or threatened them when one approached too close to him. Before the summer was over, the two immature males would be evicted from the lodge. Then they might have to travel several miles upstream or downstream in search of undefended areas of shoreline where they could try to establish a den prior to the coming winter. This would be a very difficult time for them compared with their previous life of relative leisure. The youngsters would be exposing themselves to unknown dangers such as otters and minks in the new habitats and would also have to gather enough food for the long winter ahead. They would then have to try to locate mates to help them in the arduous task of dam and lodge construction.

With the end of August, the aspens were slowly being transformed into golden torches, and the forest edges and the lakeshores were aflame with the scarlet leaves and berries of the mountain ash. The beavers would soon lose their worn summer coats and replace them with the longer and more luxuriant winter pelage. Likewise, the pine martens were gradually replacing their now rough and grizzled summer fur with their stunning winter coats of longer and more lustrous reddish-brown upper coloration, a more blackish tail and legs, and an orange-yellow throat patch.

By early September the change of seasons was evident almost everywhere. Already the snow line was progressing perceptibly down the slopes of the Grand Teton, and the golden belt of aspens around the rim of Jackson Hole filled the entire area with a radiance almost beyond credulity. The trumpeter swan cygnets on Christian Pond were nearly fledged and spent long periods flapping their wings in exercise. The sandhill crane family from the beaver pond in the willow thicket had fledged in late August. Together with cranes from elsewhere in the park, they gathered in open meadows prior to leaving for their Bear Lake fall staging areas. The heron colony on the Oxbow was likewise deserted, the last of the young having fledged in mid-August, about the same time that the ospreys on the Oxbow abandoned their eyrie.

FOURTEEN

A Yellowstone Autumn

OVER THE DECADES of the twentieth century, the populations of elk and bison in Yellowstone and Grand Teton parks progressively increased as wolves, mountain lions, and coyotes were effectively removed, the last Yellowstone wolf having been killed in 1926. The Park Service began killing Yellowstone bison during the 1920s, when the population was rising rapidly, from about 500 in 1920 to about 1,100 by 1930. In 1934 an elk-culling program also began to reduce that population by about 3,000 per year, aiming toward a goal of more ecologically sustainable numbers. Nevertheless, by the 1960s Yellowstone's northern range was being seriously overgrazed by elk and bison. In addition, worries by cattle-raisers in adjacent Montana that any Yellowstone Park bison infected with brucellosis (a disease which seems to affect these animals only slightly) might transmit it to cattle. By 1940 there were about

11,000 elk and about 600 bison on Yellowstone's northern range, a population still well above the park's goals. Over the next two decades the range continued to deteriorate, and it was decided that bison and elk numbers must be further reduced. Extensive bison trapping and removal began in the winter of 1965, resulting in a park population of 266 animals in 1966, the lowest since about 1915.

In 1967 Yellowstone Park officials also decided that they would also allow the killing of 600 elk in the park annually so that the elk population would be reduced to 5,000. Public indignation stopped the hunt soon after it began, and since then elk have not been killed within the park for the sole purpose of reducing herd size. However, by 1988 the park's elk population numbered over 19,000, and the bison population was approaching 900. Besides the major northern range herd, wintering elk herds were also centered (from north to south) in areas such as Paradise Valley of Gallatin National Forest, the Gallatin River, the Madison-Firehole River, Sunlight-Crandall Creek (in Shoshone National Forest), the North Fork of the Shoshone River, the Greybull River, and the Gros Ventre portion of the National Elk Refuge.

Legal hunting of elk outside Yellowstone Park's boundaries has long been allowed. Since the 1980s, between 500 and 4,500 elk have been legally taken from Yellowstone's northern range population annually in an effort to curb further population growth. Limited authorized hunting of bison that had wandered outside Yellowstone Park's boundaries in Montana also began in the mid-1980s. The highly publicized killing of these unsuspecting

bison was terminated after only a few years, owing to the bloody scenes showing often inept hunters fulfilling real-life roles as "the gang that couldn't shoot straight."

In spite of these efforts at population control, the elk, bison, and deer populations in Yellowstone Park continued to increase during the 1980s, the bison population most rapidly. With increasing population size and associated foraging competition, winter movements by bison out of the park to other foraging areas also increased. Over the two decades between 1985 and 2005 about 4,000 bison were killed during these frequent northward migrations out of the park into Montana. A handful of bison have migrated into Shoshone National Forest of Wyoming at the park's eastern border and into Targhee National Forest of Idaho along its western boundaries. Some bison also move south toward Grand Teton National Park to winter in the Snake River Valley.

The story of elk hunting in the Grand Teton–Jackson Hole area is similar to that of the bison. Since 1950 every licensed elk hunter (their permits having been won by lottery) serves as a "deputized warden." These hunters may drive to the Antelope Flats area between Grand Teton Park and Jackson and park daily until the elk are finally forced by the increasingly winter-like weather to "come down." About 8,000 elk annually winter at the refuge, most of them coming from southern parts of Yellowstone and northern parts of Grand Teton parks and the rest from nearby national forest lands.

An agreement made in 1975 between the National Elk Refuge and the Wyoming Game and Fish Commission stipulated that no more than 7,500 elk would be fed during winter on refuge lands, with any excess representing the number of male and female elk that could be legally killed. Then about 2,500 hunting permits were being issued annually for the Grand Teton–Jackson area. About half of these licensed hunters usually appeared to participate in the hunt, the so-called annual "Slaughter at Antelope Flats." Of this total, about half of the hunters were successful, so that 500–800 elk were then being shot annually. A few bison and moose as well as trumpeter swans have also been shot during these hunts, presumably by hunters who couldn't distinguish them from elk.

The Jackson Hole bison herd, which had first been allowed to run free in Grand Teton Park in 1969, expanded into the National Elk Refuge during the 1970s. The herd became large enough that annual culling began in 1989 in an effort to hold the combined refuge and national park bison population at about 400 animals. By 2004 the Jackson Hole bison herd had risen to about 800 animals and was being legally hunted in the nearby Bridger-Teton National Forest. Plans to also hunt bison legally in Grand Teton Park and the National Elk Refuge were then temporarily put on hold as a result of legal action by the Fund for Animals and delayed until an environmental impact statement for determining the effects of the feeding program on bison and elk had been completed.

~~

In high mountain meadows of Yellowstone and Grand Teton parks, the elk were responding to September's first signals of impending winter. Gradually, as the nights became colder and vegetation on parts of the summer range dried out, the herds began to merge and move to richer vegetation and lower areas. Since early August the males had been rubbing velvet from

FACING PAGE. *Bull elk bugling, September, Madison River, Yellowstone National Park, Wyoming*

OVERLEAF. *Mount Moran and autumn aspens reflected in the Snake River at Oxbow Bend, Grand Teton National Park, Wyoming*

their hardened antlers by thrashing shrubs and weeds, which also tended to release some of the aggressive energy building within them.

The first indication that the rut was approaching was the growing intolerance of the older bulls toward younger ones, which after a few threats moved off to the edge of the bull groups. A few spikes that had remained with their mothers began driving the older cows about, even attempting to bugle, but the cows largely ignored them. Here and there older bulls began to bugle, but the cows also avoided their efforts to gather them together and hold them in a group.

With September came the first hard frosts and the transformation of Grand Teton and Yellowstone parks into golden landscapes as the aspens on mountain slopes began to respond to the temperature changes. As the days continued to grow colder and the elk moved to progressively lower meadows, the older bulls' tempers also grew shorter. Each spent more time driving the cows, thrashing the vegetation, and wallowing in muddy or boggy areas. Although the bulls bugled throughout the day, they concentrated their bugling in the morning and evening, challenging all others within hearing. Soon, the largest and most dominant males controlled a dozen or more cows and their calves, constantly driving and patrolling them and grazing but little.

For the elk, this was the start of an intensely dangerous period. To reach the safety of their winter range in the National Elk Refuge, more than 100 miles to the south, they would have not only escape daily threats from wolves but also run the gauntlet of nearly 1,000 hunters within Grand Teton National Park and hundreds in the adjoining Bridger-Teton National Forest. The hunting season in the national forest usually begins in early September during the rut. To survive the early fall hunt, bulls must remain in the most remote high country for as long as possible. Yet, when winter finally forces them out of the high wilderness areas before the hunting season ends, most elk must face a firing line of hunters. The trip can be made safely only at night or by remaining as long as possible west of the Snake River, where hunting is not allowed. Yet, for the ultimate good of the elk and the entire ecosystem, their numbers must not be allowed to outstrip the resources of the wintering grounds. The bloody scenes reenacted every fall in parts of Grand Teton National Park are the unhappy solution adopted, for better or worse, by the state and federal agencies responsible for management of the elk and their habitat.

In such questions lies the paradox of preserving and protecting the wildlife and the complex interrelationships that hold this enormous ecosystem together. To preserve the elk from all hunting is to invite disaster by their overgrazing of grasses and overbrowsing of plants such as aspen, upon which so many other animals depend so heavily. In recent years the reintroduced wolves have taken a measurable toll on the elk, but tens of thousands remain and must try to survive the winter snows. The winter range will support only a limited population, leaving the rest to die, whether from periodic disease, starvation, or hunting.

The life of the Greater Yellowstone region is thus a continuing challenge to the intellect. Since we cannot "control" the elk without inadvertently affecting the wolves, ravens, coyotes, and aspens, so we cannot affect coyotes or aspens without also affecting mice and tree swallows. And we cannot affect tree swallows in the Yellowstone without affecting them in their wintering areas in Central America. In this way, the world is drawn ever closer together, and the

shock waves
of how we act
here and now will ema-
nate in time and space as the
ripples of the present spread out to
touch and disturb the shorelines of the
future. Thus the cranes that nest on an old
abandoned beaver lodge are as dependent upon
the now-dead beaver as the moose or swan that
forages in the beaver pond, or the osprey that fishes in its
clear waters. And a trumpeter swan that was killed by a
frustrated elk hunter who failed somehow to get his allot-
ted bull not only is gone for all time, but its lifelong mate and their
potential future broods are also effectively eliminated. And so their
pond lacks the trumpeting calls that carry with them all the majesty of
fifty million years of swan evolution and survival, leaving only the silent
mountains to endure.

For whatever values and purposes we might seek in wild animals, whether as a source
of food or of pure aesthetic enjoyment, we must ever try to comprehend them better; they
will never comprehend us. We must also love them for what they are, whether large or small,
beautiful or ugly, predator or prey, for they will never love us. And we must try to preserve
them from extinction for our own good; for better or worse we alone control the destinies
of all species in the animal kingdom. Unfortunately, our history has mostly been for the
worse, but places like Yellowstone and Grand Teton allow us to see that our own lives can
be enhanced and made more rewarding by finding and protecting natural places where species might live out their own lives without human interference. In spite of our too-frequent
management mistakes, these places allow us to hear the distant sounds of elk bugling across
mountain valleys, cherish the sight of sandhill cranes dancing in green meadows, and catch
the odors of alpine flowers on alpine meadows. These are treasures having values beyond
mortal calculations.

ABOVE. *Sandhill crane,
adults fighting*

APPENDIX 1

Observing Wildlife in the Greater Yellowstone Ecoregion

THE GREAT DIVERSITY of wildlife in both national parks ensures interesting observations any time of the year. However, some areas and seasons are far better than others. Throughout the year, early morning and late evening are the best times to see large animals and birds. Late spring (mid-May to early June) and late fall (September and early October) are also infinitely better for wildlife-watching than mid-summer, when extremely heavy traffic and associated human disturbance in Yellowstone Park keep most large animals away from well-traveled areas and make attempts at wildlife-watching a nightmare. Todd Wilkinson's *Watching Yellowstone and Grand Teton Wildlife* (2008) provides advice on finding thirty-two of the region's most charismatic mammals and sixteen of its more conspicuous and characteristic birds. Terry McEneaney's books (1988, 1993) are the best sources for bird-finding in the region.

Hooved Mammals (Ungulates)

BIGHORN SHEEP are not abundant and are most readily seen during winter in the Red Hills area along the Gros Ventre Range southeast of Grand Teton NP (about thirty are typically present on the slopes of Hoback Canyon) and in the National Elk Refuge (where about sixty winter). They also make rare appearances on Sheep Mountain year-round and in the Teton Range during summer. In Yellowstone NP they are most often seen on Mount Washburn, especially along the trail to its summit. The slopes between Mammoth and Gardiner provide other good viewing opportunities.

BISON in Yellowstone NP are widespread and numerous. They may often be seen in open meadow areas; over 4,000 were present in 2004, a record number. Hayden Valley is perhaps the best site for seeing bull bison throughout the year. The Lamar Valley and Lower Geyser Basin support large herds from fall through winter. During summer months, bulls are widespread through the geyser basins south to Yellowstone Lake. In Grand Teton NP and surrounding Jackson Hole bison number in the hundreds (about 900 in 2010) and have been steadily increasing for several decades in spite of recent efforts to control them. During summer and fall they mostly range over the sagebrush flats west of the Snake River, between Jackson Lake and Moose, and especially in the Potholes area. In the winter they move into the National Elk Refuge. They are sometimes also seen in the lower Gros Ventre Valley, particularly during early summer.

ELK are numerous in both parks. About 30,000 are present in Yellowstone NP during summer, and up to about 10,000 may remain in the park during winter, when they are concentrated on grasslands, including the Lamar and Hayden Valleys. Thousands also migrate south to winter in the National Elk Refuge. Up to about 8,000 may be seen at the National Elk Refuge from late November or early December through April. During summer, elk usually can be seen locally in Grand Teton NP, especially near sunset or sunrise along forest edges south of Signal Mountain or near Timbered Island.

MOOSE are present throughout the year in marshes and extensive willow stands of both parks, with populations of each numbering in the hundreds. They are relatively more abundant and much more easily found in Grand Teton than in Yellowstone. The willow flats east of Jackson Lake and the bottomlands of the Snake, Gros Ventre, and Buffalo Fork Rivers are favored by Grand Teton moose. In Yellowstone NP one should look for them around Pelican Creek and Hayden Valley. They also are often seen around Yellowstone Lake, such as near Fishing Bridge and Lake Village.

MOUNTAIN GOATS are very local in Yellowstone NP and are most likely to be seen in its northeastern corner on the slopes of Baronette and Abiather peaks. They have also been reported a few times in the northwestern corner of the park (Wilkinson 2008). Some also occur in the Snake River Range to the south of Grand Teton NP.

MULE DEER are widely distributed in both parks. In Yellowstone NP they are especially common around Yellowstone Lake. In Grand Teton NP they are also relatively common along the shore of Jackson Lake and on the slopes of Signal Mountain and Blacktail Butte; they are infrequently seen along the trails in the Teton Range.

OVERLEAF. *A newborn moose calf drinking from Christian Pond alongside its mother, June, Grand Teton National Park, Wyoming*

PRONGHORNS are most often seen in Grand Teton NP on Antelope Flats and east of Blacktail Butte during summer. They often are visible from US Highway 26/287 or Antelope Flats Road. They may sometimes also be observed along the Gros Ventre River east of the park. In Yellowstone NP they are common in the Lamar Valley and are found almost anywhere in the northern parts of the park where sagebrush is present. During winter they might be seen in Gardiner Basin.

WHITE-TAILED DEER are far less common in both parks than mule deer. They have moved into Yellowstone NP along Paradise Valley and are sometimes seen along the Yellowstone and Gardiner Rivers. They have also expanded into Grand Teton NP via Jackson Hole and are moving north along the Snake River. They are more adapted to woodland-edge and riverine habitats than are mule deer, and are less likely to occupy drier brushlands in broken country. They are also slightly larger than mule deer and tend to outcompete them where both coexist.

Large Carnivores

BLACK BEARS are most numerous in Yellowstone NP and are sometimes seen near campgrounds. Recent estimates put their Yellowstone NP numbers at about 650. In Grand Teton NP they are occasionally seen in the foothills and canyons of the Teton Range.

COYOTES may be seen almost anywhere but most often in open meadows during early morning and late evening. They are especially common in Yellowstone's Lamar Valley and on Antelope Flats of Grand Teton NP. During winter they concentrate on the National Elk Refuge. Their numbers declined sharply after wolves were introduced in Yellowstone NP but have since recovered.

GRIZZLY BEARS in Yellowstone NP are carefully managed to try to keep them away from most human contact. Females with cubs can be especially dangerous. The park's excessive and invasive handling of the bears, including trapping, tranquilizing, radio-collaring, and ear tagging, cause many to believe the bears are overly handled and overly managed. In addition to regular sightings in the Lamar Valley, many summer road-side observations occur along Dunraven Pass and Mount Washburn, often creating major bear jams. Grizzlies have long been rare in the Tetons but in recent years have moved into most areas of Grand Teton NP. A five-year-old grizzly (tag number 610) with two cubs-of-the-year (COYs) appeared near Signal Mountain in May 2011, followed a week later by a fifteen-year-old female with three COYs. This was grizzly number 399, the mother of number 610, and a world-famous Teton bear. Grizzly 610's sister, grizzly number 615, was shot and killed just outside Grand Teton NP in 2009 during the region's annual elk hunt. In a recent year a total of about fifty grizzlies were killed by various human-related factors, of which nearly forty were illegally killed by hunters. The grizzly population in the Yellowstone NP region was about 450 in the 1970s, prior to the elimination of open-air garbage dumps and of problem bears that habitually visited dumps, after which it dropped to about 130. As of 2012 there were about 600 grizzlies in the Greater Yellowstone region. Grizzlies regularly patrol the calving grounds of elk, such as in Antelope Valley and Willow Flats in Grand Teton, to seek out and kill the calves. The best available and most recent information on the bears of Yellowstone is that of Halfpenny (2007).

OVERLEAF. *A grizzly bear cub chewing on a wildflower blossom, June, Grand Teton National Park, Wyoming*

The decline of two of the grizzly bear's most important food sources—the cutthroat trout and whitebark pine seeds—threaten the bear's recovery. The introduction of lake trout into Yellowstone Lake has wiped out most of the cutthroat trout that spawned in its tributaries. Climate change, fungus, blister rust, and mountain pine beetle infestation has caused the loss of whitebark pine. Because of the impending loss of these important foods, many believe the grizzly populations have not and may not fully recover and continue to be threatened by these and other ongoing changes in food availability. In spite of this, there is a huge political move led by the Inter Agency Grizzly Bear Study Team (IGBST), which includes the two national parks, the U.S. Fish and Wildlife Service and the three game and fish agencies of Montana, Wyoming, and Idaho to delist the bears from the endangered species list by 2014. Grizzly bears were originally listed as "threatened" under the Endangered Species Act in the 1970s. The U.S. Department of the Interior delisted the bears in 2007. But in 2009, the Ninth Circuit Court of Appeals upheld a court-ordered reversal of the bear's status. This new proposed delisting would turn over the bear's management to the state game and fish agencies, who would then sell licenses for grizzlies to be sport hunted, like black bears, wolves, and cougars.

Large cats. MOUNTAIN LIONS, LYNX, and BOBCATS are all rarely seen. They are also very mobile, with large home ranges, so they might occur anywhere. Mountain lions specialize on deer and elk as favorite prey and are likely to occur in remote areas of open country, such as the National Elk Refuge or the Lamar Valley. Lynx prey largely on snowshoe hares, and bobcats favor cottontails, rodents, and birds. All wild felids are largely nocturnal and highly elusive, so any sightings should be cherished as probably once-in-a-lifetime events.

WOLVES are likely to be seen well away from areas subject to regular human activities, and are presently easier to view than mountain lions, lynx, or bobcats. In 2010 the largest Yellowstone packs were centered in Gibbon Meadows, the Lamar Valley, the Blacktail Deer Plateau, and near the Montana border. In Grand Teton NP the Phantom Springs area held the largest number in 2010. During the summer months the wolves move to higher altitudes wherever elk are concentrated.

Small Mammals

BADGERS might be seen in the Lamar Valley, Hayden Valley, and around Mammoth Hot Springs of Yellowstone NP and in the Antelope Flats area of Grand Teton NP, where ground squirrels or other burrowing rodents are common. The National Elk Refuge also offers potential viewing opportunities.

BATS are most likely to be seen around old buildings or feeding above lakes during twilight. SHREWS and VOLES are more rarely seen, but are most likely to be encountered in grassy meadows. All of these generally small and nocturnal mammals may be difficult or impossible to identify in the field.

BEAVERS can usually be seen during evening along the rivers or on ponds at numerous places in both parks, such as along the Snake River in Grand Teton NP and the Gardiner River in Yellowstone NP. MUSKRATS are common and often can also be seen in beaver ponds.

Bushy-tailed woodrats are relatively nocturnal, but their large stick nests might be seen along boulders or cliffs, such as Obsidian Cliff in Yellowstone or Signal Mountain in Grand Teton NP (Streubel 1995).

Miscellaneous rodents. Least chipmunks, golden-mantled ground squirrels, and Uinta ground squirrels are nearly ubiquitous and usually easy to find in rocky or grassy areas, especially around campgrounds. Red squirrels are scattered throughout the coniferous forests and are often encountered. Porcupines are seen less often and are usually found in trees.

Mountain cottontails and white-tailed jackrabbits might be found in grasslands and sage scrub, such as on Antelope Flats in Grand Teton NP and Gardiner Basin in Yellowstone NP, but both are now difficult to find. Snowshoe hares are common in open coniferous forests.

Pikas are common on talus slopes in both parks. In Yellowstone NP they are common along the Madison River and at Obsidian Cliff. In Grand Teton NP they may be seen along various mountain trails, such as the Cascade Canyon trail.

River otters are often seen in the Gibbon, Lamar, Madison, and Firehole Rivers of Yellowstone NP. They are often seen along the Snake River in Grand Teton NP and also can be found at Emma Matilda and Two Ocean Lakes.

Weasels. Ermine, long-tailed weasels, and pine martens all occur at unpredictable locations and move so rapidly that they are often seen only momentarily. However, martens are most often seen in conifers, where they hunt for red squirrels. Mink are elusive, mostly nocturnal, and infrequently seen. Wolverines and fishers are extremely rare.

Yellow-bellied marmots are commonly seen on talus slopes or meadows in both parks. In Yellowstone NP look for them around Storm Point or the Old Faithful overlook. In Grand Teton NP they may often be seen along the Cascade Canyon trail. Some marmots in the region have a melanistic (blackish) pelage.

Birds

Birding opportunities in the Yellowstone region have been very well documented. Terry McEneaney (1988) suggested promising birding sites for 20 especially characteristic or charismatic Yellowstone birds and listed "best birding" locations for all of the 279 total species that then had been reported from the park. He later (1993) outlined three birding routes in northern Yellowstone NP and several bird-rich locations in Red Rock Lakes NWR. O. K. Scott (1993) outlined eleven routes or sites in Jackson Hole. Bert Raynes (1984) described 57 Jackson Hole birds and suggested places for finding them (out of 293 total species reported in the overall Grand Teton–Jackson Hole and Bridger-Teton Forest region). He and Darwin Wile (1994) provided extensive advice for birding in the Jackson Hole region in their *Finding the Birds of Jackson Hole,* suggesting five driving loops and seventeen foot routes and providing an annotated list of about 320 regularly occurring to accidental species.

OVERLEAF. *Adult black-pelaged wolf, February, Lamar Valley, Yellowstone National Park, Wyoming*

AMERICAN DIPPERS are limited to fairly small, rapid streams, such as the Gibbon, Firehole and Gardiner in Yellowstone NP and Cascade Creek in Grand Teton NP. Their rounded and moss-covered nests are often placed on the undersides of bridges, so looking under bridges for nests may allow one to find an active territory.

BALD EAGLES can usually be found around Yellowstone Lake and along the Yellowstone River; up to fifteen pairs have nested in the park (McEneaney 1988). They are most often seen around Yellowstone Lake and along rivers such as the Yellowstone and Madison. In Grand Teton NP they may be seen from the highway along the Snake River and are often seen on float trips down the river. Nestings often occur along the Snake River, and eagles are regularly seen along the Gros Ventre River. Disturbing their nests is prohibited, and river floaters are not allowed to land near nesting birds. During fall many eagles migrate to overwinter at the National Elk Refuge, and they are also common year-round at Red Rock Lakes NWR.

COMMON LOONS are most likely to be seen on Yellowstone and Jackson Lakes outside the breeding season. Loons nest in small numbers in both parks, typically on lakes with good fish populations and in remote bays with shoreline vegetation. Mary Bay and Steamboat Point on Yellowstone Lake are good places to search for them in Yellowstone NP (McEneaney 1988). In Grand Teton NP they may sometimes be found on Two Ocean Lake, Jenny Lake, and along the Oxbow. They are occasional visitors at Red Rock Lakes NWR and at the National Elk Refuge. In 2006 there were thirty-nine adult loons in Yellowstone NP, nine nests, and two fledged young (McEneaney 2007a).

Corvids. COMMON RAVENS are widespread throughout the entire Yellowstone ecosystem and are usually found around campgrounds and major tourist concentrations (e.g., Old Faithful and Grand Canyon overlooks), where they are on the constant lookout for food scraps. Other widespread corvids that might occur in these same areas are GRAY JAYS, STELLER'S JAYS, and BLACK-BILLED MAGPIES. Ravens and magpies also regularly gather at large mammal carcasses to scavenge scraps after the wolves, coyotes, and eagles have left. CLARK'S NUTCRACKERS are more likely to be found at higher elevations, typically subalpine areas during summer and especially among the whitebark and limber pines, the seeds of which the birds consume throughout the year.

DUSKY GROUSE (previously named the "blue grouse") are widespread and common. In Yellowstone NP the one-way loop road south of Mammoth is an excellent location for hearing or seeing dusky grouse, as is the road to Mount Washburn. In Grand Teton NP some promising areas for seeing the species are the west shore of Jenny Lake, the trail from String Lake to Leigh Lake, and the upper slopes of Signal Mountain (Raynes 1984). They are also common in the National Elk Refuge and uncommon at Red Rock Lakes NWR and Grays Lake NWR. Dusky grouse are sometimes seen in sagebrush scrub near conifers during the spring display period, but for much of the year they are closely associated with fairly dense coniferous forests. They winter at fairly high altitudes, feeding on conifer needles. The males' spring territorial drumming (mainly during May and June) carries for great distances, but is very low in both volume and pitch and thus very often goes unnoticed by park visitors.

Falcons. Peregrines and prairie falcons are relatively common in both parks, the former having recovered from near extirpation during the middle of the twentieth century. Nesting of both species occurs on steep cliffsides. Prairie falcons have often nested on Blacktail Butte in Grand Teton NP, and may nest on Miller Butte in the National Elk Refuge. Peregrines may sometimes be seen at the Grizzly Overlook, along the Hayden Valley in Yellowstone NP, or along the rocky slopes of the Teton Range west of Jackson Lake. The Alaska Basin west of Yellowstone and Grand Teton parks also supports peregrines. Both species are common at Red Rock Lakes NWR, and the prairie falcon is uncommon at Grays Lake NWR, but seeing them is largely a matter of luck.

Golden eagles are uncommon nesters in both parks but are regular visitors during migration and winter. They are also uncommon residents at Grays Lake NWR and Red Rock Lakes NWR (especially along Blacktail Road and Lima Road and in the Alaska Basin to the east of the refuge) and are occasionally found in the National Elk Refuge (in the vicinity of Lower Slide Lake).

Greater sage-grouse occur commonly in the sage habitats of Jackson Hole and are local in Grand Teton NP. A famous display ground at Jackson Airport is now nearly abandoned as a result of development, with only a few males present in 2010. Sage-grouse commonly occur in the National Elk Refuge and along the Gros Ventre Valley. They are uncommon at Grays Lake NWR, occasional at Red Rock Lakes NWR, and rare in Yellowstone NP.

Greater sandhill cranes can be easily seen and heard on the National Elk Refuge from the highway north of Jackson. In Yellowstone NP they are often visible from the Wildlife Overlook above the Yellowstone River, between Fishing Bridge and Canyon, or along Fountain Flats, north of Old Faithful. Other good crane habitats exist at Willow Park, Swan Lake Flats, Blacktail Ponds, and Antelope Creek. In Grand Teton NP they also frequent the Oxbow area of the Snake River, the marshes around Two Ocean Lake, and the willow flats east of Jackson Lake. They often nest in and around beaver ponds, among vegetation low enough to provide panoramic visibility but some protective surrounding cover, and where there is little or no human activity. They are common nesters at Grays Lake NWR (where the species' greatest known breeding density occurs), Red Rock Lakes NWR, and the National Elk Refuge.

Grebes. The greatest regional grebe diversity is at Red Rock Lakes NWR, where one might find western, Clark's, and eared grebes on Lower Red Rock Lake or near the campground beside Upper Red Rock Lake. Eared grebes are common nesters at Grays Lake NWR. In Yellowstone NP grebes are often seen at Alum Creek, Junction Butte Ponds, and along Slough Creek. In Grand Teton NP Oxbow Bend and Jackson Lake are good viewing locations for migrant grebes.

Harlequin ducks are always very hard to find, but a few occur during spring below Fishing Bridge at LeHardy Rapids, their historic Yellowstone stronghold. They might also

OVERLEAF. *Male greater sage-grouse below the Tetons, February, Grand Teton National Park, Wyoming*

be searched for elsewhere along the Yellowstone River or from Yellowstone Bridge. They are rare in Grand Teton NP but have sometimes been seen in Cascade Canyon. They are occasional nesters at the National Elk Refuge and are unreported from Red Rock Lakes NWR or Grays Lake NWR.

Hawks. The summer-resident SWAINSON'S HAWK and the almost ubiquitous and year-round RED-TAILED HAWK are very common at both refuges and parks. Red Rock Lakes NWR and Grays Lake NWR probably offer the best chances of seeing the FERRU-GINOUS HAWK, which often nests in close association with ground squirrel or prairie dog colonies. Northern goshawks are perhaps most common in Grand Teton NP, but like all accipiters it is elusive and usually seen only in rapid flight in or near coniferous forest.

Herons. GREAT BLUE HERONS may usually be seen during summer from the Rockefeller Highway (US 287/191) at the Oxbow Bend stretch of the Snake River. Herons are also often seen along the Snake River north of Moose and near the Blacktail Pond overlook. They also breed commonly at Red Rock Lakes NWR and the National Elk Refuge. AMERICAN BITTERNS and BLACK-CROWNED NIGHT-HERONS are also most likely to be found at Red Rock Lakes NWR or Grays Lake NWR, as is the otherwise rare WHITE-FACED IBIS.

Hummingbirds. CALLIOPE HUMMINGBIRDS are common in both parks and refuges. RUFOUS HUMMINGBIRDS are uncommon in Yellowstone NP and at Jackson and Red Rock Lakes and are occasional in Grand Teton NP and the National Elk Refuge. BROAD-TAILED HUMMINGBIRDS are common in Jackson Hole and the National Elk Refuge, uncommon at Red Rock Lakes NWR, common at Grays Lake NWR, and occasional to rare elsewhere. All hummingbirds are most often seen in flower-rich meadows, especially where red to orange nectar-rich flowers (such as gilia and Indian paintbrush) are blooming.

OSPREYS may be seen in Yellowstone NP from viewpoints along the Grand Canyon, where they regularly nest on rock pinnacles. They also nest in trees along rivers such as the Madison and around some of the lakes. Up to sixty pairs typically nest in the park. In 2006 there were only fourteen nests in Yellowstone NP, and three young fledged (McEneaney 2007a). In Grand Teton NP they may be seen around Jackson Lake and along the Snake River as well as along the Buffalo Fork and Gros Ventre Rivers. They are only occasional to rare nesters at Red Rock Lakes NWR and Grays Lake NWR.

Owls. GREAT GRAY OWLS are widespread but never easy to find. They may sometimes be found at the edges of coniferous woods bordering open meadows, in quiet locations where auditory hunting for small rodents may effectively be done. In both parks look (and especially listen) for these owls along the edges of forested meadows, such as those south of Canyon Village in Yellowstone NP, or the meadows southwest of Moose in Grand Teton NP. These owls have long nested in an area bounded by the Moose-Wilson Road, the Taggart Lake Trail, the Valley Trail, and the Whitegrass Ranger Station (W. E. Harper, in Scott 1993). They are occasional nesters at Red Rock Lakes NWR and the National Elk

Refuge and are rare at Grays Lake NWR. The great horned owl is the only owl likely to be seen by most visitors in the Greater Yellowstone region; the others are nearly all nocturnal and very difficult to detect without special effort.

Rosy-finches. BLACK ROSY-FINCHES have limited breeding ranges centering on alpine tundra in the Greater Yellowstone Ecosystem and are very local in Yellowstone NP. These finches may be searched for above timberline on Mount Washburn (10,243 feet), which can be reached by trails from parking areas at Dunraven Pass or the Antelope Creek Overlook. Outside the park the alpine zone of the Red Lodge–Cooke City highway provides excellent viewing possibilities for both rosy-finches and water pipits. Rosy-finches also occur in the alpine zones of Grand Teton NP, but alpine areas in the Tetons must be reached by trails. From Jackson they can most easily be seen by taking the tramway at Teton Village to an alpine area at the top of Rendezvous Mountain (10,000 feet). Other more easily accessible subalpine to lower alpine locations in the Teton–Jackson Hole region that might support rosy-finches, especially just prior to or after their breeding season, include Teton Pass (8,400 feet) and Togwotee Pass (9,600 feet). During late fall and winter the birds spread out widely over much lower altitudes, when they often occur together with the other two rosy-finch species.

RUFFED GROUSE commonly occur in both parks, especially in aspen groves. In Yellowstone NP the Blacktail Plateau drive and Floating Island Lake area are good locations for finding both ruffed and dusky grouse (McEneaney 1993). In Grand Teton NP the trail up Death Canyon (off the Moose-Wilson Road) often has ruffed grouse. Ruffed grouse are most easily found by listening for the sounds of drumming males in early morning or late afternoon hours between May and early July. Ruffed grouse are also common in the National Elk Refuge and at Red Rock Lakes NWR and Grays Lake NWR.

Shorebirds. LONG-BILLED CURLEWS are sometimes visible near Flat Creek in the National Elk Refuge and are common breeders at Red Rock Lakes NWR and Grays Lake NWR. The latter two refuges also offer the best chances of seeing some other large shorebirds, such as AMERICAN AVOCETS and WILLETS, and MARBLED GODWITS are most likely to be seen at Red Rock Lakes NWR.

TRUMPETER SWANS are frequently seen in the Lamar Valley and along the Madison River during summer months in Yellowstone NP. During summer in Grand Teton NP they might be found on Christian Pond (a traditional nesting site that was nearly dry in 2010), Sawmill Pond, and several of the more inaccessible beaver ponds or lakes throughout the valley areas of Jackson Hole. They can be observed on Jackson Lake and the Snake River during the nonbreeding season as well as in Buffalo Valley during spring. Usually at least one nesting pair as well as small groups of nonbreeders can be seen at the National Elk Refuge. At Red Rock Lakes NWR trumpeter swans often nest at Shambo Pond, about a half mile west of the Upper Red Rock Lake campground. Trumpeter swans are in a serious long-term regional decline in the Greater Yellowstone region; up to seventy were present in Yellowstone NP during the late 1960s, but by 2006 there were only fourteen pairs in Yellowstone NP, with only three nestings and no young fledged (McEneaney 2007a).

Waterfowl. Many waterfowl are distinctive and widespread in both parks and refuges. Among the most visually appealing breeding ducks in the region are the BARROW'S GOLDEN-EYE, BUFFLEHEAD, and COMMON MERGANSER, all of which nest along wooded lakes and streams in both parks as well as at Red Rock Lakes NWR. With great luck, during July one might see a female of one of these species carrying several young ducklings on her back. The greatest diversity and number of summer regional waterfowl may be found at Red Rock Lakes NWR (twenty-one breeders) and Grays Lake NWR (sixteen breeders). CANADA GEESE are common breeders throughout the region.

Woodpeckers. AMERICAN THREE-TOED and BLACK-BACKED WOODPECKERS are both attracted to recently burned (within five years) forests and other areas of recent forest disturbance, so any specific location advice is soon outdated. Black-backed woodpeckers are far rarer than three-toed and are thus much harder to find. LEWIS'S WOODPECKERS may also often be found in burned-over forest habitats but remain in them for longer periods following fires. All three species prefer very recently burned forests over older burn sites or other disturbed areas where dead conifers have bark that is peeling away from the wood, helping to expose bark beetles. NORTHERN FLICKERS, DOWNY WOODPECKERS, and HAIRY WOODPECKERS are all easily seen. SAPSUCKERS are often attracted to aspens because of their fairly soft wood and relatively accessible, abundant sap. Local species include the WILLIAMSON'S SAPSUCKER, which is much harder to find than the more common RED-NAPED SAPSUCKER. Only a few hundred pairs of Williamson's sapsucker are believed to be present in Yellowstone NP, whereas the population of red-naped sapsuckers probably numbers in the thousands (McEneaney 2007a). Williamson's sapsuckers are only occasional nesters at Red Rock Lakes NWR and the National Elk Refuge. Aspen groves and mature stands of Douglas-fir with scattered aspens provide good areas in which to search for both sapsuckers and typical woodpeckers.

FACING PAGE. *Lewis's woodpecker perched in an aspen, Grand Teton National Park, Wyoming*

Appendix 2

Birds of the Greater Yellowstone Ecoregion

Birds of the Greater Yellowstone Ecoregion

		Wyoming (Statewide)		Grand Teton NP	Yellowstone NP	Jackson Hole	Red Rock Lakes NWR
	Status	Abundance	Habitats				
Greater White-fronted Goose	M (Arctic)	1	WL	x		x	x
Snow Goose	M (Arctic)	2	WL, AG	O	R	O	U
Ross's Goose	M (Arctic)	1	WL			R	x
Canada Goose	R & M	4	WL, ME, AG	C*	A*	C*	C*
Trumpeter Swan	R	2	WL	C*	C*	C*	C*
Tundra Swan	M (Arctic)	2	WL	O	U	O	U
Wood Duck	S	2	RI, WL	U	R	O*	O
Gadwall	R	4	WL	U*	C*	C*	C*
American Wigeon	R	4	WL	U	C*	C*	C*
Mallard	R	4	WL	C*	A*	C*	C*
Blue-winged Teal	S	3	WL	O	U*	O*	C*
Cinnamon Teal	S	3	WL	U*	C*	O*	C*
Northern Shoveler	S	3	WL	O	U*	R*	C*
Northern Pintail	R	4	WL	U*	U*	O*	C*
Green-winged Teal	R	4	WL	C*	C*	C*	C*
Canvasback	S	2	WL	O	U*	R*	C*
Redhead	S	3	WL	U*	U*	C	C*
Ring-necked Duck	S	3	WL	C*	C*	C*	U*

continued on next page

Birds of the Greater Yellowstone Ecoregion—*continued*

	Wyoming (Statewide)			Grand Teton NP	Yellowstone NP	Jackson Hole	Red Rock Lakes NWR
	Status	*Abundance*	*Habitats*				
Greater Scaup	M (Boreal)	1	WL			x	x
Lesser Scaup	S	2	WL	O	C*	O*	C*
Harlequin Duck	S	2	WL	O	R*	O*	x
Surf Scoter	M (Boreal)	1	WL	x		x	x
White-winged Scoter	M (Boreal)	2	WL	x		x	x
Bufflehead	R	2	WL, RI	O*	U*	C*	U*
Common Goldeneye	R	3	WL, RI		U	O	O*?
Barrow's Goldeneye	R	3	WL, RI	C*	A*	C*	O*
Hooded Merganser	S	2	WL	R	R	O	O*
Red-breasted Merganser	S	2	WL	O	R	O	O*?
Common Merganser	R	3	WL, RI	C*	C*	C*	C*
Ruddy Duck	S	3	WL	O*	U*	O*	C*
Gray Partridge	R	2	SH, RI, PR, AG		R*	O*	O*
Dusky (Blue) Grouse	R	3	FO(C), RI, SF	C*	C*	C*	C*
Ruffed Grouse	R	3	FO(D), SH, RI, SF	C*	U*	C*	U*
Greater Sage-grouse	R	3	SH, ME, AG	C*		C*	O*
Sharp-tailed Grouse	R	3	PR, SH, AG			O	
Pacific Loon	M (Arctic)	1	WL		x	x	
Common Loon	S	2	WL	O*	U*	O*	O
Pied-billed Grebe	S	3	WL	U*	U*	C*	C*
Horned Grebe	S	2	WL	x	R?	R	O*
Red-necked Grebe	S	1	WL	x	R*	x	O*
Eared Grebe	S	3	WL	O	U*	O*	C*
Western Grebe	S	3	WL	R	U*	O*	C*
Clark's Grebe	S	2	WL		R	O	U*
American White Pelican	S	3	WL	U	C*	C	C*
Double-crested Cormorant	S	3	WL	O	U*	C*	C*
American Bittern	S	2	WL	U*	R*	O*	U*
Great Blue Heron	S	3	WL	U*	U*	C*	C*
Great Egret	S	1	WL	x		O	x
Snowy Egret	S	2	WL	R	R	O	O
Black-crowned Night-Heron	S	2	WL	x	R	R	C*
White-faced Ibis	S	2	WL, ME, AG	O	R	O	U*
Turkey Vulture	S	3	ALL	x	R	C*	x
Osprey	S	3	RI	C*	C*	C*	O*
Bald Eagle	R	2	FO, RI	C*	U*	C*	C*
Northern Harrier	S	3	SH, PR, WL	O	U*	C*	C*
Sharp-shinned Hawk	S	3	FO, SH, RI	O	U*	O*	U
Cooper's Hawk	S	3	FO	O	U*	O*	U*
Northern Goshawk	R	3	FO(C)	C*	U*	O*	U*
Swainson's Hawk	S (NM)	3	PR, ME, SH, AG, SF	C*	C*	C*	C*
Red-tailed Hawk	R	3	ALL	C*	C*	C*	C*

continued on next page

	Wyoming (Statewide)			Grand Teton NP	Yellowstone NP	Jackson Hole	Red Rock Lakes NWR
	Status	*Abundance*	*Habitats*				
Ferruginous Hawk	R	3	RI, SH.PR, SF	R	R	R*	U*
Rough-legged Hawk	WM (Arctic)	3	SH, PR, AG	C	U	C	C
Golden Eagle	R	3	FO, SH, PR, AG, SF	O	U*	C*	U*
American Kestrel	S	3	PR, ME, AG, SF, RI	C*	C*	C*	C*
Merlin	R	2	FO, RI, SH, SF	O	R	O	O*
Prairie Falcon	R	3	SF, PR, ME, SH	O*	U*	O*	C*
Peregrine Falcon	R	2	SF, PR, ME, RI, FO	R	R*	O*	U*
Gyrfalcon	WM (Arctic)	1	SH, PR, AG			x	x
Virginia Rail	S	4	WL	x	R*	O*	O*
Yellow Rail	S	1	WL		R	x	
Sora	S	3	WL, RI, AG	O	C*	C*	U*
American Coot	S	4	WL	U*	C*	C*	A*
Sandhill Crane	S	3	ME, AG, WL	U*	U*	C*	C*
Whooping Crane	S	1	ME, AG, WL	x	R	R	x
Black-bellied Plover	M (Arctic)	2	SF, WL	x	R	x	
Semipalmated Plover	M (Arctic)	2	SF, WL	x	R	O	O
Killdeer	S	4	SF, WL	C*	C*	C*	C*
Mountain Plover	S	3	PR			x	
Black-necked Stilt	S	3	WL, SF		R	R	O
American Avocet	S	3	ME, WL, AG, SF	O	U	O*	C*
Spotted Sandpiper	S	3	SF, WL	C*	C*	C*	C*
Solitary Sandpiper	M (Boreal)	3	SF, WL	R	R	O	O
Greater Yellowlegs	M (Boreal)	3	SF, WL	O	R	O	U
Willet	S	3	SF, WL	O	U*	O*	C*
Lesser Yellowlegs	M (Boreal)	3	SF, WL	O	R	O	U
Upland Sandpiper	S (NM)	2	PR, AG			x	O
Long-billed Curlew	S	2	SH, PR, ME, AG, SF	O	R*	C*	C*
Marbled Godwit	S	2	ME, WL, SF, AG	R	R	R	U*
Sanderling	M (Arctic)	1	SF, WL	x	R	R	O
Semipalmated Sandpiper	M (Arctic)	2	SF, WL	x	U	O	O
Western Sandpiper	M (Arctic)	2	SF, WL	R	R	R	O
Least Sandpiper	M (Arctic)	3	SF, WL	O	R	R	O
White-rumped Sandpiper	M (Arctic)	1	SF, WL				O
Baird's Sandpiper	M (Arctic)	3	SF, WL	R	R	O	O
Pectoral Sandpiper	M (Arctic)	2	SF, WL	R	R	R	
Stilt Sandpiper	M (Arctic)	2	SF, WL	R	R	x	
Long-billed Dowitcher	M (Arctic)	3	SF, WL	O	U	O	U
Wilson's Snipe	S	3	ME, WL, AG, RI	C*	C*	C*	A*
Wilson's Phalarope	S	3	SF, WL	U	U*	C*	C*
Red-necked Phalarope	M (Arctic)	2	SF, WL	O	R	R	
Bonaparte's Gull	M (Boreal)	2	WL	O	R	R	
Franklin's Gull	S	3	WL, AG	O	R	C	A*

continued on next page

	Wyoming (Statewide)			Grand Teton NP	Yellowstone NP	Jackson Hole	Red Rock Lakes NWR
	Status	*Abundance*	*Habitats*				
Ring-billed Gull	M (Regional)	S	WL	O	U*	C	U*
California Gull	S	3	WL	C	A*	C	A*
Caspian Tern	S	2	WL	R	U*	O	x
Black Tern	S	3	WL	R	R*?	R	O
Common Tern	S	2	WL	R	U*	O	x
Forster's Tern	S	3	WL		R	O	C*
Rock Pigeon	R	4	AG, UR	U	U*	C*	x
Band-tailed Pigeon	M (Regional)	1	FO(C), SH	x		x	x
Eurasian Collared-Dove	R	3	UR	R	x	O	
Mourning Dove	S	4	ALL	O	U*	C*	U*
Black-billed Cuckoo	S (NM)	2	FO(D), RI, SF	x	x	R	x
Yellow-billed Cuckoo	S (NM)	2	FO(D), RI, SF			x	x
Western Screech-Owl	R	2	FO(D), SF, RI	R	R*?	R*	x
Great Horned Owl	R	3	FO, RI, ME, PR, SF	O	U*	C*	C*
Northern Pygmy-Owl	R	1	FO(C)	R	R*	O*	O
Burrowing Owl	S	2	SH, PR, AG	R	R	R*	O
Great Gray Owl	R	1	FO(C), PR	O*	U*	O*	C*
Long-eared Owl	R	3	FO, RI, SF	O	R*	O*	O*
Short-eared Owl	R	3	SH, PR, WL, AG	O	R*	O*	U*
Boreal Owl	R	2	FO(C)	x	R*	O*	
Northern Saw-whet Owl	R	2	FO(C), RI	R	R*	O*	O*
Common Nighthawk	S (NM)	4	R, ME, SH, AG, UR	C*	C*	C*	O
Common Poorwill	S (NM)	2	SH, PR, AG, FO			R*	
White-throated Swift	S (NM)	3	SF	O	U*	O*	O
Black-chinned Hummingbird	S (NM)	2	SH, RI	R		O	O
Calliope Hummingbird	S (NM)	3	SH, RI, PR, FO	C*	C*	C*	U*
Broad-tailed Hummingbird	S (NM)	3	RI, FO, ME	O	R*	C*	U*
Rufous Hummingbird	S (NM)	3	RI, FO, ME	O	U*	C*	U*
Belted Kingfisher	R	3	WL, RI	C*	U*	C*	C*
Acorn Woodpecker	Ac	1	FO	x		x	
Lewis's Woodpecker	S	2	FO(D), RI	O	R*	O*	O
Red-headed Woodpecker	S	2	FO(D), RI	x	x	x	x
Williamson's Sapsucker	S	2	FO(C)	O	U*	O*	O*
Red-naped Sapsucker	S	3	FO(C)	C*	C*	C*	C*
Downy Woodpecker	R	3	FO(D)	C*	U*	C*	C*
Hairy Woodpecker	R	2	FO	C*	C*	C*	C*
American Three-toed Woodpecker	R	2	FO(C)	O*	U*	O*	O
Black-backed Woodpecker	R	2	FO(C)	O*	R*	O*	O*
Northern Flicker	R	3	FO, RI, SH, SF	U	C*	C*	C*
Pileated Woodpecker	R	1	FO		x	x	
Olive-sided Flycatcher	S (NM)	3	FO(C), RI	C	U*	C*	U*
Western Wood-Pewee	S (NM)	3	FO(C), RI	C*	U*	C*	C*

continued on next page

	Wyoming (Statewide)			Grand Teton NP	Yellowstone NP	Jackson Hole	Red Rock Lakes NWR
	Status	*Abundance*	*Habitats*				
Willow Flycatcher	S (NM)	3	RI	U*	U*	O*	C*
Least Flycatcher	S (NM)	3	FO(D)	x	x	O	x
Hammond's Flycatcher	S (NM)	2	FO(C), RI	O	U*	C*	U*
Dusky Flycatcher	S (NM)	3	FO(C), RI, SH	C	C*	C*	C
Cordilleran Flycatcher	S (NM)	3	FO(D), RI	R*	R*	O*	U*
Say's Phoebe	S (NM)	3	SH, PR	R	R	R	O
Western Kingbird	S (NM)	3	SH, PR, AG, FO, RI	R	R	R	U
Eastern Kingbird	S (NM)	3	SH, PR, AG, FO, RI	O	R	O*	U
Northern Shrike	WM (Boreal)	3	SH	O	U	O	U
Loggerhead Shrike	S	3	FO, SH	R	R	O*	U*
Plumbeous Vireo	S (NM)	2	FO(D), RI	R	R	O	U
Warbling Vireo	S (NM)	4	FO, RI	C	C*	A*	C*
Red-eyed Vireo	S (NM)	2	FO(D), SF	O*	R	R	x
Gray Jay	R	3	FO(C)	C*	C*	C*	U*
Steller's Jay	R	3	FO(C), SH, UR	C*	U*	C*	O*
Blue Jay	R	3	FO(D), RI			x	x
Pinyon Jay	R	2	FO(C), SH	R	R	x	O
Clark's Nutcracker	R	3	FO(C), SF, SH	C*	A*	C*	C*
Black-billed Magpie	R	4	ALL	C*	C*	C*	A*
American Crow	R	3	ALL	O	R*	C*	C*
Common Raven	R	3	ALL	C*	A*	C*	C*
Horned Lark	R	4	SH, PR	O	U*	C*	C*
Tree Swallow	S (NM)	3	FO, RI	A*	A*	A*	C*
Violet-green Swallow	S (NM)	3	ALL	O	C*	C*	O*
Northern Rough-winged Swallow	S (NM)	3	RI, WL	O	U*	C*	U*
Bank Swallow	S (NM)	3	RI, WL.ME	C	U*	C*	C*
Cliff Swallow	S (NM)	3	ALL	A*	A*	A*	C*
Barn Swallow	S (NM)	3	ALL	C*	U*	C*	C*
Black-capped Chickadee	R	3	FO, RI, UR	C*	U*	C*	C*
Mountain Chickadee	R	3	FO(C)SH	C*	A*	C*	C*
Red-breasted Nuthatch	R	3	FO(C), RI	U	C*	C*	C*
White-breasted Nuthatch	R	3	FO(C), RI	C*	U*	O*	U*
Pygmy Nuthatch	R	2	FO(C)		R	x	O*
Brown Creeper	R	3	FO(C)	O	R*	O*	U*
Rock Wren	S	3	SF, SH, PR	U	C*	C*	U*
Canyon Wren	S	3	SF, SH			x	O
House Wren	S	3	RI, FO	U*	C*	C*	C*
Winter Wren	M (Regional)	1	FO(C)			R	x
Marsh Wren	S	3	WL	O	R*	C*	C*
American Dipper	R	3	WL	C	C*	C*	C*
Golden-crowned Kinglet	R	2	FO(C)	O	U*	O*	U
Ruby-crowned Kinglet	R	3	FO(C), SH, SF	U*	C*	C*	C*

continued on next page

	Wyoming (Statewide)			Grand Teton NP	Yellowstone NP	Jackson Hole	Red Rock Lakes NWR
	Status	*Abundance*	*Habitats*				
Western Bluebird	S	2	FO, SH	R		x	O
Mountain Bluebird	S	3	ME, PR, SH, AG	C*	C*	C*	A*
Townsend's Solitaire	R	3	FO(C)	O	U*	C*	C*
Veery	S (NM)	2	FO(D), RI	O	R	R	U*
Swainson's Thrush	S (NM)	3	FO(C), RI, SH	C*	C*	C*	U*
Hermit Thrush	S	3	FO(C), SH	C*	C*	C*	C*
American Robin	R	3	FO, RI, WL, AG, UR	C*	A*	A*	C*
Varied Thrush	M (Regional)	1	FO(C), RI		x	x	
Gray Catbird	S	3	RI, UR	O	R*	O*	O
Northern Mockingbird	S	2	RI, SH, SF	x	x	x	x
Sage Thrasher	S	3	SH	O	U*	C*	U*
European Starling	R	4	RI, AG, UR	C*	C*	C*	C*
American Pipit	S	3	ME	C	C*	C*	U
Sprague's Pipit	M (Regional)	2	SH, RI	x	x	x	
Bohemian Waxwing	WM (Boreal)	3	FO, RI, SH, SF	O	U	O	O
Cedar Waxwing	R	2	FO, RI, SH, SF	O	U*	C*	U*
McCown's Longspur	S	3	PR, SH, AG	x	R	x	
Lapland Longspur	WM (Arctic)	3	PR, AG	x	R	x	U
Snow Bunting	WM (Arctic)	2	SH, PR	O	R	O	C
Tennessee Warbler	M (Boreal)	2	FO, SF	R	R	R	O
Orange-crowned Warbler	S (NM)	2	FO, RI	O	R*	O*	O*
Nashville Warbler	M (Regional)	1	FO, SF, SH	x	x	x	
Yellow Warbler	S(NM)	4	RI, SF	C*	C*	A*	C*
Yellow-rumped Warbler	S(NM)	3	FO, RI	A*	A*	A*	C*
Townsend's Warbler	S(NM)	2	FO(C), SF	R	R	R	O
Blackburnian Warbler	M (Regional)	1	RI, SF	x		x	
Palm Warbler	M (Boreal)	1	RI, SF		x	x	
American Redstart	S (NM)	2	RI		R	O*	U*
Northern Waterthrush	M (Boreal)	2	FO, RI	R	R*	O*	O
MacGillivray's Warbler	S (NM)	3	FO, RI	C*	C*	C*	C*
Common Yellowthroat	S(NM)	3	RI	C*	C*	C*	C*
Wilson's Warbler	S(NM)	3	RI	C*	U*	C*	C*
Yellow-breasted Chat	S(NM)	3	RI, WL	x	x	x	x
Green-tailed Towhee	S	3	SH, RI	C*	U*	C*	O*
Spotted Towhee	S	3	FO, SH, RI		R	O	
American Tree Sparrow	WM (Arctic)	2	RI, AG, UR	O	U	O	O
Chipping Sparrow	S	2	FO, RI, SH	C*	C*	C*	C*
Clay-colored Sparrow	S	2	FO, RI, SH, AG	R	x	O*	
Brewer's Sparrow	S	3	SH	C	C*	A*	C*
Vesper Sparrow	S	3	SH, PR, AG	C*	C*	A*	C*
Lark Sparrow	S	3	SH, PR, AG, FO	O	R	R	O*
Sage Sparrow	S	3	SH	x		x	

continued on next page

Birds of the Greater Yellowstone Ecoregion—*continued*

	Wyoming (Statewide)			*Grand Teton NP*	*Yellowstone NP*	*Jackson Hole*	*Red Rock Lakes NWR*
	Status	*Abundance*	*Habitats*				
Lark Bunting	S	4	SH, PR, AG	R	R	R	O
Savannah Sparrow	S	4	RI, ME, PR, WL, AG	C*	C*	C*	A*
Grasshopper Sparrow	S	3	SH, PR, ME, AG		R	R	
Fox Sparrow	R	3	RI, FO, SH, SF	O	R*	C*	O
Song Sparrow	R	3	RI, WL	C*	U*	C*	C*
Lincoln's Sparrow	S	3	RI, WL	C*	C*	C*	C*
White-throated Sparrow	M (Boreal)	2	RI, UR	R		R	
Harris's Sparrow	WM (Arctic)	2	RI, AG, UR	R		R	
White-crowned Sparrow	S	3	RI	A*	C*	A*	C*
Dark-eyed Junco	R	3	F, UR	A*	A*	C*	
Western Tanager	S (NM)	3	FO	C*	C*	C*	C*
Rose-breasted Grosbeak	S (NM)	2	FO(D), RI, UR	O	x	R	x
Black-headed Grosbeak	S (NM)	3	FO, RI, UR	O	R	C*	U
Lazuli Bunting	S (NM)	3	FO(D), SH, RI	O	C*	O*	U*
Indigo Bunting	S (NM)	2	RI	x		x	
Dickcissel	S (NM)	2	PR			x	
Bobolink	S (NM)	2	SH, PR, AG	R	x	O*	O*
Red-winged Blackbird	S	4	RI, WL, AG	C*	C*	A*	C*
Western Meadowlark	S	4	SH, PR, AG	U	C*	C*	C*
Yellow-headed Blackbird	S	3	WL	C	C*	C*	C*
Brewer's Blackbird	S	4	ALL	A*	C*	C*	C*
Common Grackle	S	3	RI, SH, WL, AG, UR		R	C*	x
Brown-headed Cowbird	S	3	RI, SH, PR, AG, UR	C	C*	C*	C*
Orchard Oriole	S (NM)	2	RI, , UR	x		x	
Bullock's Oriole	S (NM)	3	RI, UR	O	R	C*	x
Gray-crowned Rosy-Finch	R	3	ME, SF, AG	U	U	C	?
Black Rosy-Finch	R	2	ME, SF, AG	U*	U*	C*	O*
Pine Grosbeak	R	2	FO(C)	O	U*	C*	C*
Cassin's Finch	R	3	FO(C).UR	C*	C*	C*	C*
House Finch	R	3	FO, SH, SP, UR	R	R*	C	
Red Crossbill	R	3	FO(C), SF	O*	U*	C*	U*
White-winged Crossbill	R	2	FO(C)	x	R*	O	
Common Redpoll	WM (Arctic)	2	SH, PR, SF	R	R	O	C
Hoary Redpoll	WM (Arctic)	1	SH, PR, SF		R	x	
Pine Siskin	R	3	FO(C), RI, UR	C*	C*	C*	C*
American Goldfinch	R	3	RI, UR	O	R	O*	U*
Evening Grosbeak	R	3	FO(C), UR	O	U*	O*	O
House Sparrow	R	4	AG, UR	C*	R*	C*	O*

Note: This list of 266 regularly occurring Greater Yellowstone birds excludes all species considered Wyoming accidentals or those reported from only one of the four listed locations. Wyoming species' status, abundance, and habitat affiliations are mostly after the *Wyoming Bird Checklist* (Wyoming Game & Fish Department 2008). The Grand Teton National Park bird list is based partly on Johnsgard (1982) and Follett (1986). The Yellowstone National Park list is mainly based on McEneaney (1988, 2008). The Jackson Hole regional list is based on Raynes (2000) and Raynes and Raynes (2008); an online list can be found at http://www.npwrc.usgs.gov/resource/birds/chekbird/ r6/jackhole.htm. The Red Rock Lakes National Wildlife Refuge list is based on http://www.npwrc.usgs.gov/resource/birds/chekbird/r6/redrock.htm. Asterisks indicate reported breeding. Taxonomy and species sequence are based on American Ornithologists' Union, *Check-List of North American Birds,* 7th ed. (1998), with supplements to 2010.

Statewide Wyoming Status Codes

M: Migrant, present during spring and/or fall (Arctic, Boreal Forest, or Regional breeders)
NM: Neotropic Migrant, wintering primarily from Mexico southward
R: Resident year-round
S: Summer resident, presumed or known to breed regionally
WM: Wintering Migrant (Arctic and Boreal Forest breeders)

Local Abundance Codes (summer abundance for breeders; otherwise when most abundant)

A: Abundant
C: Common
U: Uncommon
O: Occasional
R: Rare
x: Accidental
*: One or more breeding records

Habitats (those indicated may relate to Wyoming generally)

AG: Agricultural lands (pastures, croplands, irrigated meadows, shelterbelts)
ALL: All major terrestrial habitats used
FO: Forests; (C) = mainly coniferous, (D) = mainly deciduous
ME: Meadows (wet to moist meadows and grasslands)
PR: Prairie grasslands with native vegetation
RI: Riparian habitats (streams, reservoirs, lakes)
SF: Special Features (caves, cliffs, barren shores, roadsides, mines, burned or logged sites, etc.)
SH: Shrublands (especially sage-dominated and pinyon-juniper shrublands)
UR: Urban (city habitats, including buildings and other structures)
WL: Wetlands (aquatic habitats with emergent vegetation, usually also with open water)

Wyoming Statewide Abundance Codes

1: Rare
2: Uncommon
3: Common
4: Abundant

APPENDIX 3

Vertebrates of the Greater Yellowstone Ecoregion

Mammals

The following list is organized in the taxonomic sequence of Clark and Stromberg (1987); species' status information is mostly from Streubel (1995) and Luce et al. (1997, 2004). Yellowstone NP population estimates are mostly from the US National Park Service's website, but see also McEneaney (2008). Red Rock Lakes NWR records are also based on that refuge's website.

MASKED SHREW (*Sorex cinereus*). Common throughout western Wyoming and reported at Red Rock Lakes NWR. Occupies diverse forest and grassland and shrubland habitats as well as rock outcrops and talus fields.

PREBLE'S SHREW (*Sorex preblei*). Documented in Wyoming only for Lamar Ranger Station, Yellowstone NP. Associated with moist meadows and forests.

VAGRANT SHREW (*Sorex vagrans*). Documented only from northwestern Lincoln County (in Jackson Hole region south of Grand Teton NP). Associated with riparian habitats.

DUSKY SHREW (*Sorex monticolus*). Widespread in the Greater Yellowstone Ecoregion and common in Yellowstone and Grand Teton NP. Often found in moist montane or spruce-fir forests but also in shrubland and grassland habitats as well as in rock outcrops and talus fields.

DWARF SHREW (*Sorex nanus*). Documented but little studied in the Greater Yellowstone Ecoregion. Apparently rare in Yellowstone and Grand Teton NP. Often found in montane coniferous forests but also in shrubland and grassland habitats as well as rock outcrops and talus fields.

NORTHERN WATER SHREW (*Sorex palustris*). Widespread in the Greater Yellowstone Ecoregion. Common in Yellowstone and Grand Teton NP and at Red Rock Lakes NWR. Often found in coniferous forests, riparian shrub, alpine grasslands, and wetlands.

WESTERN SMALL-FOOTED MYOTIS. (*Myotis ciliolabrum*). Of uncertain status in the Greater Yellowstone Ecoregion. Reported but not documented from Jackson Hole region (Wyoming latilong #8, Luce et al. 1997) and rare, if present, in Yellowstone NP. Usually found in montane forest, sage steppes, or shortgrass prairie near rock outcrops. Roosts and hibernates in caves or other rocky areas.

LITTLE BROWN MYOTIS (*Myotis lucifugus*). Widespread in the Greater Yellowstone Ecoregion. Common in Yellowstone and Grand Teton NP and at Red Rock Lakes NWR. Found in forests, sagebrush grasslands, riparian shrubland, and urban areas, often close to water. Roosts and hibernates in caves, buildings, trees.

LONG-LEGGED MYOTIS (*Myotis volans*). Probably widespread but poorly documented in the Greater Yellowstone Ecoregion. Common in Yellowstone NP and reported from Grand Teton NP. Generally common in forests, basin-prairie, mountain foothills, shrublands, and riparian habitats above 3,500–4,000 feet. Roosts in caves, buildings, and trees.

FRINGE-TAILED MYOTIS (*Myotis thysanodes*). Status uncertain. Reported by the National Park Service as uncommon in Yellowstone NP but not known from elsewhere in the Greater Yellowstone Ecoregion; otherwise known only from eastern Wyoming. Roosting and hibernation occur on cliffs and large snags.

LONG-EARED MYOTIS (*Myotis evotis*). Widespread in the Greater Yellowstone Ecoregion; uncommon in Yellowstone NP. Often found among ponderosa pines, usually near water, but rarely occurs as high as spruce-fir forests.

SILVER-HAIRED BAT (*Lasionycterus noctivagans*). Apparently present throughout in the Greater Yellowstone Ecoregion. Common in Yellowstone NP and documented from Jackson Hole. Usually found in coniferous or deciduous forests, often near water. Roosts in trees, mines, caves, houses, and under tree bark.

BIG BROWN BAT (*Eptesicus fuscus*). Common in Yellowstone NP, but apparently not reported from Grand Teton NP or Jackson Hole. Found in coniferous and deciduous forests, open country, and urban areas. Roosts and hibernates in buildings, caves, crevices, etc.

HOARY BAT (*Lasiurus cinereus*). Documented from Grand Teton NP; uncommon in Yellowstone NP. Found in coniferous or deciduous forests, sagebrush grasslands, riparian shrublands, and urban areas. Roosts solitarily in trees. Migratory.

TOWNSEND'S BIG-EARED BAT (*Plecotus townsendii*). Uncommon in Yellowstone NP; also reported from Jackson Hole. Found in forests, shrublands, grasslands, and juniper woodlands; hibernates in caves or mines.

PIKA (*Ochotona princeps*). Widespread in the Greater Yellowstone Ecoregion. Common in Yellowstone and Grand Teton NP and reported from Red Rock Lakes NWR. Often found on talus slopes from about 8,000 feet up to the alpine zone.

WHITE-TAILED JACKRABBIT (*Lepus townsendii*). Local in the Greater Yellowstone Ecoregion. Reported from grasslands in Jackson Hole and northern Yellowstone NP (from Mammoth to Gardiner Basin). Occupies sagebrush grasslands, and other open habitats at lower elevations, but sometimes reaches alpine tundra.

MOUNTAIN (NUTTALL'S) COTTONTAIL (*Sylvilagus nuttallii*). Widespread in the Greater Yellowstone Ecoregion. Occupies open, often brushy, habitats from 3,900 to 8,850 feet.

DESERT COTTONTAIL (*Sylvilagus audubonii*). Rare in the Greater Yellowstone Ecoregion. Reported near Gardiner in northern Yellowstone NP. Very similar to the mountain cottontail but paler and larger with longer ears. Occupies more grassy habitats at lower altitudes than the mountain cottontail.

SNOWSHOE HARE (*Lepus americanus*). Widespread in the Greater Yellowstone Ecoregion. Common in Yellowstone and Grand Teton NP; also reported from Jackson Hole and Red Rock Lakes NWR. Occupies coniferous forests, aspens, and willow thickets.

LEAST CHIPMUNK (*Eutamias minimus*). Widespread in the Greater Yellowstone Ecoregion. Common in Yellowstone and Grand Teton NP; reported from Jackson Hole and Red Rock Lakes NWR. Occupies sagebrush, shrublands, badlands, and forest openings.

YELLOW PINE CHIPMUNK (*Eutamias amoenus*). Widespread in the Greater Yellowstone Ecoregion. Common in Yellowstone and Grand Teton NP; reported from Jackson Hole and Red Rock Lakes NWR. Common in coniferous forests, especially lodgepole pine, but also in aspen or juniper woodlands and other near-forested habitats.

UINTA CHIPMUNK (*Tamias umbrinus*). Widespread in the Greater Yellowstone Ecoregion. Uncommon in Yellowstone and Grand Teton NP; present in Jackson Hole. Frequents edges of clearings in dense spruce-fir forest and, elsewhere in Wyoming, rocky habitats from the ponderosa pine to subalpine zones.

YELLOW-BELLIED MARMOT (*Marmota flaviventris*). Widespread in the Greater Yellowstone Ecoregion. Common in Yellowstone and Grand Teton NP and in Jackson Hole. Favors rock outcrops, but also found in other somewhat open habitats from valleys to alpine tundra and forest edges.

WYOMING GROUND SQUIRREL (*Spermophilus elegans*). Rare or very local in the Greater Yellowstone Ecoregion. Reported only from Red Rock Lakes NWR. Occurs from sagebrush grasslands to alpine meadows.

UINTA GROUND SQUIRREL (*Spermophilus annutus*). Widespread in the Greater Yellowstone Ecoregion. Common in Yellowstone and Grand Teton NP, Jackson Hole, and at Red Rock Lakes NWR. Found in grasslands, meadows, sagebrush grasslands, and open areas in forests.

GOLDEN-MANTLED GROUND SQUIRREL (*Citellus lateralis*). Widespread in the Greater Yellowstone Ecoregion. Common in Yellowstone and Grand Teton NP; reported from Jackson Hole and Red Rock Lakes NWR. Often found on rock outcrops, but also occupies lowland meadows, forest openings, and tundra.

RED SQUIRREL (*Tamiasciurus hudsonicus*). Widespread in the Greater Yellowstone Ecoregion. Common in Yellowstone and Grand Teton NP, Jackson Hole, and at Red Rock Lakes NWR. Abundant in coniferous forests and aspens.

NORTHERN FLYING SQUIRREL (*Glaucomys sabrinus*). Widespread in the Greater Yellowstone Ecoregion, but rarely seen because of its nocturnality. Occasional in Yellowstone and Grand Teton NP. Found in coniferous forests and aspen woods.

NORTHERN POCKET GOPHER (*Thomomys talpoides*). Widespread in the Greater Yellowstone Ecoregion. Common in Yellowstone and Grand Teton NP; reported from Jackson Hole and Red Rock Lakes NWR. Favors loose, deep soils with few rocks.

BEAVER (*Castor canadensis*). Widespread in the Greater Yellowstone Ecoregion. Common in Yellowstone NP (estimated 500 animals), Grand Teton NP, Jackson Hole, and at Red Rock Lakes NWR. Associated with aquatic habitat close to aspen, willow, or cottonwood stands.

DEER MOUSE (*Perornyscus maniculatus*). Widespread in the Greater Yellowstone Ecoregion. Abundant in Yellowstone and Grand Teton NP, Jackson Hole, and at Red Rock Lakes NWR. Occupies nearly all terrestrial habitats.

BUSHY-TAILED WOODRAT (*Neotoma cinerea*). Widespread in the Greater Yellowstone Ecoregion. Common in Yellowstone and Grand Teton NP, Jackson Hole, and at Red Rock Lakes NWR. Often found in habitats with rock outcrops but also occupies abandoned buildings.

SOUTHERN (BOREAL) RED-BACKED VOLE (*Clethrionomys gapperi*). Widespread in the Greater Yellowstone Ecoregion. Common in Yellowstone and Grand Teton NP; also reported from Jackson Hole and Red Rock Lakes NWR. Found in coniferous and mixed forests with abundant litter, logs, and windfall, often in damp sites near water.

HEATHER (MOUNTAIN) VOLE (*Phenacomys intermedius*). Widespread in the Greater Yellowstone Ecoregion. Common in Yellowstone and Grand Teton NP; reported from Jackson Hole. Occurs in conifers, aspens, sagebrush grasslands, and alpine meadows.

MEADOW VOLE (*Microtus pennsylvanicus*). Widespread in the Greater Yellowstone Ecoregion. Common in Yellowstone and Grand Teton NP; reported from Jackson Hole and Red Rock Lakes NWR. Abundant in moist to wet meadows, grasslands, and other grassy habitats.

MOUNTAIN VOLE (*Microtus montanus*). Widespread in the Greater Yellowstone Ecoregion and common in Yellowstone and Grand Teton NP and Jackson Hole. Typically found in grassy habitats, usually occurring at higher elevations than the meadow vole.

LONG-TAILED VOLE (*Microtus longicaudus*). Widespread in the Greater Yellowstone Ecoregion. Common in Yellowstone and Grand Teton NP, Jackson Hole, and at Red Rock Lakes NWR. Occupies grasslands, meadows, and streamsides lined with deciduous trees.

WATER (RICHARDSON) VOLE (*Microtus richardsoni*). Widespread in the Greater Yellowstone Ecoregion. Present but poorly documented in Yellowstone and Grand Teton NP. Frequents alpine and subalpine meadows with watercourses and overhanging banks.

SAGEBRUSH VOLE (*Lemniscus curtatus levidensis*). Rare in Grand Teton NP and not reported in Yellowstone NP. Occupies sagebrush grasslands.

MUSKRAT (*Ondatra zibethicus*). Widespread in the Greater Yellowstone Ecoregion. Common in Yellowstone and Grand Teton NP, Jackson Hole, and at Red Rock Lakes NWR. Occupies marshy habitats such as beaver ponds.

WESTERN JUMPING MOUSE (*Zapus princeps*). Widespread in the Greater Yellowstone Ecoregion. Common in Yellowstone and Grand Teton NP and Jackson Hole; uncommon at Red Rock Lakes NWR. Typically found in grassy areas near water.

PORCUPINE (*Erethizon dorsatum*). Widespread in the Greater Yellowstone Ecoregion. Common in Yellowstone and Grand Teton NP, Jackson Hole, and at Red Rock Lakes NWR. Occurs in most habitats, especially deciduous and coniferous forests.

COYOTE (*Canis latrans*). Widespread in the Greater Yellowstone Ecoregion. Common in Yellowstone and Grand Teton NP, Jackson Hole, and at Red Rock Lakes NWR. Occupies most open habitats, such as the sagebrush grasslands of the Lamar and Hayden Valleys (Yellowstone NP) and Antelope Flats (Grand Teton NP).

GRAY WOLF (*Canis lupus*). Reintroduced successfully into Yellowstone NP in 1995 and 1996. Wolves had reached Grand Teton NP and the National Elk Refuge by 1999. By 2011 there were packs in the Gros Ventre part of the Elk Refuge, in Antelope Flats, along Pacific Creek, and near Hoback Junction. There are both historic and probable recent records at Red Rock Lakes NWR. The Greater Yellowstone region population exceeded 300 individuals by the end of 2003, and by the end of 2008 the three northern Rocky Mountain states (Wyoming, Montana, and Idaho) held more than 1,650 wolves. The Yellowstone NP population has declined greatly since the early 2000s. In 2010, the year that legal killing of wolves in the Greater Yellowstone region began, the Yellowstone NP population consisted of about 85 individuals, or about half its peak numbers of 175 individuals. Canine distemper has also been a serious cause of mortality in young. Occurs in diverse habitats, usually near elk herds.

RED FOX (*Vulpes fulva*). Widespread in the Greater Yellowstone Ecoregion. Occasional in Yellowstone and Grand Teton NP and Jackson Hole; reported from Red Rock Lakes NWR. Occupies most open and mixed habitats, especially near riparian habitats.

BLACK BEAR (*Ursus americanus*). Widespread in the Greater Yellowstone Ecoregion. The population of Yellowstone NP is typically 500–650 individuals. Also occurs in Grand Teton NP and at Red Rock Lakes NWR. Common in coniferous forests, aspen, riparian scrublands, and grasslands.

GRIZZLY BEAR (*Ursus horribilis*). Widespread but rare in the Greater Yellowstone Ecoregion, where the population consisted of about 600 individuals in 2010; recent counts range from 280 to 610. Also reported from Grand Teton NP and Red Rock Lakes NWR. Occupies coniferous forests, aspen, riparian scrublands, and grasslands, from valleys up to the alpine zone.

RACCOON (*Procyon lotor*). Local in the Greater Yellowstone Ecoregion. Occasional in Grand Teton NP, rare in Yellowstone NP, and very rare at Red Rock Lakes NWR. Occupies diverse habitats, but especially common along wooded riverbottoms.

MARTEN (*Martes americana*). Widespread in the Greater Yellowstone Ecoregion. Common in Yellowstone and Grand Teton NP; reported from Red Rock Lakes NWR. Usually found in coniferous forests but also in cottonwood riparian woods.

ERMINE (SHORT-TAILED WEASEL) (*Mustela erminea muricus*). Widespread in the Greater Yellowstone Ecoregion. Common in Yellowstone and Grand Teton NP; reported from Red Rock Lakes NWR. Occupies most habitats, especially coniferous forests.

LONG-TAILED WEASEL (*Mustela frenata*). Widespread in the Greater Yellowstone Ecoregion. Common in Yellowstone and Grand Teton NP; reported from Red Rock Lakes NWR. Occupies diverse habitats, from willows to subalpine spruce-fir.

MINK (*Mustela vison*). Widespread in the Greater Yellowstone Ecoregion. Occasional in Yellowstone and Grand Teton NP; reported from Red Rock Lakes NWR. Frequents most habitats near water.

WOLVERINE (*Gulo luscus*). Nearly extirpated from the Rocky Mountain region. Rare in Yellowstone and Grand Teton NP; also reported from Red Rock Lakes NWR. Frequents remote locations, especially coniferous forests and alpine or subalpine meadows.

BADGER (*Taxidea taxus*). Widespread in the Greater Yellowstone Ecoregion. Common in Yellowstone NP (especially the Lamar Valley) and Grand Teton NP (Antelope Flats); also at Red Rock Lakes NWR. Typically found in grasslands, sagebrush, and grass-alder scrub with deep soils.

STRIPED SKUNK (*Mephitis mephitis*). Widespread in the Greater Yellowstone Ecoregion. Uncommon to rare in Yellowstone and Grand Teton NP; common at Red Rock Lakes NWR. Occupies diverse habitats, especially riparian woodlands.

RIVER OTTER (*Lutra canadensis*). Local and generally rare in the Greater Yellowstone Ecoregion. Uncommon in Yellowstone NP (especially Yellowstone Lake) and Grand Teton NP (especially the Snake River, Two Ocean and Emma Matilda Lakes). Occasional at Red Rock Lakes NWR. Associated with lakes and rivers having good fish populations.

MOUNTAIN LION (*Felis concolor*). Rare in the Greater Yellowstone Ecoregion. The Yellowstone NP population typically has fifteen to seventeen individuals; also reported from Jackson Hole, the National Elk Refuge, and Red Rock Lakes NWR. Mostly occurs in habitats that support good deer populations.

LYNX (*Lynx canadensis*). Rare in the Greater Yellowstone Ecoregion, but probably occurs in both parks; rare at Red Rock Lakes NWR. Associated with dense subalpine coniferous forests.

BOBCAT (*Lynx rufus*). Widespread in the Greater Yellowstone Ecoregion. Uncommon but possibly widespread in Yellowstone and Grand Teton NP; occasional at Red Rock Lakes NWR. Mostly found in open, broken country, meadows, and mixed habitats.

ELK (*Cervus canadensis*). Abundant and widespread in the Greater Yellowstone Ecoregion. The Yellowstone NP population has at times exceeded 30,000 individuals during summer and as many as to 19,000 (in 1994) during winter. In 2010 the estimated park population was 15,000–25,000. Winter severity greatly affects elk numbers; in recent years the winter park estimates have been as low as about 5,000. Also common in Grand Teton NP and at Red Rock Lakes NWR. Abundant at the National Elk Refuge during winter and common in the northern range of Yellowstone NP. Occupies coniferous forests, meadows, and grasslands.

MULE DEER (*Odocoileus hemionus*). Widespread in the Greater Yellowstone Ecoregion. The population of Yellowstone NP is typically 2,300–2,500 individuals; also common in Grand Teton NP, Jackson Hole, and at Red Rock Lakes NWR. Found in grasslands, scrublands, and open forests, especially in broken country.

WHITE-TAILED DEER (*Odocoileus virginianus*). Local and rare in the Greater Yellowstone Ecoregion. Uncommon and still very local in both parks, but increasing in numbers and range after entering Yellowstone NP from the north and moving up the Yellowstone and Gardner Valleys and probably expanding into Grand Teton NP from Idaho. More typical of riparian edges, cultivated lands, and moister climates than the mule deer, but slightly larger and likely to outcompete it where both are present.

MOOSE (*Alces alces*). Widespread in the Greater Yellowstone Ecoregion. The Yellowstone NP population is typically over 500 individuals, but in 2010 the estimated population was less than 500. Several hundred are also in Grand Teton NP and adjacent Jackson Hole. Also occurs at Red Rock Lakes NWR. Occupies coniferous forests and meadows, mostly near water.

PRONGHORN (*Antilocapra americana*). Local in the Greater Yellowstone Ecoregion. The Yellowstone NP population is typically 200–250 individuals, and the Grand Teton NP population averages somewhat larger. Also common in the National Elk Refuge and at Red Rock Lakes NWR. Associated with sagebrush grasslands.

BISON (*Bison bison*). Local in the Greater Yellowstone Ecoregion. The Yellowstone NP population typically averages over 3,500 individuals, mostly centered in the northern grasslands (the Lamar and Hayden Valleys). The Grand Teton NP population consisted of a few dozen animals in the early 1980s but by 2010 had increased to a few hundred, mostly scattered between Kelly and Moose; during winter several hundred are present in the National Elk Refuge. Strays sometimes have appeared at Red Rock Lakes NWR. Occupies sagebrush grasslands, meadows, and other grassland habitats.

BIGHORN SHEEP (*Ovis canadensis*). Local in montane topography of the Greater Yellowstone Ecoregion. The Yellowstone NP population was 150–225 individuals in the early 2000s; in 2010 the estimated population was 250–275. Also present locally in Grand Teton NP and Jackson Hole (Gros Ventre and Teton Ranges). Historically reported from Red Rock Lakes NWR. Occupies mountainous, rimrock, and generally rugged habitats, especially those having grasses and rocky outcrops.

MOUNTAIN GOAT (*Oreamnos americana*). Local in alpine habitats of the Greater Yellowstone Ecoregion. Introduced and still very local in northern Yellowstone NP. This population consisted of 200–250 individuals as of 2010. Limited to areas of alpine topography and steep cliffs.

OVERLEAF. *Cow elk and calves crossing the Buffalo Fork River, Grand Teton National Park, Wyoming*

Birds

Taxonomy in the following list is according to American Ornithologists' Union, *Check-List of North American Birds,* 7th ed. (1998), with supplements to 2010. Species known from only one of the two national parks and considered accidentals are excluded from this list. The "Grand Teton–Jackson Hole" designation is largely based on Raynes and Wile (1994) and Raynes (2000) and encompasses Grand Teton NP, the Jackson Hole valley, the National Elk Refuge, the eastern parts of Targhee National Forest, and much of the Bridger-Teton National Forest. A recent regional Jackson Hole hard-copy check-list of 340 species is available (Raynes and Raynes 2008). The Yellowstone NP list is mostly based on McEneaney's (2007b) list of 323 species. Online checklists are available for Red Rock Lakes NWR (http://www.npwrc.usgs.gov/resource/birds/chekbird/r6/redrock.htm) and Grays Lake NWR (http://www.npwrc.usgs.gov/resource/birds/chekbird/r1/graylake.htm).

GREATER WHITE-FRONTED GOOSE (*Anser albifrons*). Accidental fall migrant.

SNOW GOOSE (*Chen caerulescens*). Occasional fall migrant, rare during winter.

TRUMPETER SWAN (*Cygnus buccinator*). Common permanent resident. Breeding has been reported in Grand Teton–Jackson Hole and Yellowstone NP and at Red Rock Lakes NWR and Grays Lake NWR, with populations well documented at Red Rock Lakes NWR and in Yellowstone NP (McEneaney 2008).

TUNDRA SWAN (*Cygnus columbianus*). Occasional migrant during spring, fall, and winter.

CACKLING GOOSE (*Branta hutchinsii*). Records for the recently (2004) recognized and arctic-breeding species are still too limited to judge its relative abundance, but it is probably an occasional spring and fall migrant.

CANADA GOOSE (*Branta canadensis*). Common permanent resident. Breeding has been reported in Grand Teton–Jackson Hole and Yellowstone NP and at Grays Lake NWR and Red Rock Lakes NWR.

WOOD DUCK (*Aix sponsa*). Occasional summer resident at Red Rock Lakes NWR.

GADWALL (*Anus strepera*). Uncommon summer resident, common spring and fall migrant, rare in winter. Breeding has been reported in Grand Teton–Jackson Hole and Yellowstone NP.

AMERICAN WIGEON (*Anas americana*). Uncommon summer resident, common in spring and fall, rare in winter. Breeding has been reported in Grand Teton–Jackson Hole and Yellowstone NP and at Grays Lake NWR and Red Rock Lakes NWR.

MALLARD (*Anas platyrhynchos*). Common to abundant permanent resident. Breeding has been reported in Grand Teton–Jackson Hole and Yellowstone NP and at Grays Lake NWR and Red Rock Lakes NWR.

AMERICAN BLACK DUCK (*Anas rubripes*). Accidental migrant in Yellowstone NP.

BLUE-WINGED TEAL (*Anas discors*). Uncommon to occasional summer resident. Breeding has been reported in Yellowstone NP and at Red Rock Lakes NWR.

CINNAMON TEAL (*Anas cyanoptera*). Uncommon summer resident. Breeding has been reported in Grand Teton–Jackson Hole and Yellowstone NP and at Red Rock Lakes NWR.

NORTHERN SHOVELER (*Anus clypeata*). Rare to occasional permanent resident. Breeding has been reported in Grand Teton–Jackson Hole and Yellowstone NP and at Grays Lake NWR and Red Rock Lakes NWR.

Northern Pintail (*Anas acuta*). Uncommon summer resident, and common spring and fall migrant, uncommon in winter. Breeding has been reported in Yellowstone NP and at Grays Lake NWR and Red Rock Lakes NWR.

Green-winged Teal (*Anas crecca*). Common to uncommon permanent resident. Breeding has been reported in Grand Teton–Jackson Hole and Yellowstone NP and at Grays Lake NWR and Red Rock Lakes NWR.

Canvasback (*Aythya valisineria*). Occasional spring and fall migrant. Breeding has been reported in Grand Teton–Jackson Hole and Yellowstone NP and at Grays Lake NWR and Red Rock Lakes NWR.

Redhead (*Aythya americana*). Uncommon summer resident, common to rare migrant in spring and fall. Breeding has been reported in Grand Teton–Jackson Hole and Yellowstone NP and at Grays Lake NWR and Red Rock Lakes NWR.

Ring-necked Duck (*Aythya collaris*). Common to uncommon permanent resident. Breeding has been reported in Grand Teton–Jackson Hole and Yellowstone NP and at Grays Lake NWR and Red Rock Lakes NWR.

Lesser Scaup (*Aythya affinis*). Occasional spring and fall migrant. Breeding has been reported in Grand Teton–Jackson Hole and Yellowstone NP and at Grays Lake NWR and Red Rock Lakes NWR.

Harlequin Duck (*Histrionicus histrionicus*). Occasional from spring to fall. Breeding has been reported in Grand Teton–Jackson Hole and Yellowstone NP. During the early 2000s there were twenty to twenty-six pairs in Yellowstone NP, a relatively stable population (McEneaney 2007a).

Common Goldeneye (*Bucephala americana*). Occasional permanent resident. Reportedly has bred at Red Rock Lakes NWR, but confirmed breeding in Wyoming is still lacking (Faulkner 2010).

Barrow's Goldeneye (*Bucephala islandica*). Common to uncommon permanent resident. Breeding has been reported in Grand Teton–Jackson Hole and Yellowstone NP and at Grays Lake NWR and Red Rock Lakes NWR.

Bufflehead (*Bucephala albeola*). Rare to occasional permanent resident. Breeding has been reported in Grand Teton–Jackson Hole and Yellowstone NP and at Red Rock Lakes NWR.

Surf Scoter (*Melanitta perspicillata*). Accidental fall migrant.

White-winged Scoter (*Melanitta fusca*). Accidental fall migrant.

Hooded Merganser (*Lophodytes cucullatus*). Rare from fall to spring. Reported breeding at Grays Lake NWR and Red Rock Lakes NWR.

Red-breasted Merganser (*Mergus serrator*). Occasional in spring and fall. Reported breeding at Red Rock Lakes NWR.

Common Merganser (*Mergus merganser*). Common permanent resident. Breeding has been reported in Grand Teton–Jackson Hole and Yellowstone NP and at Red Rock Lakes NWR.

Ruddy Duck (*Oxyura jamaicensis*). Occasional from late spring to fall. Breeding has been reported in Grand Teton–Jackson Hole and Yellowstone NP and at Grays Lake NWR and Red Rock Lakes NWR.

Chukar (*Alectoris chukar*). Accidental in fall and winter. Breeding has been reported in Grand Teton–Jackson Hole; some records may be from game-farm birds.

Gray Partridge (*Perdix perdix*). Rare resident. Breeding has been reported in Grand Teton–Jackson Hole and Yellowstone NP and at Grays Lake NWR.

DUSKY GROUSE (*Dendragapus obscurus*). Common permanent resident. Breeding has been reported in Grand Teton–Jackson Hole and Yellowstone NP and at Grays Lake NWR and Red Rock Lakes NWR.

RUFFED GROUSE (*Bonasa umbellus*). Common permanent resident. Breeding has been reported in Grand Teton–Jackson Hole and Yellowstone NP and at Grays Lake NWR and Red Rock Lakes NWR.

GREATER SAGE-GROUSE (*Centrocercus urophasianus*). Common permanent resident. Breeding has been reported in Grand Teton–Jackson Hole and at Grays Lake NWR and Red Rock Lakes NWR. A rapidly declining species worthy of nationally threatened status.

SHARP-TAILED GROUSE (*Tympanuchus phasianellus*). Rarely reported in Jackson Hole, fall to spring. Reported as breeding at Grays Lake NWR, but rare and declining throughout the region.

COMMON LOON (*Gavia immer*). Occasional to uncommon in spring and fall, rare in summer. Breeding has been reported in Grand Teton–Jackson Hole and Yellowstone NP.

PIED-BILLED GREBE (*Podilymbus podiceps*). Common summer resident and breeder in Grand Teton NP and Yellowstone NP and at Red Rock Lakes NWR.

HORNED GREBE (*Podiceps auritus*). Occasional to rare during migration, rare in summer. Reported breeding at Red Rock Lakes NWR; a hypothetical breeder in Yellowstone NP.

RED-NECKED GREBE (*Podiceps grisegena*). Rare or accidental in spring and fall. Reported breeding in Yellowstone NP and at Red Rock Lakes NWR.

EARED GREBE (*Podiceps nigricollis*). Common to occasional in spring and fall; occasional during summer. Breeding has been reported in Grand Teton–Jackson Hole and at Grays Lake NWR and Red Rock Lakes NWR.

WESTERN GREBE (*Aechmophorus occidentalis*). Occasional to rare from spring to fall. Breeding has been reported in Grand Teton–Jackson Hole and Yellowstone NP and at Grays Lake NWR and Red Rock Lakes NWR.

CLARK'S GREBE (*Aechmophorus clarkii*). Rare during summer in Yellowstone NP. Reported breeding at Red Rock Lakes NWR.

AMERICAN WHITE PELICAN (*Pelecanus erythrorhynchus*). Variably common from spring to fall. Breeds regularly in Yellowstone NP and at Red Rock Lakes NWR. In 2006 there were 427 nests on the Molly Islands in Yellowstone Lake, and 362 young were fledged (McEneaney 2007a).

DOUBLE-CRESTED CORMORANT (*Phalacrocorax auritus*). Uncommon to occasional from spring to fall. Breeding has been reported in Grand Teton–Jackson Hole and Yellowstone NP. In 2006 there were 110 nests on the Molly Islands in Yellowstone Lake, and 261 young were fledged (McEneaney 2007a). Also reported breeding at Red Rock Lakes NWR.

AMERICAN BITTERN (*Botaurus lentiginosus*). Uncommon to rare from spring to fall. Breeding has been reported in Grand Teton–Jackson Hole and Yellowstone NP and at Grays Lake NWR and Red Rock Lakes NWR.

GREAT BLUE HERON (*Ardea herodias*). Common from spring to fall but rare in winter. Breeding has been reported in Grand Teton–Jackson Hole and Yellowstone NP and at Grays Lake NWR and Red Rock Lakes NWR.

GREAT EGRET (*Egretta alba*). Accidental or very rare migrant in spring in Grand Teton–Jackson Hole.

SNOWY EGRET (*Egretta thula*). Occasional to rare from spring to fall.

BLACK-CROWNED NIGHT HERON (*Nycticorax nycticorax*). Accidental or rare from spring to fall. Reported breeding at Grays Lake NWR.

WHITE-FACED IBIS (*Plegadis chihi*). Occasional to rare from spring to fall. Reported breeding at Grays Lake NWR.

TURKEY VULTURE (*Cathartes aura*). Rare from spring to fall.

OSPREY (*Pandion haliaetus*). Common from spring through fall but rare in winter. Breeds regularly in Grand Teton–Jackson Hole and Yellowstone NP. In 2006 there were forty-one nesting pairs in Yellowstone NP, and twenty-nine young were fledged (McEneaney 2007a).

BALD EAGLE (*Haliaeetus leucocephala*). Common permanent resident. Breeds regularly in Grand Teton–Jackson Hole and Yellowstone NP.

NORTHERN HARRIER (*Circus cyaneus*). Occasional to uncommon from spring through fall, rare in winter. Breeding has been reported in Grand Teton–Jackson Hole and Yellowstone NP (about fifteen pairs typically present) and at Red Rock Lakes NWR.

SHARP-SHINNED HAWK (*Accipiter striatus*). Occasional to uncommon from spring to fall. Breeding has been reported in Grand Teton–Jackson Hole and Yellowstone NP.

COOPER'S HAWK (*Accipiter cooperi*). Occasional to uncommon from spring to fall. Breeding has been reported in Grand Teton–Jackson Hole and Yellowstone NP and at Grays Lake NWR.

NORTHERN GOSHAWK (*Accipiter gentilis*). Common to uncommon permanent resident. Breeding has been reported in Grand Teton–Jackson Hole and Yellowstone NP and at Grays Lake NWR and Red Rock Lakes NWR.

SWAINSON'S HAWK (*Buteo swainsoni*). Common from spring to fall. Breeding has been reported in Grand Teton–Jackson Hole and Yellowstone NP and at Grays Lake NWR and Red Rock Lakes NWR. About twenty-eight to thirty-six nesting pairs occur in Yellowstone NP annually (McEneaney 2007a).

RED-TAILED HAWK (*Buteo jamaicensis*). Common from spring to fall but rare in winter. Breeding has been reported in Grand Teton–Jackson Hole and Yellowstone NP and at Grays Lake NWR and Red Rock Lakes NWR. An estimated 126–39 birds are present in Yellowstone NP annually (McEneaney 2007a).

FERRUGINOUS HAWK (*Buteo regalis*). Rare from spring to fall. Breeding has been reported in Grand Teton–Jackson Hole and at Grays Lake NWR and Red Rock Lakes NWR.

ROUGH-LEGGED HAWK (*Buteo lagopus*). Common to uncommon winter visitor.

GOLDEN EAGLE (*Aquila chrysaetos*). Occasional to uncommon permanent resident. Breeding has been reported in Grand Teton–Jackson Hole and Yellowstone NP and at Grays Lake NWR and Red Rock Lakes NWR.

AMERICAN KESTREL (*Falco sparverius*). Common from spring to fall; rare in winter. Breeding has been reported in Grand Teton–Jackson Hole and Yellowstone NP and at Grays Lake NWR and Red Rock Lakes NWR.

MERLIN (*Falco columbarius*). Occasional in spring and fall; rare in summer. Breeding has been reported in Grand Teton–Jackson Hole and at Red Rock Lakes NWR; a hypothetical breeder in Yellowstone NP.

PRAIRIE FALCON (*Falco mexicanus*). Occasional to uncommon from spring through fall; rare in winter. Breeding has been reported in Grand Teton–Jackson Hole and Yellowstone NP and at Grays Lake NWR and Red Rock Lakes NWR.

PEREGRINE FALCON (*Falco peregrinus*). Locally uncommon permanent resident. Breeding has been reported in Grand Teton–Jackson Hole and Yellowstone NP and at Red Rock Lakes NWR. In 2006 there were thirty-one nesting pairs in Yellowstone NP, and fifty young were fledged (McEneaney 2007a).

VIRGINIA RAIL (*Rallus limicola*). Rare to accidental from spring to fall. Breeding has been reported in Yellowstone NP and at Grays Lake NWR and Red Rock Lakes NWR.

SORA (*Porzana carolina*). Common to occasional from spring to fall. Breeding has been reported in Grand Teton–Jackson Hole and Yellowstone NP and at Grays Lake NWR and Red Rock Lakes NWR.

AMERICAN COOT (*Fulica americana*). Uncommon from spring to fall. Breeding has been reported in Grand Teton–Jackson Hole and Yellowstone NP and at Grays Lake NWR and Red Rock Lakes NWR.

SANDHILL CRANE (*Grus canadensis*). Uncommon from spring to fall. Breeds regularly in Grand Teton–Jackson Hole and Yellowstone NP and at Grays Lake NWR and Red Rock Lakes NWR.

WHOOPING CRANE (*Grus americanus*). Accidental migrant in spring and fall. The experimentally introduced Rocky Mountain population that migrated through Wyoming died out during the 1990s.

SEMIPALMATED PLOVER (*Charadrius semipalmatus*). Rare migrant in spring and fall.

BLACK-BELLIED PLOVER (*Pluvialis squatarola*). Rare migrant in spring and fall.

KILLDEER (*Charadrius vociferans*). Common from spring to fall; rare in winter. Breeds in Grand Teton–Jackson Hole and Yellowstone NP and at Grays Lake NWR and Red Rock Lakes NWR.

SPOTTED SANDPIPER (*Actitis macularia*). Common from spring to fall. Breeds in Grand Teton–Jackson Hole and Yellowstone NP and at Grays Lake NWR and Red Rock Lakes NWR.

SOLITARY SANDPIPER (*Tringa solitaria*). Occasional to rare migrant in spring and fall.

GREATER YELLOWLEGS (*Tringa melanoleuca*). Occasional migrant in spring and fall.

WILLET (*Tringa semipalmatus*). Occasional to uncommon in spring and fall; rare summer resident. Breeding has been reported in Yellowstone NP and at Grays Lake NWR and Red Rock Lakes NWR.

LESSER YELLOWLEGS (*Tringa flavipes*). Occasional to rare migrant in spring and fall.

LONG-BILLED CURLEW (*Numenius americana*). Occasional migrant and summer resident from spring to fall. Breeding has been reported in Grand Teton NP, Jackson Hole; and Yellowstone NP and at Grays Lake NWR and Red Rock Lakes NWR.

MARBLED GODWIT (*Limosa fedoa*). Rare to occasional spring and fall migrant; rare summer resident. It may have once bred in Yellowstone NP (McEneaney 1988).

SANDERLING (*Calidris alba*). Rare spring and fall migrant.

SEMIPALMATED SANDPIPER (*Calidris pusilla*). Uncommon to rare fall migrant.

WESTERN SANDPIPER (*Calidris mauri*). Rare fall migrant.

LEAST SANDPIPER (*Calidris minutilla*). Occasional to rare fall migrant.

BAIRD'S SANDPIPER (*Calidris bairdii*). Rare fall migrant.

PECTORAL SANDPIPER (*Calidris melanotos*). Rare fall migrant.

STILT SANDPIPER (*Calidris himantopus*). Rare spring migrant.

LONG-BILLED DOWITCHER (*Limnodromus scolopaceus*). Occasional spring and fall migrant.

WILSON'S SNIPE (*Gallinago delicata*). Common resident from spring to fall; rare in winter. Breeding has been reported in Grand Teton–Jackson Hole and Yellowstone NP and at Grays Lake NWR and Red Rock Lakes NWR.

AMERICAN AVOCET (*Recurvirostra americana*). Occasional to uncommon from spring to fall, but not yet known to breed in either park. Reported breeding at Grays Lake NWR and Red Rock Lakes NWR.

BLACK-NECKED STILT (*Himantopus mexicanus*). Rare to accidental summer visitor; not yet known to breed in either park. Reported breeding at Grays Lake NWR.

WILSON'S PHALAROPE (*Phalaropus tricolor*). Uncommon spring and fall migrant, uncommon to occasional summer resident. Breeding has been reported in Grand Teton–Jackson Hole and Yellowstone NP and at Grays Lake NWR and Red Rock Lakes NWR.

RED-NECKED PHALAROPE (*Phalaropus lobatus*). Rare to occasional spring and fall migrant.

BONAPARTE'S GULL (*Larus philadelphia*). Occasional to rare spring and fall migrant.

FRANKLIN'S GULL (*Larus pipixcan*). Occasional to rare from spring to fall; not yet known to breed in either park. Reported breeding at Grays Lake NWR and Red Rock Lakes NWR.

RING-BILLED GULL (*Larus delawarensis*). Rare to uncommon spring and fall migrant; uncommon summer resident. Breeding has been reported in Yellowstone NP (Yellowstone Lake) and at Red Rock Lakes NWR.

CALIFORNIA GULL (*Larus californicus*). Common to abundant from spring to fall. Breeds in Yellowstone NP (Yellowstone Lake) and at Red Rock Lakes NWR. In 2006 there were seventy-eight nests on the Molly Islands in Yellowstone Lake, and eighty-one young were fledged (McEneaney 2007a).

CASPIAN TERN (*Sterna caspia*). Uncommon spring and fall migrant; occasional (Grand Teton NP and Jackson Hole) to uncommon (Yellowstone NP) summer resident. Breeding has often been reported on the Molly Islands in Yellowstone Lake, but in 2006 there were no nests (McEneaney 2007a).

BLACK TERN (*Chlidonias niger*). Rare to occasional from spring to fall; reported breeding in Yellowstone NP and at Grays Lake NWR and Red Rock Lakes NWR.

COMMON TERN (*Sterna hirundo*). Uncommon to rare summer visitor and fall migrant.

FORSTER'S TERN (*Sterna forsteri*). Occasional during summer at Jackson Hole; reported breeding at Red Rock Lakes NWR.

ROCK PIGEON (*Columba livia*). Local permanent resident. Breeding has been reported in Grand Teton–Jackson Hole and Yellowstone NP.

BAND-TAILED PIGEON (*Columba fasciata*). Accidental or very rare in spring and summer in Grand Teton–Jackson Hole.

MOURNING DOVE (*Zenaida macroura*). Occasional to uncommon from spring to fall. Breeding has been reported in Grand Teton–Jackson Hole and Yellowstone NP and at Grays Lake NWR and Red Rock Lakes NWR.

EURASIAN COLLARED-DOVE (*Streptopelia decaocto*). A self-introduced species that is rapidly increasing. As of 2011, a locally common permanent resident in Grand Teton–Jackson Hole. Also reported recently from Yellowstone NP (Faulkner 2010); likely eventually to occupy all lower elevation habitats in the region.

BLACK-BILLED CUCKOO (*Coccyzus erythropthalmus*). Occasional from spring to fall in Grand Teton–Jackson Hole. A rapidly declining species nationally.

WESTERN SCREECH-OWL (*Otus kennicottii*). Rare permanent resident. Breeding has been reported in Jackson Hole.

GREAT HORNED OWL (*Bubo virginianus*). Occasional to uncommon permanent resident. Breeding has been reported in Grand Teton–Jackson Hole and Yellowstone NP and at Grays Lake NWR and Red Rock Lakes NWR.

NORTHERN PYGMY-OWL (*Glaucidium gnoma*). Rare permanent resident. Breeding has been reported in Grand Teton–Jackson Hole and Yellowstone NP.

OVERLEAF. *Great gray owl listening intently for voles and mice under the snow, December, Grand Teton National Park, Wyoming*

BURROWING OWL (*Athene cunicularia*). Rare from spring to fall. Reported breeding at Grays Lake NWR; a hypothetical breeder in Yellowstone NP.

GREAT GRAY OWL (*Strix nebulosa*). Occasional to uncommon permanent resident. Breeding has been reported in Grand Teton–Jackson Hole and Yellowstone NP and at Grays Lake NWR and Red Rock Lakes NWR.

LONG-EARED OWL (*Asio otus*). Occasional to rare from summer to fall. Breeding has been reported in Grand Teton–Jackson Hole and Yellowstone NP and at Grays Lake NWR and Red Rock Lakes NWR.

SHORT-EARED OWL (*Asio flammeus*). Occasional in summer and fall; rare in winter and spring. Breeding has been reported in Grand Teton–Jackson Hole and Yellowstone NP and at Grays Lake NWR and Red Rock Lakes NWR.

BOREAL OWL (*Aegolius funereus*). Rare permanent resident in Grand Teton–Jackson Hole. The species' status in Yellowstone NP is uncertain, but it was recently reported as a breeder (McEneaney 2008).

NORTHERN SAW-WHET OWL (*Aegolius acadicus*). Rare permanent resident. Breeding has been reported in Grand Teton–Jackson Hole and Yellowstone NP and at Red Rock Lakes NWR.

COMMON NIGHTHAWK (*Chordeiles minor*). Common resident from spring to fall. Breeding has been reported in Grand Teton–Jackson Hole and Yellowstone NP and at Grays Lake NWR.

WHITE-THROATED SWIFT (*Aeronautes saxatalis*). Uncommon in summer in Yellowstone NP; accidental in Grand Teton–Jackson Hole. Breeding has been reported in Yellowstone NP.

BLACK-CHINNED HUMMINGBIRD (*Archilochus alexandri*). Occasional in spring and summer in Grand Teton–Jackson Hole; not yet reported from Yellowstone NP. Reported breeding at Grays Lake NWR.

CALLIOPE HUMMINGBIRD (*Stellula calliope*). Common from spring to fall. Breeding has been reported in Grand Teton–Jackson Hole and Yellowstone NP and at Grays Lake NWR and Red Rock Lakes NWR.

BROAD-TAILED HUMMINGBIRD (*Selasphorus platycercus*). Common to rare from spring to fall. Breeding has been reported in Grand Teton–Jackson Hole and Yellowstone NP and at Grays Lake NWR and Red Rock Lakes NWR.

RUFOUS HUMMINGBIRD (*Selasphorus rufus*). Common to occasional from spring to fall. Breeding has been reported in Grand Teton–Jackson Hole and Yellowstone NP and at Grays Lake NWR and Red Rock Lakes NWR.

BELTED KINGFISHER (*Ceryle alcyon*). Common from spring to fall; occasional in winter. Breeding has been reported in Grand Teton–Jackson Hole and Yellowstone NP and at Grays Lake NWR and Red Rock Lakes NWR.

LEWIS'S WOODPECKER (*Asyndesmus lewis*). Occasional to rare from spring to fall. Breeding has been reported in Grand Teton–Jackson Hole and Yellowstone NP.

RED-NAPED SAPSUCKER (*Sphyrapicus nuchalis*). Common from spring to fall. Breeding has been reported in Grand Teton–Jackson Hole and Yellowstone NP.

WILLIAMSON'S SAPSUCKER (*Sphyrapicus thyroideus*). Occasional to uncommon from spring to fall. Breeding has been reported in Grand Teton–Jackson Hole and Yellowstone NP and at Red Rock Lakes NWR.

DOWNY WOODPECKER (*Dendrocopus pubescens*). Common permanent resident. Breeding has been reported in Grand Teton–Jackson Hole and Yellowstone NP and at Grays Lake NWR and Red Rock Lakes NWR.

HAIRY WOODPECKER (*Dendrocopus villosus*). Common permanent resident. Breeding has been reported in Grand Teton–Jackson Hole and Yellowstone NP and at Grays Lake NWR and Red Rock Lakes NWR.

AMERICAN THREE-TOED WOODPECKER (*Picoides dorsalis*). Occasional from spring to fall; rare in winter. Breeding has been reported in Grand Teton–Jackson Hole and Yellowstone NP and at Grays Lake NWR.

BLACK-BACKED WOODPECKER (*Picoides arcticus*). Occasional (Grand Teton NP) to common (Yellowstone NP) in spring and summer; rare in fall. Breeding has been reported in Grand Teton–Jackson Hole and Yellowstone NP and at Red Rock Lakes NWR.

NORTHERN FLICKER (*Colaptes auritus*). Common summer resident. Breeding has been reported in Grand Teton–Jackson Hole and Yellowstone NP and at Grays Lake NWR and Red Rock Lakes NWR.

OLIVE-SIDED FLYCATCHER (*Nuttallornis borealis*). Common to uncommon from spring to fall. Breeding has been reported in Grand Teton–Jackson Hole and Yellowstone NP and at Red Rock Lakes NWR.

WESTERN WOOD-PEWEE (*Contopus sordidulus*). Common to uncommon from spring to fall. Breeding has been reported in Grand Teton–Jackson Hole and Yellowstone NP and at Grays Lake NWR and Red Rock Lakes NWR.

WILLOW FLYCATCHER (*Empidonax traillii*). Uncommon to occasional from spring to fall. Breeding has been reported in Grand Teton–Jackson Hole and Yellowstone NP and at Grays Lake NWR and Red Rock Lakes NWR.

HAMMOND'S FLYCATCHER (*Empidonax hammondii*). Occasional to uncommon from spring to fall. Breeding has been reported in Grand Teton–Jackson Hole and Yellowstone NP and at Red Rock Lakes NWR.

DUSKY FLYCATCHER (*Empidonax oberholseri*). Common from spring to fall. Breeding has been reported in Grand Teton–Jackson Hole and Yellowstone NP.

CORDILLERAN FLYCATCHER (*Empidonax occidentalis*). Occasional to rare from spring to fall. Breeding has been reported in Grand Teton–Jackson Hole and Yellowstone NP and at Red Rock Lakes NWR.

SAY'S PHOEBE (*Sayornis saya*). Rare from spring to fall. Breeding has been reported in Grand Teton–Jackson Hole; a hypothetical breeder in Yellowstone NP.

EASTERN KINGBIRD (*Tyrannus tyrannus*). Occasional to rare from spring to fall. Breeding has been reported in Grand Teton–Jackson Hole and at Red Rock Lakes NWR; a hypothetical breeder in Yellowstone NP.

WESTERN KINGBIRD (*Tyrannus verticalis*). Rare from spring to fall. A hypothetical breeder in Yellowstone NP.

SCISSOR-TAILED FLYCATCHER (*Tyrannus forficatus*). Accidental in Grand Teton–Jackson Hole and Yellowstone NP.

NORTHERN SHRIKE (*Lanius excubitor*). Occasional to uncommon migrant from fall to spring.

LOGGERHEAD SHRIKE (*Lanius ludovicianus*). Uncommon (Grand Teton NP) to rare (Yellowstone NP) in spring and summer. Breeding has been reported in Grand Teton–Jackson Hole and Yellowstone NP and at Red Rock Lakes NWR.

PLUMBEOUS VIREO (*Vireo plumbeus*). Rare from spring to fall in Grand Teton–Jackson Hole. Previously known as part of the solitary vireo population complex, now recognized as consisting of three species, of which the plumbeous breeder is the local, presumably breeding, form. The other two newly recognized species include the blue-headed vireo (*V. solitarius*), a possible very rare migrant, and Cassin's vireo (*V. cassinii*), also not yet reported from the ecoregion but possibly present.

RED-EYED VIREO (*Vireo olivaceus*). Occasional to rare from spring to fall.

WARBLING VIREO (*Vireo gilvus*). Uncommon to abundant from spring to fall. Breeding has been reported in Grand Teton–Jackson Hole and Yellowstone NP and at Grays Lake NWR and Red Rock Lakes NWR.

GRAY JAY (*Perisoreus canadensis*). Common permanent resident. Breeding has been reported in Grand Teton–Jackson Hole and Yellowstone NP and at Grays Lake NWR.

STELLER'S JAY (*Cyanocitta stelleri*). Common permanent resident. Breeding has been reported in Grand Teton–Jackson Hole and Yellowstone NP and at Grays Lake NWR.

PINYON JAY (*Gymnorhinus cyanocephalus*). Rare or accidental in summer, fall, and winter.

CLARK'S NUTCRACKER (*Nucifraga columbiana*). Common to abundant permanent resident. Breeding has been reported in Grand Teton–Jackson Hole and Yellowstone NP and at Red Rock Lakes NWR.

BLACK-BILLED MAGPIE (*Pica pica*). Common permanent resident. Breeding has been reported in Grand Teton–Jackson Hole and Yellowstone NP and at Grays Lake NWR and Red Rock Lakes NWR. The Yellowstone NP population is probably about a hundred birds (McEneaney 2007a).

AMERICAN CROW (*Corvus brachyrhynchus*). Occasional to rare permanent resident. Breeding has been reported in Grand Teton–Jackson Hole and Yellowstone NP and at Grays Lake NWR and Red Rock Lakes NWR.

COMMON RAVEN (*Corvus corax*). Common to abundant permanent resident. Breeding has been reported in Grand Teton–Jackson Hole and Yellowstone NP and at Grays Lake NWR and Red Rock Lakes NWR. The Yellowstone NP population is about 100–150 birds (McEneaney 2007a).

HORNED LARK (*Eremophila alpestris*). Occasional to uncommon permanent resident. Breeding has been reported in Grand Teton–Jackson Hole and Yellowstone NP and at Grays Lake NWR and Red Rock Lakes NWR.

TREE SWALLOW (*Iridoprocne bicolor*). Abundant from spring to fall. Breeding has been reported in Grand Teton–Jackson Hole and Yellowstone NP and at Grays Lake NWR and Red Rock Lakes NWR.

VIOLET-GREEN SWALLOW (*Tachycineta thalassina*). Common from spring to fall. Breeding has been reported in Grand Teton–Jackson Hole and Yellowstone NP and at Grays Lake NWR and Red Rock Lakes NWR.

ROUGH-WINGED SWALLOW (*Stelgidopteryx ruficollis*). Uncommon to occasional from spring to fall. Breeding has been reported in Grand Teton–Jackson Hole and Yellowstone NP and at Grays Lake NWR and Red Rock Lakes NWR.

BANK SWALLOW (*Riparia riparia*). Common in spring and summer. Breeding has been reported in Grand Teton–Jackson Hole and Yellowstone NP and at Grays Lake NWR and Red Rock Lakes NWR.

CLIFF SWALLOW (*Petrochelidon pyrrhonota*). Abundant in spring and summer; common in fall. Breeding has been reported in Grand Teton–Jackson Hole and Yellowstone NP and at Grays Lake NWR and Red Rock Lakes NWR.

BARN SWALLOW (*Hirundo rusticola*). Common to uncommon from spring to fall. Breeding has been reported in Grand Teton–Jackson Hole and Yellowstone NP and at Grays Lake NWR and Red Rock Lakes NWR.

Black-capped Chickadee (*Parus atricapillus*). Common to uncommon permanent resident. Breeding has been reported in Grand Teton–Jackson Hole and Yellowstone NP and at Grays Lake NWR and Red Rock Lakes NWR.

Mountain Chickadee (*Parus gambeli*). Common to abundant permanent resident. Breeding has been reported in Grand Teton–Jackson Hole and Yellowstone NP and at Grays Lake NWR and Red Rock Lakes NWR.

Red-breasted Nuthatch (*Sitta canadensis*). Common to uncommon permanent resident. Breeding has been reported in Grand Teton–Jackson Hole and Yellowstone NP and at Grays Lake NWR and Red Rock Lakes NWR.

White-breasted Nuthatch (*Sitta carolinensis*). Common to uncommon permanent resident. Breeding has been reported in Grand Teton–Jackson Hole and Yellowstone NP and at Red Rock Lakes NWR.

Brown Creeper (*Certhia familiaris*). Occasional to rare permanent resident. Breeding has been reported in Grand Teton–Jackson Hole and Yellowstone NP and at Grays Lake NWR and Red Rock Lakes NWR.

House Wren (*Troglodytes aedon*). Uncommon to common from spring to fall. Breeding has been reported in Grand Teton–Jackson Hole and Yellowstone NP and at Grays Lake NWR and Red Rock Lakes NWR.

Winter Wren (*Troglodytes hiemalis*). Rare to very rare summer resident in Grand Teton–Jackson Hole, where it has reportedly bred. Rare to very rare in Yellowstone NP.

Rock Wren (*Salpinctes obsoletus*). Common from spring to fall. Breeding has been reported in Grand Teton–Jackson Hole and Yellowstone NP and at Grays Lake NWR and Red Rock Lakes NWR.

Marsh Wren (*Cistothorus palustris*). Occasional to rare from spring to fall. Breeding has been reported in Grand Teton–Jackson Hole and Yellowstone NP and at Red Rock Lakes NWR.

American Dipper (*Cinclus mexicanus*). Common permanent resident. Breeding has been reported in Grand Teton–Jackson Hole and Yellowstone NP and at Grays Lake NWR and Red Rock Lakes NWR.

Golden-crowned Kinglet (*Regulus satrapa*). Occasional to uncommon from spring to fall; rare in winter. Breeding has been reported in Grand Teton–Jackson Hole and Yellowstone NP.

Ruby-crowned Kinglet (*Regulus calendula*). Common to occasional from spring to fall; rare in winter. Breeding has been reported in Grand Teton–Jackson Hole and Yellowstone NP and at Grays Lake NWR and Red Rock Lakes NWR.

Blue-gray Gnatcatcher (*Polioptila caeruleus*). Accidental or very rare fall migrant in Grand Teton–Jackson Hole and Yellowstone NP.

Western Bluebird (*Sialia mexicana*). Occasional in spring and fall in Grand Teton–Jackson Hole and Yellowstone NP.

Mountain Bluebird (*Sialia currucoides*). Common from spring to fall. Breeding has been reported in Grand Teton–Jackson Hole and Yellowstone NP and at Grays Lake NWR and Red Rock Lakes NWR.

Townsend's Solitaire (*Myadestes townsendi*). Occasional to uncommon permanent resident. Breeding has been reported in Grand Teton–Jackson Hole and Yellowstone NP and at Red Rock Lakes NWR.

Veery (*Catharus fuscescens*). Occasional to rare from spring to fall. Breeding has been reported in Grand Teton–Jackson Hole and at Red Rock Lakes NWR; a hypothetical breeder in Yellowstone NP.

OVERLEAF. *Common ravens fly from an elk carcass as a coyote approaches, February, Yellowstone National Park, Wyoming*

SWAINSON'S THRUSH (*Catharus ustulatus*). Common in spring and summer; occasional in fall. Breeding has been reported in Grand Teton–Jackson Hole and Yellowstone NP and at Grays Lake NWR and Red Rock Lakes NWR.

HERMIT THRUSH (*Catharus guttatus*). Common from spring to fall. Breeding has been reported in Grand Teton–Jackson Hole and Yellowstone NP and at Red Rock Lakes NWR.

AMERICAN ROBIN (*Turdus migratorius*). Abundant from spring to fall; rare in winter. Breeding has been reported in Grand Teton–Jackson Hole and Yellowstone NP and at Grays Lake NWR and Red Rock Lakes NWR.

VARIED THRUSH (*Ixoreus naevius*). Accidental or very rare migrant in spring and fall.

GRAY CATBIRD (*Dumetella carolinensis*). Rare to occasional from spring to fall. Breeding has been reported in Grand Teton–Jackson Hole and Yellowstone NP and at Grays Lake NWR.

NORTHERN MOCKINGBIRD (*Mimus polyglottos*). Accidental or very rare migrant in spring and fall.

SAGE THRASHER (*Oreoscoptes montanus*). Occasional to uncommon from spring to fall. Breeding has been reported in Grand Teton–Jackson Hole and Yellowstone NP and at Grays Lake NWR and Red Rock Lakes NWR.

EUROPEAN STARLING (*Sturnus vulgaris*). Common from spring to fall; occasional in winter. Breeding has been reported in Grand Teton–Jackson Hole and Yellowstone NP and at Grays Lake NWR and Red Rock Lakes NWR.

AMERICAN PIPIT (*Anthus spinoletta*). Common from spring to fall; rare in winter. Breeding has been reported in Grand Teton–Jackson Hole and Yellowstone NP.

SPRAGUE'S PIPIT (*Anthus spragueii*). Accidental or very rare migrant in spring and fall.

BOHEMIAN WAXWING (*Bombycilla garrulus*). Occasional to uncommon migrant in winter and spring. Reported breeding at Red Rock Lakes NWR.

CEDAR WAXWING (*Bombycilla cedrorum*). Occasional to uncommon from spring to fall; overwintering reported at Grand Teton–Jackson Hole. Reported breeding in Grand Teton–Jackson Hole and Yellowstone NP and at Red Rock Lakes NWR.

MCCOWN'S LONGSPUR (*Calcarius mccownii*). Accidental or very rare migrant in spring and fall.

LAPLAND LONGSPUR (*Calcarius lapponicus*). Accidental or very rare winter migrant.

SNOW BUNTING (*Plectrophenax nivalis*). Rare to occasional migrant from fall to spring.

TENNESSEE WARBLER (*Oreothlypis peregrina*). Rare to occasional migrant in spring and fall.

ORANGE-CROWNED WARBLER (*Oreothlypis celata*). Occasional to rare from spring to fall. Breeding has been reported in Grand Teton–Jackson Hole; a hypothetical breeder in Yellowstone NP. Also reported breeding at Grays Lake NWR and Red Rock Lakes NWR.

NASHVILLE WARBLER (*Oreothlypis ruficapilla*). Accidental or very rare migrant in spring and fall.

YELLOW WARBLER (*Dendroica petechia*). Common to abundant from spring to fall. Breeding has been reported in Grand Teton–Jackson Hole and Yellowstone NP and at Grays Lake NWR and Red Rock Lakes NWR.

YELLOW-RUMPED WARBLER (*Dendroica coronata*). Common to abundant from spring to fall. Breeding has been reported in Grand Teton–Jackson Hole and Yellowstone NP and at Grays Lake NWR and Red Rock Lakes NWR.

TOWNSEND'S WARBLER (*Dendroica townsendi*). Rare in summer and fall. Breeding has been reported in Yellowstone NP (McEneaney 1988).

AMERICAN REDSTART (*Setophaga ruticilla*). Occasional to rare in spring and summer; a hypothetical breeder in Yellowstone NP. Reported breeding at Red Rock Lakes NWR.

NORTHERN WATERTHRUSH (*Parksiana noveboracensis*). Rare from spring to fall.

MACGILLIVRAY'S WARBLER (*Oporornis tolmiei*). Common from spring to fall. Breeding has been reported in Grand Teton–Jackson Hole and Yellowstone NP and at Grays Lake NWR and Red Rock Lakes NWR.

COMMON YELLOWTHROAT (*Geothlypis trichas*). Common from spring to fall. Breeding has been reported in Grand Teton–Jackson Hole and Yellowstone NP and at Grays Lake NWR and Red Rock Lakes NWR.

WILSON'S WARBLER (*Wilsonia citrina*). Common to uncommon from spring to fall. Breeding has been reported in Grand Teton–Jackson Hole and Yellowstone NP and at Red Rock Lakes NWR.

GREEN-TAILED TOWHEE (*Chlorura chlorura*). Common to uncommon from spring to fall. Breeding has been reported in Grand Teton–Jackson Hole and Yellowstone NP and at Grays Lake NWR and Red Rock Lakes NWR.

SPOTTED TOWHEE (*Pipilo maculatus*). Rare from spring to fall.

AMERICAN TREE SPARROW (*Spizella arborea*). Occasional to uncommon from fall to spring.

CLAY-COLORED SPARROW (*Spizella pallida*). Rare in summer in Grand Teton–Jackson Hole; it has reportedly bred in the vicinity of Jackson.

CHIPPING SPARROW (*Spizella passerina*). Common from spring to fall. Breeding has been reported in Grand Teton–Jackson Hole and Yellowstone NP and at Grays Lake NWR and Red Rock Lakes NWR.

BREWER'S SPARROW (*Spizella breweri*). Common from spring to fall. Breeding has been reported in Grand Teton–Jackson Hole and Yellowstone NP and at Grays Lake NWR and Red Rock Lakes NWR.

VESPER SPARROW (*Pooecetes gramineus*). Common from spring to fall. Breeding has been reported in Grand Teton–Jackson Hole and Yellowstone NP and at Grays Lake NWR and Red Rock Lakes NWR.

LARK SPARROW (*Chondestes grammicus*). Occasional to rare in summer and fall. Reported breeding at Red Rock Lakes NWR; a hypothetical breeder in Yellowstone NP.

SAGE SPARROW (*Amphispiza belli*). Accidental or very rare in spring and summer in Grand Teton–Jackson Hole.

LARK BUNTING (*Calamospiza melanocorys*). Rare in spring and summer.

SAVANNAH SPARROW (*Passerculus sandwichensis*). Common from spring to fall. Breeding has been reported in Grand Teton–Jackson Hole and Yellowstone NP and at Grays Lake NWR.

GRASSHOPPER SPARROW (*Ammodramus savannarum*). Rare from spring to fall.

FOX SPARROW (*Passerella iliaca*). Occasional to rare from spring to fall. Breeding has been reported in Grand Teton–Jackson Hole and Yellowstone NP and at Grays Lake NWR.

SONG SPARROW (*Melospiza melodia*). Common to uncommon from spring to fall; occasional in winter. Breeding has been reported in Grand Teton–Jackson Hole and Yellowstone NP and at Grays Lake NWR and Red Rock Lakes NWR.

SWAMP SPARROW (*Melospiza georgiana*). Accidental or very rare in fall in Grand Teton–Jackson Hole.

LINCOLN'S SPARROW (*Melospiza melodia*). Common from spring to fall. Breeding has been reported in Grand Teton–Jackson Hole and Yellowstone NP and at Grays Lake NWR and Red Rock Lakes NWR.

Dark-eyed Junco (*Junco hyemalis*). Common to abundant from spring to fall; occasional in winter. Breeding has been reported in Grand Teton–Jackson Hole and Yellowstone NP and at Grays Lake NWR and Red Rock Lakes NWR.

Harris's Sparrow (*Zonotrichia querula*). Rare fall to spring resident.

White-crowned Sparrow (*Zonotrichia leucophrys*). Common to abundant from spring to fall; rare in winter. Breeding has been reported in Grand Teton–Jackson Hole and Yellowstone NP and at Grays Lake NWR and Red Rock Lakes NWR.

White-throated Sparrow (*Zonotrichia albicollis*). Rare spring and fall migrant in Grand Teton–Jackson Hole.

Rose-breasted Grosbeak (*Pheucticus ludovicianus*). Occasional to accidental from spring to fall.

Black-headed Grosbeak (*Pheucticus melanocephalus*). Common to rare from spring to fall. Breeding has been reported in Grand Teton–Jackson Hole and at Grays Lake NWR.

Lazuli Bunting (*Passerina amoena*). Common to occasional to rare from spring to fall. Breeding has been reported in Grand Teton–Jackson Hole and Yellowstone NP and at Grays Lake NWR and Red Rock Lakes NWR.

Indigo Bunting (*Passerina cyaneus*). Accidental or very rare in spring and summer.

Western Tanager (*Piranga ludovicianus*). Common from spring to fall. Breeding has been reported in Grand Teton–Jackson Hole and Yellowstone NP and at Grays Lake NWR and Red Rock Lakes NWR.

Bobolink (*Dolichonyx oryzivorus*). Occasional in spring and summer. Breeding has been reported in Grand Teton–Jackson Hole and at Grays Lake NWR and Red Rock Lakes NWR.

Red-winged Blackbird (*Agelaius phoeniceus*). Common from spring to fall; rare in winter. Breeding has been reported in Grand Teton–Jackson Hole and Yellowstone NP and at Grays Lake NWR and Red Rock Lakes NWR.

Western Meadowlark (*Sturnella neglecta*). Common (Yellowstone NP) to occasional (Grand Teton–Jackson Hole) from spring to fall. Breeding has been reported in Grand Teton–Jackson Hole and Yellowstone NP and at Grays Lake NWR and Red Rock Lakes NWR.

Yellow-headed Blackbird (*Xanthocephala xanthocephala*). Common from spring to fall. Breeding has been reported in Grand Teton–Jackson Hole and Yellowstone NP and at Grays Lake NWR and Red Rock Lakes NWR.

Brewer's Blackbird (*Euphagus cyanocephalus*) Common to abundant from spring to fall; rare in winter. Breeding has been reported in Grand Teton–Jackson Hole and Yellowstone NP and at Grays Lake NWR and Red Rock Lakes NWR.

Brown-headed Cowbird (*Molothrus ater*). Common from spring to fall. Breeding has been reported in Grand Teton–Jackson Hole and Yellowstone NP and at Grays Lake NWR and Red Rock Lakes NWR.

Orchard Oriole (*Icterus spurius*). Accidental or very rare in spring and summer in Grand Teton–Jackson Hole, where it has reportedly bred.

Bullock's Oriole (*Icterus bullockii*). Occasional to rare from spring to fall. Breeding has been reported in Grand Teton–Jackson Hole and at Grays Lake NWR; a hypothetical breeder in Yellowstone NP.

Gray-crowned Rosy-Finch (*Leucosticte tephrocotis*). Common to rare resident from fall to spring.

Black Rosy-Finch (*Leucosticte atratus*). Common to occasional permanent resident. Breeding has been reported in Grand Teton–Jackson Hole and Yellowstone NP and at Red Rock Lakes NWR.

PINE GROSBEAK (*Pinicola enucleator*). Occasional to uncommon permanent resident. Breeding has been reported in Grand Teton–Jackson Hole and Yellowstone NP and at Red Rock Lakes NWR.

CASSIN'S FINCH (*Carpodacus cassinii*). Common from spring to fall; rare in winter. Breeding has been reported in Grand Teton–Jackson Hole and Yellowstone NP and at Grays Lake NWR and Red Rock Lakes NWR.

HOUSE FINCH (*Carpodacus mexicana*). Accidental or very rare permanent resident. Breeding has been reported in Yellowstone NP (McEneaney 1988); a hypothetical breeder in Grand Teton–Jackson Hole.

RED CROSSBILL (*Loxia curvirostra*). Occasional to uncommon permanent resident. Breeding has been reported in Grand Teton–Jackson Hole and Yellowstone NP and at Red Rock Lakes NWR.

WHITE-WINGED CROSSBILL (*Loxia leucoptera*). Accidental to rare migrant from fall to spring.

COMMON REDPOLL (*Carduelis flammea*). Common to occasional migrant from fall to spring.

PINE SISKIN (*Carduelis pinus*). Common from spring to fall; occasional in winter. Breeding has been reported in Grand Teton–Jackson Hole and Yellowstone NP and at Grays Lake NWR and Red Rock Lakes NWR.

AMERICAN GOLDFINCH (*Carduelis tristis*). Occasional to rare from spring to fall. Breeding has been reported in Grand Teton–Jackson Hole and at Grays Lake NWR and Red Rock Lakes NWR; a hypothetical breeder in Yellowstone NP.

EVENING GROSBEAK (*Cocothraustes vespertina*). Uncommon to occasional permanent resident. Breeding has been reported in Grand Teton–Jackson Hole and Yellowstone NP and at Grays Lake NWR and Red Rock Lakes NWR.

HOUSE SPARROW (*Passer domesticus*). Common permanent resident near human activity. Breeding has been reported in Grand Teton–Jackson Hole and at Grays Lake NWR and Red Rock Lakes NWR.

Amphibians and Reptiles

Taxonomy and status information in the following list are from Koch and Peterson (1995) and Luce et al. (1997, 2004).

AMPHIBIANS

BLOTCHED TIGER SALAMANDER (*Ambystoma tigrinum melanostictum*). Widespread in Yellowstone NP; especially common in the Lamar Valley and also abundant in Grand Teton NP. Occurs in a wide variety of habitats.

BOREAL (WESTERN) TOAD (*Bufo boreas boreas*). Common and widespread in meadows, woodlands, and wetlands of both parks, from the lowest elevations to about 9,400 feet (near Togwotee Pass).

BOREAL (WESTERN) CHORUS FROG (*Pseudacris triseriata*). Common to abundant in Grand Teton NP and Yellowstone NP, but far more often heard than seen. Occurs in marshes and ponds as high as the lower alpine zone.

BULLFROG (*Bufo catesbiana*). Observed in Kelly Warm Springs area of Jackson Hole, where introduced. Occupies permanent warm waters at lower elevations.

COLUMBIA SPOTTED FROG (*Rana luteoventris*; previously regarded as part of *R. pretiosa*). The most commonly seen amphibian in Grand Teton NP and Yellowstone NP. Occupies many wetlands, from foothills to montane forests.

NORTHERN LEOPARD FROG (*Rana pipiens*). Documented in Grand Teton NP (Jenny, String, and Leigh Lakes), but not found in recent decades and perhaps extirpated. Occupies swampy marshes and ponds at lower altitudes.

SPADEFOOT (*Spea* sp.). Documented historically from the Firehole River of Yellowstone NP.

REPTILES

EASTERN SHORT-HORNED LIZARD (*Phrynosoma douglasii brevirostre*). Documented historically from Jackson Hole and near the west entrance of Yellowstone NP. Widespread in Wyoming generally, in grasslands and sagebrush below 6,500 feet.

NORTHERN SAGEBRUSH LIZARD (*Sceloperus g. graciosus*). Documented from Grand Teton NP and Yellowstone NP. Occupies rock outcrops in sagebrush, usually below 6,500 feet but occurs up to 8,300 feet in warm hydrothermal areas of Yellowstone NP.

RUBBER BOA (*Charina bottae*). Documented from Yellowstone NP and observed in Grand Teton NP. Present in foothills and lower montane zones up to about 2,600 meters. Nocturnal and rarely seen.

BULLSNAKE (*Pituophis catenifer*). Documented only from northern Yellowstone NP, mostly at elevations below 6,700 feet. Occurs in diverse plains, foothills, and lower montane habitats. Most common in warmer, drier areas of Yellowstone NP, such as around Mammoth Hot Springs.

WANDERING GARTER SNAKE (*Thamnophis elegans vagrans*). The most common reptile in Grand Teton NP and Yellowstone NP. Common in all zones except alpine, usually near water, at elevations up to about 8,300 feet.

WESTERN PLAINS GARTER SNAKE (*Thamnophis radix haydeni*). Observed in the Jackson Hole region (Wyoming latilong #8, Luce et al. 1997). Usually seen near water, but also occurs in dry grasslands and sandhills.

VALLEY GARTER SNAKE (*Thamnophis sirtalis fitchi*). Documented in Grand Teton NP and reported from southwestern Yellowstone NP along Fall River. Occurs in plains, foothills, and mountains as high as about 6,900 feet. Usually found near water.

EASTERN YELLOW-BELLY RACER (*Coluber constrictor flaviventris*). Documented historically from the lower Yellowstone River near Gardiner, Montana.

PRAIRIE RATTLESNAKE (*Crotalis v. viridus*). Documented only from the lower Yellowstone River area of extreme northern Yellowstone NP. Occupies open, often rocky habitats.

Fishes

Taxonomy and status information in this list are based mainly on Baxter and Simon (1970).

MOUNTAIN WHITEFISH (*Prosopium williamsoni*). Occurs on upper Snake River tributaries in Grand Teton NP and in the Madison and Yellowstone drainages of Yellowstone NP.

BROWN TROUT (*Salmo trutta*). Introduced into Yellowstone NP in the 1930s and later widely elsewhere in Wyoming. Uncommon.

CUTTHROAT TROUT (*Salmo clarki*). Wyoming's only native trout; abundant in all Western Slope drainages and the Madison and Yellowstone drainages. Three local cutthroat variants are recognized in Yellowstone NP: the Snake River fine-spotted, the Yellowstone, and the West Slope.

RAINBOW TROUT (*Salmo gairdneri*). Introduced into Yellowstone NP in the 1930s and later widely elsewhere in Wyoming. Uncommon.

Brook Trout (*Salvelinus frontinalis*). Introduced into Yellowstone NP in the 1930s and later widely elsewhere in Wyoming. Common.

Lake Trout (*Salvelinus numaycush*). Introduced into Wyoming in the 1930s; now common in many lakes, including Jackson Lake. Introduced illegally into Yellowstone Lake during the 1980s, where it has adversely impacted native cutthroat trout populations.

Arctic Grayling (*Thymallus arcticus*). Reported historically from Yellowstone NP (Madison, Gibbon, Firehole, and Gallatin Rivers and the headwaters of Yellowstone River). This rare Pleistocene relict species now probably occurs in only a few headwater lakes in Yellowstone NP; its limited range extends into southern Montana.

Lake Chub (*Couesius plumbeus*). Reported from Yellowstone Lake.

Utah Chub (*Gila atraria*). Reported as abundant from Heart Lake, Witch Creek, and the upper Snake River tributaries.

Leatherside Chub (*Gilia copei*). Reported as rare from the upper Snake River.

Bonneville Redside Shiner (*Richardsonius balteatus hydrophlox*). Reported as abundant from Yellowstone Lake and the upper Snake River.

Longnose Dace (*Rhinichthys cataractae*). Reported as common from Yellowstone Lake and the upper Snake River.

Speckled Dace (*Rhinichthys osculus*). Reported as common from Yellowstone Lake and the upper Snake River.

Utah Sucker (*Catostomus ardens*). Reported as abundant from Yellowstone Lake and the upper Snake River.

Mountain Sucker (*Catostomus platyrhynchus*). Reported as common from Yellowstone Lake and the upper Snake River.

June Sucker (*Chasmistes liorus*). Known only from a specimen at Jackson Lake or the Snake River adjacent to Jackson Lake Dam.

Mottled Sculpin (*Cottus bairdi*). Common in the upper Snake River and the Madison and Gibbon Rivers.

Piute Sculpin (*Cottus beldingi*). Common at the headwaters of the Snake River.

APPENDIX 4

Dragonflies and Damselflies of the Greater Yellowstone Ecoregion

THE INFORMATION IN THE FOLLOWING LIST is arranged alphabetically within families by genera and species and is adapted from B. C. Kondratieff, coord., *Dragonflies and Damselflies (Odonata) of the United States* (2000), and D. Paulson, *Dragonflies and Damselflies of the West* (2009).

Damselflies

CALOPTERYGIDAE: BROAD-WINGED DAMSELFLIES

RIVER JEWELWING (*Calopteryx aequabilis*). May occur in region (edge of range).

LESTIDAE: SPREAD-WINGED DAMSELFLIES

SPOTTED SPREADWING (*Lestes congener*). Occurs throughout region.

COMMON SPREADWING (*Lestes disjunctus*). Occurs throughout region.

EMERALD SPREADWING (*Lestes dryas*). Occurs throughout region.

COENAGRIONIDAE: NARROW-WINGED DAMSELFLIES

PAIUTE DANCER (*Argia alberta*). Occurs throughout region.

VIVID DANCER (*Argia vivida*). Occurs throughout region.

TAIGA BLUET (*Coenagrion resolutum*). Occurs throughout region.

RIVER BLUET (*Enallagma anna*). May occur in region (edge of range).

BOREAL BLUET (*Enallagma boreale*). Occurs throughout region.

NORTHERN BLUET (*Enallagma annexum*). Occurs throughout region.

PACIFIC FORKTAIL (*Ischnura cervula*). Occurs throughout region.

EASTERN FORKTAIL (*Ischnura verticalis*). May occur in region (edge of range).

Dragonflies

AESHNIDAE: DARNERS

LANCE-TIPPED DARNER (*Aeshna constricta*). Occurs throughout region.

LAKE DARNER (*Aeshna eremita*). Occurs throughout region.

VARIABLE DARNER (*Aeshna interrupta*). Occurs throughout region.

SEDGE DARNER (*Aeshna juncea*). Occurs throughout region.

BLUE-EYED DARNER (*Aeshna multicolor*). Occurs throughout region.

PADDLE-TAILED DARNER (*Aeshna palmata*). Occurs throughout region.

ZIGZAG DARNER (*Aeshna sitchensis*). Occurs throughout region.

SHADOW DARNER (*Aeshna umbrosa*). Occurs throughout region.

COMMON GREEN DARNER (*Anax junius*). Occurs throughout region.

GOMPHIDAE: CLUBTAILS

PALE SNAKETAIL (*Ophiogomphus severus*). Occurs throughout region.

CORDULIIDAE: EMERALDS

AMERICAN EMERALD (*Cordulia shurtleffii*). Occurs throughout region.

HUDSONIAN EMERALD (*Somatochlora hudsonica*). Occurs throughout region.

OCELLATED EMERALD (*Somatochlora minor*). May occur in region (edge of range).

MOUNTAIN EMERALD (*Somatochlora semicircularis*). Occurs throughout region.

LIBELLULIDAE: SKIMMERS

WESTERN PONDHAWK (*Erythemis collocata*). May occur in region (edge of range).

BOREAL WHITEFACE (*Leucorrhinia borealis*). Occurs throughout region.

HUDSONIAN WHITEFACE (*Leucorrhinia hudsonica*). Occurs throughout region.

DOT-TAILED WHITEFACE (*Leucorrhinia intacta*). Occurs throughout region.

RED-WAISTED WHITEFACE (*Leucorrhinia proxima*). Occurs throughout region.

EIGHT-SPOTTED SKIMMER (*Libellula forensis*). Occurs throughout region.

COMMON WHITETAIL (*Libellula* [*Plathemis*] *lydia*). Occurs throughout region.

FOUR-SPOTTED SKIMMER (*Libellula quadrimaculata*). Occurs throughout region.

FLAME SKIMMER (*Libellula saturata*). May occur in region (edge of range).

VARIEGATED MEADOWHAWK (*Sympetrum corruptum*). Occurs throughout region.

SAFFRON-WINGED MEADOWHAWK (*Sympetrum costiferum*). May occur in region (edge of range).

BLACK MEADOWHAWK (*Sympetrum danae*). Occurs throughout region.

CHERRY-FACED MEADOWHAWK (*Sympetrum internum*). Occurs throughout region.

WHITE-FACED MEADOWHAWK (*Sympetrum obtrusum*). Occurs throughout region.

STRIPED MEADOWHAWK (*Sympetrum pallipes*). Occurs throughout region.

APPENDIX 5

Butterflies of the Greater Yellowstone Ecoregion

INFORMATION IN THE FOLLOWING LIST is arranged alphabetically within families and subfamilies by genera and species. Distribution statements are based on *Butterflies and Moths of North America* (Opler et al. 2010) and *Butterflies of North America* (Brock and Kaufmann 2003).

Parnassians and Swallowtails (*Papilionidae*)

PARNASSIANS (*PARNASSIINAE*)

CLODIUS PARNASSIAN (*Parnassius clodius*). Occurs throughout region.

ROCKY MOUNTAIN PARNASSIAN (*Parnassius smintheus*). Occurs throughout region.

SWALLOWTAILS (*PAPILIONINAE*)

PALE SWALLOWTAIL (*Papilio eurymedon*). Occurs throughout region.

INDRA SWALLOWTAIL (*Papilio indra*). Occurs throughout region.

OLD WORLD SWALLOWTAIL (*Papilio machaon*). Occurs throughout region.

TWO-TAILED SWALLOWTAIL (*Papilio multicaudata*). Occurs throughout region.

BLACK SWALLOWTAIL (*Papilio polyxenes*). Occurs throughout region.

WESTERN TIGER SWALLOWTAIL (*Papilio rutulus*). Occurs throughout region.

ANISE SWALLOWTAIL (*Papilio zelicaon*). Occurs throughout region.

Whites and Sulfurs (*Pieridae*)

SARA ORANGETIP (*Anthocharis sara*). Occurs throughout region.

QUEEN ALEXANDRA'S SULFUR (*Colinas alexandra*). Occurs throughout region.

ORANGE SULFUR (*Colinas eurytheme*). Occurs throughout region.

CLOUDED SULFUR (*Colinas philodice*). Occurs throughout region.

LARGE MARBLE (*Euchloe ausonidae*). Occurs throughout region.

PEARLY MARBLE (*Euchloe hyantis*). Occurs throughout region.

PINE WHITE (*Neophasia monpia*). Occurs throughout region.

MUSTARD WHITE (*Pieris napi*). Occurs throughout region.

CABBAGE WHITE (*Pieris rapae*). Occurs throughout region.

BECKER'S WHITE (*Pontia beckerii*). Occurs throughout region.

CHECKERED WHITE (*Pontia protodice*). Occurs throughout region.

SPRING WHITE (*Pontia sisymbri*). Occurs throughout region.

Gossamer-winged Butterflies (*Lycaenidae*)

COPPERS (*LYCAENINAE*)

LUSTROUS COPPER (*Lycaena cupreus*). Occurs throughout region.

GRAY COPPER (*Lycaena dione*). Occurs throughout region.

EDITH'S COPPER (*Lycaena editha*). Occurs throughout region.

PURPLISH COPPER (*Lycaena heloides*). Occurs throughout region.

BLUE COPPER (*Lycaena heteronea*). Occurs throughout region.

BRONZE COPPER (*Lycaena hyllus*). Occurs throughout region.

MARIPOSA COPPER (*Lycaena mariposa*). Occurs throughout region.

LILAC-BORDERED COPPER (*Lycaena nivalis*). Occurs throughout region.

AMERICAN COPPER (*Lycaena phloeas*). Occurs throughout region.

RUDDY COPPER (*Lycaena rubidus*). Occurs throughout region.

HAIRSTREAKS (*THECLINAE*)

BROWN ELFIN (*Callophrys augustinus*). Local in region.

WESTERN PINE ELFIN (*Callophrys eryphon*). Occurs throughout region.

JUNIPER HAIRSTREAK (*Callophrys gryneus*). Occurs throughout region.

BRAMBLE HAIRSTREAK (*Callophrys perplexa*). Occurs throughout region.

HOARY ELFIN (*Callophrys polios*). Local in region.

SHERIDAN'S HAIRSTREAK (*Callophrys sheridanii*). Occurs throughout region.

THICKET HAIRSTREAK (*Callophrys spinetorum*). Occurs throughout region.

CALIFORNIA HAIRSTREAK (*Satyrium californica*). Local in region.

SYLVAN HAIRSTREAK (*Satyrium sylvinus*). Local in region.

CORAL HAIRSTREAK (*Satyrium titus*). Occurs throughout region.

GRAY HAIRSTREAK (*Strymon melinus*). Occurs throughout region.

BLUES (*POLYOMMATINAE*)

ARCTIC BLUE (*Agriades glandon*). Occurs throughout region.

SPRING AZURE (*Celastrina ladon*). Occurs throughout region.

DOTTED BLUE (*Euphilotes enoptes*). Occurs throughout region.

WESTERN TAILED BLUE (*Everes amyntula*). Occurs throughout region.

SILVERY BLUE (*Glaucopsyche lygdamus*). Occurs throughout region.

ARROWHEAD BLUE (*Glaucopsyche piasus*). Occurs throughout region.

NORTHERN BLUE (*Lycaeides idas*). Occurs throughout region.

MELISSA BLUE (*Lycaeides melissa*). Occurs throughout region.

ACMON BLUE (*Plebejus acmon*). Occurs throughout region.

BOISDUVAL'S BLUE (*Plebejus icarioides*). Occurs throughout region.

GREENISH BLUE (*Plebejus saepiolus*). Occurs throughout region.

SHASTA BLUE (*Plebejus shasta*). Occurs throughout region.

Brush-footed Butterflies (*Nymphalidae*)
LONGWINGS (*HELICONIINAE*)

MEADOW FRITILLARY (*Boloria bellona*). Occurs throughout region.

ARCTIC FRITILLARY (*Boloria chariclea*). Occurs throughout region.

BOG FRITILLARY (*Boloria eunomia*). Occurs throughout region.

FREIJA FRITILLARY (*Boloria freija*). Occurs throughout region.

FRIGGA FRITILLARY (*Boloria frigga*). Occurs throughout region.

RELICT FRITILLARY (*Boloria kriemhild*). Occurs throughout region.

DINGY FRITILLARY (*Boloria improba*). Local in region.

SILVER-BORDERED FRITILLARY (*Boloria selene*). Occurs throughout region.

VARIEGATED FRITILLARY (*Euptoieta claudia*). Occurs throughout region.

APHRODITE FRITILLARY (*Speyeria aphrodite*). Local in region.

CALLIPPE FRITILLARY (*Speyeria callippe*). Occurs throughout region.

CORONIS FRITILLARY (*Speyeria coronis*). Occurs throughout region.

GREAT SPANGLED FRITILLARY (*Speyeria cybele*). Occurs throughout region.

EDWARDS' FRITILLARY (*Speyeria edwardsii*). Occurs throughout region.

GREAT BASIN FRITILLARY (*Speyeria egleis*). Occurs throughout region.

NORTHWESTERN FRITILLARY (*Speyeria hesperis*). Occurs throughout region.

HYDASPE FRITILLARY (*Speyeria hydaspe*). Occurs throughout region.

MORMON FRITILLARY (*Speyeria mormonia*). Occurs throughout region.

ZERENE FRITILLARY (*Speyeria zerene*). Occurs throughout region.

TRUE BRUSHFOOTS (*NYMPHALINAE*)

MILBERT'S TORTOISESHELL (*Aglais milberti*). Occurs throughout region.

SAGEBRUSH CHECKERSPOT (*Chlosyne acastus*). Occurs throughout region.

GORGONE CHECKERSPOT (*Chlosyne gorgone*). Local in region.

NORTHERN CHECKERSPOT (*Chlosyne palla*). Occurs throughout region.

ROCKSLIDE CHECKERSPOT (*Chlosyne whitneyi*). Occurs throughout region.

VARIABLE CHECKERSPOT (*Euphydryas chalcedona*). Occurs throughout region.

EDITH'S CHECKERSPOT (*Euphydryas editha*). Occurs throughout region.

GILLETTE'S CHECKERSPOT (*Euphydryas gillettii*). Occurs throughout region.

MOURNING CLOAK (*Nymphalis antiopa*). Occurs throughout region.

CALIFORNIA TORTOISESHELL (*Nymphalis californica*). Occurs throughout region.

COMPTON TORTOISESHELL (*Nymphalis vaualbum*). Occurs throughout region.

NORTHERN CRESCENT (*Phyciodes cocyta*). Occurs throughout region.

MYLITTA CRESCENT (*Phyciodes mylitta*). Occurs throughout region.

FIELD CRESCENT (*Phyciodes pulchellus*). Occurs throughout region.

PALE CRESCENT (*Phyciodes pallida*). Occurs throughout region.

GREEN COMMA (*Polygonia faunus*). Occurs throughout region.

HOARY COMMA (*Polygonia gracilis*). Occurs throughout region.

GRAY COMMA (*Polygonia progne*). Occurs throughout region.

SATYR COMMA (*Polygonia satyrus*). Occurs throughout region.

WEST COAST LADY (*Vanessa annabella*). Occurs throughout region.

PAINTED LADY (*Vanessa cardui*). Occurs throughout region.

RED ADMIRAL (*Vanessa atalanta*). Occurs throughout region.

ADMIRALS AND RELATIVES (*LIMENITIDINAE*)

VICEROY (*Limenitis archippus*). Local in region.

WHITE ADMIRAL (*Limenitis arthemis arthemis*). Occurs throughout region.

WEIDEMEYER'S ADMIRAL (*Limenitis weidemeyerii*). Occurs throughout region.

MILKWEED BUTTERFLIES (*DANAINAE*)

MONARCH (*Danaus plexippus*). Occurs throughout region.

Skippers (*Hesperidae*)

SPREAD-WING SKIPPERS (*PYRGINAE*)

SILVER-SPOTTED SKIPPER (*Epargyreus clarus*). Occurs throughout region.

AFRANIUS DUSKYWING (*Erynnis afranius*). Occurs throughout region.

DREAMY DUSKYWING (*Erynnis icelus*). Occurs throughout region.

PERSIUS DUSKYWING (*Erynnis persius*). Occurs throughout region.

COMMON SOOTYWING (*Pholisora catullus*). Occurs throughout region.

COMMON CHECKERED-SKIPPER (*Pyrgus communis*). Occurs throughout region.

TWO-BANDED CHECKERED-SKIPPER (*Pyrgus ruralis*). Occurs throughout region.

NORTHERN CLOUDYWING (*Thorybes pylades*). Occurs throughout region.

SKIPPERLINGS (*HETEROPTERINAE*)

ARCTIC SKIPPERLING (*Carterocephalus palaemon*). Occurs throughout region.

COMMON BRANDED SKIPPER (*Hesperia comma*). Occurs throughout region.

JUBA SKIPPER (*Hesperia juba*). Occurs throughout region.

NEVADA SKIPPER (*Hesperia nevada*). Occurs throughout region.

UNCAS SKIPPER (*Hesperia uncas*). Occurs throughout region.

GARRITA SKIPERLING (*Oarisma garita*). Occurs throughout region.

DRACO SKIPPER (*Polites draco*). Occurs throughout region.

LONG DASH (*Polites mystic*). Local in region.

PECK'S SKIPPER (*Polites peckius*). Local in region.

SONORAN SKIPPER (*Polites sonora*). Occurs throughout region.

TAWNY-EDGED SKIPPER (*Polites themistocles*). Occurs throughout region.

EUROPEAN SKIPPER (*Thymelicus lineola*). Local in region (introduced).

APPENDIX 6

Latin Names of Plants Mentioned in the Text

FOR INFORMATION ON THESE AND OTHER Rocky Mountain plants, see Kershaw, MacKinnon, and Polar (1998).

Coniferous Trees

COLORADO BLUE SPRUCE (*Picea pungens*)

DOUGLAS-FIR (*Pseudotsuga menzeisii*)

ENGELMANN SPRUCE (*Picea engelmannii*)

LIMBER PINE (*Pinus flexilis*)

LODGEPOLE PINE (*Pinus contorta*)

PONDEROSA PINE (*Pinus ponderosa*)

ROCKY MOUNTAIN JUNIPER (*Juniperus scopulorum*)

SUBALPINE FIR (*Abies lasiocarpa*)

WHITEBARK PINE (*Pinus albicaulis*)

Deciduous Trees

MOUNTAIN ALDER (*Alnus incana*)

NARROW-LEAF COTTONWOOD (*Populus angustifolia*)

QUAKING ASPEN (*Populus tremuloides*)

WILLOW (*Salix* spp.)

Shrubs

BIG SAGEBRUSH (*Artemisia tridentata*)

COMMON RABBITBRUSH (*Chrysothamnus* [*Ericameria*] *nauseosus*)

RUSTY-LEAF MENZIESIA (*Menziesia ferruginea*)

THIMBLEBERRY (*Rubus parviflorus*)

Forbs

WHITE FLOWERS

CALTHA (*Caltha leptosepala*)

WATER CROWFOOT (*Ranunculus aquatilis*)

WHITE TO PALE PINK FLOWERS

SPRINGBEAUTY (*Claytonia lanceolata*)

RED TO PINK FLOWERS

FIREWEED (*Epilobium angustifolium*)

GILIA (*Ipomopsis aggregata*)

RED TO YELLOW FLOWERS

INDIAN PAINTBRUSH (*Castilleja* spp.)

SPATTERDOCK OR PONDLILY (*Nuphar polysepalum*)

RED CLOVER (*Trifolium pratense*)

YELLOW FLOWERS

AVALANCHE LILY (*Erythronium grandiflorum*)

BALSAMROOT (*Balsamorhiza sagittata*)

HEARTLEAF ARNICA (*Arnica cordifolia*)

GREEN FLOWERS

PONDWEED (*Potamogeton* spp.)

SEDGES

BULRUSH (*Scirpus acutus*)

RUSH (*Juncus* spp.)

SEDGE (*Carex* spp.)

Grasses

BLUEBUNCH WHEATGRASS (*Agropyron spicatum*)

IDAHO FESCUE (*Festuca idahoensis*)

WHEATGRASS (*Agropyron* [*Pseudoroegeneria*] spp.)

OVERLEAF. *Aspen grove and approaching storm, September, Lamar Valley, Yellowstone National Park, Wyoming*

Bibliographic Notes and References

History of the Greater Yellowstone Region

A very good and up-to-date geology reference is R. B. Smith and L. J. Siegel's *Windows into the Earth: The Geologic Story of Yellowstone and Grand Teton National Parks* (New York: Oxford University Press, 2000). Much of the information on the Grand Teton area is based on the classic booklet *Creation of the Teton Landscape*, by J. D. Love and J. C. Reed Jr. (Moose, WY: Grand Teton Natural History Association, 1971). A more recent reference is *The Atlas of Yellowstone*, edited by A. W. Marcus, J. E. Meachan, A. W. Rodman, A. Y. Steingisser, S. Allan, and R. West (Berkeley: University of California Press, 2012). A fairly nontechnical road-based guidebook is W. J. Fritz and R. C. Thomas's *Roadside Geology of Yellowstone Country* (Missoula, MT: Mountain Press Publishing, 2011). J. Aschenbach summarized the volcanic history of Yellowstone in "Will Yellowstone Blow Again?" *National Geographic* 216, no. 2 (2009): 56–79. An older but very useful geologic history of Yellowstone is W. R. Keefer's *The Geologic Story of Yellowstone National Park*, Geological Survey Bulletin 1347 (1979). A more general reference is A. W. Snoke, J. R. Steidtmann, and S. M. Roberts, eds., *Geology of Wyoming*, Memoir No. 5, 2 vols. (Cheyenne: Geological Society of Wyoming, 1993).

A history of early regional human activity is presented in G. C. Fison's "Prehistoric Occupations of the Grand Teton National Park," *Naturalist* 22, no. 1 (1971): 35–37. The nineteenth-century history of the region was documented in R. D. Dorn's *The Wyoming Landscape, 1805–1878* (Cheyenne, WY: Mountain West Publishing, 1986). The seasonal phenology of natural events in the region is described by F. C. Craighead Jr. in *For Everything There Is a Season:*

The Sequence of Natural Events in the Grand Teton–Yellowstone Area (Nashville, TN: Falcon Press, 1994). J. Turner's *Travels in the Greater Yellowstone* (New York: St. Martins Press, 2009) is an evocative account of the region's history and natural history by a longtime resident.

The Gros Ventre Valley

The classic but badly outdated reference on the plant communities of Wyoming is M. Cary's *Life Zone Investigations in Wyoming*, Bureau of Biological Survey (now US Fish and Wildlife Service), North American Fauna No. 42 (1917). More specifically related to the Gros Ventre region is J. F. Reed's "The Vegetation of the Jackson Hole Wildlife Park, Wyoming," *American Midland Naturalist* 48 (1952): 700–29. The ecology of the region's forested areas is discussed in L. Loope's "Dynamics of Forest Communities in Grand Teton National Park," *Naturalist* 22, no. 1 (1971): 39–47. Another important ecological study is E. T. Oswold's "A Synecological Study of the Forested Moraines of the Valley Floor of Grand Teton National Park, Wyoming" (PhD diss., Montana State University, Bozeman, 1966).

The birds of Grand Teton National Park and Jackson Hole were first inventoried by Bert Raynes and later by B. Raynes and D. Wile (see references below). A relevant ecological study is by G. W. Salt, "An Analysis of Avifauna in the Teton Mountains and Jackson Hole, Wyoming," *Condor* 59 (1957): 373–93.

The classic study of elk is O. J. Murie's *The Elk of North America* (Mechanicsburg, PA: Stackpole, 1951). Major regional references are C. C. Anderson, "The Elk of Jackson Hole: A Review of Jackson Hole Elk Studies," *Wyoming Game and Fish Commission Bulletin* 10 (1958), and G. F. Cole, "The Elk of Grand Teton and Southern Yellowstone National Parks," National Park Service Research Report GRTE-N-1 (1969). A photographic essay of the elk in the Tetons is *Season of the Elk*, by Dean Krakel II (Kansas City, MO: Lowell Press, 1976).

The migration of pronghorns from the Gros Ventre Valley to the Green River Basin is discussed by David Quammen in "Great Migrations," *National Geographic* 218, no. 8 (2010): 28–51. A detailed monograph on the pronghorn is J. A. Byers's *American Pronghorn* (Chicago: University of Chicago Press, 1997); a nontechnical account is J. Van Wormer's *The World of the Pronghorn* (Philadelphia: J. B. Lippencott, 1969).

For an account of the behavior and biology of the dusky (previously "blue") grouse, see my book *Grouse and Quails of North America* (Lincoln: University of Nebraska Press, 1973). This title is also accessible online through the University of Nebraska's DigitalCommons website: http://digitalcommons.unl.edu/bioscigrouse/1. See also the species account of the dusky grouse in *The Birds of North America* (see "Supplemental References" below).

The Sagebrush Sea

The ecology of sagebrush in Wyoming has been described by A. A. Beetle in "A Study of Sagebrush," *Wyoming Agricultural Experiment Station Bulletin* 368 (1960), and its ecology in the park is covered by D. W. Sabinske and D. H. Knight in "Variation within the Sagebrush Vegetation of Grand Teton National Park," *Northwest Science* 52, no. 3 (1978): 195–204.

There is a large amount of literature on the ecology and behavior of coyotes, including several recent books. Especially relevant to Wyoming is the study by Adolph Murie, *Ecology of the Coyote in the Yellowstone*, US National Park Service, Fauna Series No. 4 (1940), and O. J. Murie's *Food Habits of the Coyote in Jackson Hole, Wyoming*, U.S. Department of Agriculture Circular No. 362 (1935). Most of my description of coyote whelping behavior is based on C. J. Snow's "Some Observations on the Behavioral and Morphological Development of Coyote Pups," *American Zoologist* 14 (1967): 353–55, and M. Beckoff's "Social Play and Play-Soliciting in Infant Canids," *American Zoologist* 14 (1967): 323–40. I have also used H. Silver and W. T. Silver's "Growth and Behavior of the Coyote-Like Canid of New England," *Wildlife Monographs* 17 (1969). Coyote behavior and ecology on the National Elk Refuge is described by Franz Camenzind in *Coyotes: Biology, Behavior and Management*, edited by Mark Beckoff (New York: Academic Press, 1978). For further information on coyote biology, see F. Leydet's *The Coyote: Defiant Songdog of the West* (Norman: University of Oklahoma Press, 1988) and W. Grady's *The Nature of Coyotes* (Vancouver, BC: Douglas & McIntyre, 1994).

Sources of information on pronghorn behavior primarily include D. W. Kitchen's "Social Behavior and Ecology of the Pronghorn," *Wildlife Monographs* 38 (1974), and R. E. Autenrieth and E. Fichter's "On the Behavior and Socialization of Pronghorn Fawns," *Wildlife Monographs* 42 (1975). Of related interest are "The Antelope of Colorado," Colorado Department of Fish and Game Technical Bulletin No. 4 (1959), and "Some Behavior Patterns of the Pronghorn," Colorado Department of Game, Fish and Parks Special Report No. 17 (1968). Relevant books include G. Turbak's *Pronghorn: Portrait of the American Antelope* (Flagstaff, AZ: Northland Publishing, 1995), J. A. Byers's *American Pronghorn* (Chicago: University of Chicago Press, 1997), and V. Geist's *Antelope Country: Pronghorns; the Last Americans* (Fairfield, OH: Krause Publications, 2001). The most complete summary of pronghorn ecology is B. W. O'Gara and J. D. Yoakum's *Pronghorn: Ecology and Management* (Boulder: University Press of Colorado; Washington, DC: Wildlife Management Institute, 2004).

The Lamar Valley

Historic changes in vegetation in Yellowstone's northern range are described by D. B. Houston's *The Northern Yellowstone Elk: Ecology and Management* (New York: Macmillan, 1983). Another useful reference is *Yellowstone's Northern Range: Complexity and Change in a Wildland Ecosystem* (Mammoth Hot Springs, WY: US National Park Service, 1997). The ecology of large grazing mammals on this range is summarized in *Ecological Dynamics on Yellowstone's Northern Range*, produced by the Committee on Ungulate Management in Yellowstone National Park (Washington, DC: National Academy Press, 2002).

The history of Yellowstone's wolf population is described by J. L. Weaver in *The Wolves of Yellowstone*, US National Park Service National Research Report 14 (1978): 1–38. The reintroduction of wolves into Yellowstone Park has been described in many books, but one of the best first-person accounts is in M. K. Phillips and D. W. Smith's *The Wolves of Yellowstone* (Minneapolis, MN: Voyageur Press, 1996). Thomas McNamee's excellent account, *The Return of the Wolf to Yellowstone* (New York: Henry Holt, 1997), has over 400 references. Another account of early restoration efforts is H. Fischer's *Wolf Wars: The Remarkable Inside Story of the Restoration of Wolves to Yellowstone* (Nashville, TN: Falcon Press, 1995). A more recent account is D. W. Smith and G. Ferguson's *Decade of the Wolf: Returning the Wolf to Yellowstone* (Gullford, CT: Lyons Press, 2005). For a detailed account of the wolves' postintroduction survival, behavior, and ecology though 2002, see J. Halfpenny's *Yellowstone Wolves in the Wild* (Helena, MT: Riverbend Publishing, 2003). This book is the source of most of what I wrote on the history of the Druid Peak pack. It also provides a helpful list of recommended reading that include twelve books on wolves and seventeen websites relevant to wolf biology and conservation. Douglas Chadwick's "Wolf Wars," *National Geographic* 217, no. 3 (2010): 34–55, was my source for the summary of recent wolf distribution, numbers, and predation on livestock in the three-state northern Rocky Mountain region through 2008.

A beautifully illustrated general introduction to wolf biology is Candace Savage's *The World of the Wolf* (San Francisco: Sierra Club Books, 1986). A more technical summary is Erick Klinghammer's edited volume, *The Behavior and Ecology of Wolves* (New York: Garland STPM Press, 1979). Other important works on wolf biology include David Mech's *The Wolves of Isle Royale*, National Park Service, Fauna Series No. 7 (1966), and his later book, *The Wolf: The Ecology and Behavior of an Endangered Species* (New York: American Museum of Natural History; Garden City Press, 1970). The description of the wolf burrow is based on Adolf Murie's classic and seminal work, *The Wolves of Mount McKinley*, National Park Service, Fauna Series No. 5 (1941).

The general biology of Yellowstone's bears is documented in P. Scullery's *The Bears of Yellowstone* (Boulder, CO: Roberts Rinehart, 1986), in J. J. Craighead, J. S. Sumner, and J. A. Mitchell's *The Grizzly Bears of Yellowstone: Their Ecology in the Yellowstone Ecosystem, 1959–1992* (Washington, DC: Island Press, 1995), and most recently in J. Halfpenny's excellent *Yellowstone Bears in the Wild* (Helena, MT: Riverbend Publishing, 2007). Other useful grizzly bear sources are Thomas McName's *The Grizzly Bear* (New York: A. A. Knopf, 1982) and Chuck Neal's *Grizzlies in the Mist* (Bel Air, MD: Homestead Publishing, 2003). Grizzly bear foods are discussed in D. J. Mattson, K. C. Kendall, and D. P. Rinehart's "Food Habits of Yellowstone Grizzly Bears," *Canadian Journal of Zoology* 69 (1991): 1619–1629.

Earlier historic information on bison biology and populations in Yellowstone has been summarized through 1968 by Mary M. Meagher in *The Bison of Yellowstone National Park*, Monograph Series 1 (Washington, DC: National Park Service, 1973). Historic as well as more recent information on bison populations in the park and problems associated with bison conservation, hunting, and the brucellosis-related rancher-environmentalist debate is also provided by Mary A. Franke in *To Save the Wild Bison: Life on the Edge in Yellowstone* (Norman: University of Oklahoma Press, 2005).

For two regional accounts of the jumping mouse, see L. N. Brown's "Seasonal Activity Patterns and Breeding of Western Jumping Mice (*Zapus princeps*) in Wyoming," *American Midland Naturalist* 78 (1967): 460–70, and T. W. Clark's "Ecology of the Western Jumping Mouse in Grand Teton National Park," *Northwest Science* 45 (1971): 229–38.

The Canyon

The ecology and social behavior of the yellow-bellied marmot have been described in several papers by K. B. Armitage (*Animal Behaviour* 10 [1962]: 3129–3331; 13 [1965]:

59–68; *Journal of Mammalogy* 79 [1998]: 385–93). See also G. H. Waring's "Sounds and Communication in the Yellow-Bellied Marmot (*Marmota flaviventris*)," *Animal Behaviour* 14 (1966): 177–83. The general biology of marmots is described in D. F. Barash's *Marmots* (Stanford, CA: Stanford University Press, 1989); that of the golden eagle is summarized in my *Hawks, Eagles, and Falcons of North America: Biology and Natural History* (Washington, DC: Smithsonian Institution Press, 1990) and in the *Birds of North America* species account (see "Supplemental References" below).

The best regional reference on great gray owl biology in the Greater Yellowstone region is A. Franklin's "Breeding Biology of the Great Gray Owl (*Strix nebulosa*) in Southeastern Idaho and Northwestern Wyoming" (master's thesis, Humboldt State College, 1987). I summarized the ecology and behavior of the great gray owl in *North American Owls: Biology and Natural History* (Washington, DC: Smithsonian Institution Press, 1988), as did Robert Nero in *The Great Gray Owl: Phantom of the Northern Forest* (Washington, DC: Smithsonian Institution Press, 1980). See also the *Birds of North America* species account of the great gray owl (see "Supplemental References" below). For some field observations on the golden-mantled ground squirrel in California, see S. McKeever's "The Biology of the Golden-Mantled Ground Squirrel," *Ecological Monographs* 34 (1964): 382–402.

For a comprehensive account of the Williamson's sapsucker, see A. B. Crockett's "Ecology and Behavior of the Williamson's Sapsucker in Colorado" (PhD diss., University of Colorado, Boulder, 1975). Also relevant are A. B. Crockett and P. L. Hansley's "Coition, Nesting, and Postfledging Behavior of Williamson's Sapsucker in Colorado," *Living Bird* 16 (1978): 7–20, and A. B. Crockett and H. H. Hadow's "Nest Site Selection by Williamson and Red-Naped Sapsuckers," *Condor* 77 (1975): 365–68. The biology of Lewis's woodpecker is described in C. E. Bock's "The Ecology and Behavior of the Lewis Woodpecker (*Asyndesmus lewis*)," *University of California Publications in Zoology* 92 (1970): 1–100. See also the *Birds of North America* species accounts of the Lewis's woodpecker and Williamson's sapsucker (see "Supplemental References" below).

The Geyser Basin

General information on the Yellowstone fires of 1988 can be found in D. Patent's *Yellowstone Fires: Flames and Rebirth* (New York: Holiday House, 1990) and in C. Vogel and K. A. Goldner's *The Great Yellowstone Fire* (New York: Little, Brown, 1990). Postfire ecological changes are thoroughly described in L. L. Wallace's *After the Fires: The Ecology of Change in Yellowstone National Park* (New Haven, CT: Yale University Press, 2004). The description of bird and forest succession following the fire at Old Faithful was based on the account by D. L. Taylor and W. J. Barmore Jr., "Post-Fire Succession of Avifauna in Coniferous Forests of Yellowstone and Grand Teton National Parks, Wyoming," in *Management of Western Forests and Grasslands for Nongame Birds*, edited by R. M. DeGraaf and N. G. Tilghman, USDA Forest Service General Technical Report INT-86 (1980), 130–44.

For more information on the American three-toed, black-backed, and hairy woodpeckers, see the individual species accounts in *The Birds of North America* (see "Supplemental

References" below). Also relevant is C. E. Bock and J. H. Bock's "On the Geographical Ecology of the Three-Toed Woodpeckers, *Picoides tridactylus* and *P. arcticus*," *American Midland Naturalist* 92 (1974): 397–405.

For information on seed-storing and seed recovery in the Clark's nutcracker, see D. F. Tomback's "How Nutcrackers Find Their Seed Stores," *Condor* 82 (1980): 10–19, and S. B. Vander Wall's "An Experimental Analysis of Cache Recovery in Clark's Nutcracker," *Animal Behaviour* 30 (1982): 80–94. Information on the black-billed magpie's social behavior can be found in R. E. Jones's "Activities of the Magpie during the Breeding Period in Southern Idaho," *Northwest Science* 34 (1960): 18–25. Food-storing adaptations in the gray jay are described in W. J. Bock's "Salivary Glands in the Gray Jays (*Perisoreus*)," *Auk* 78 (1961): 355–65. See also the species accounts of the Clark's nutcracker, black-billed magpie, and gray jay in *The Birds of North America* (see "Supplemental References" below).

Much of the bison material used in this section was based on Mary M. Meagher's *The Bison of Yellowstone National Park*, National Park Service Monograph Series 1 (1973). Also relevant is Tom McHugh's "Social Behavior of the American Buffalo (*Bison Bison Bison*)," *Zoologica* 43 (1958): 1–40, and his book *The Time of the Buffalo* (New York: A. A. Knopf, 1972). There is a vast literature on bison biology and behavior, including many recent books. Some of these include H. P. Danz's *Of Bison and Man* (Niwot: University Press of Colorado, 1997), D. Fitzgerald's *Bison: Monarch of the Plains* (Portland, OR: Graphic Arts Center Publishing, 1998), F. Haines's *The Buffalo* (Norman: University of Oklahoma Press, 1995), and D. F. Lott's *American Buffalo: A Natural History* (Berkeley: University of California Press, 2002).

The Willow Flats

The ecological relationships between moose and willows in Jackson Hole is documented in D. B. Houston's "The Shiras Moose in Jackson Hole, Wyoming," Grand Teton Natural History Association Technical Bulletin No. 1 (1968). More general accounts include V. Geist's *Moose: Behavior, Ecology, Conservation* (Minneapolis, MN: Voyageur Press, 1999) and A. W. Franzman and C. C. Schwartz's *Ecology and Management of North American Moose* (Washington, DC: Smithsonian Institution Press, 1997).

The breeding biology of the greater sandhill crane has been documented at Grays Lake National Wildlife Refuge in R. C. Drewien's "Ecology of Rocky Mountain Greater Sandhill Cranes" (PhD diss., University of Idaho, Moscow, 1973). The account of the crane attacking a moose is based on a note by M. Altmann (*Journal of Mammalogy* 41 [1960]: 525). The observations of the nest at the time of hatching are my own. The description of plumage and behavior development in young cranes is largely derived from Lawrence Walkinshaw's *The Sandhill Cranes*, Cranbrook Institute of Science Bulletin 29 (1949). For more recent accounts, see my books *Crane Music: A Natural History of American Cranes* (Washington, DC: Smithsonian Institution Press, 1991) and *The Sandhill and Whooping Cranes: Ancient Voices over America's Wetlands* (Lincoln: University of Nebraska Press, 2011). See also the species account of the sandhill crane in *The Birds of North America* (see "Supplemental References" below).

The Pond

Most of the observations on nesting trumpeter swans and associated species are my own. A separate account of trumpeter swans in the Tetons was also published in *Natural History* (November [1978]: 72–77). A useful report on the breeding biology of trumpeter swans is R. D. Page's "The Ecology of the Trumpeter Swan on Red Rock Lakes National Wildlife Refuge, Montana," (PhD diss., University of Montana, Missoula, 1974). This work updates the earlier studies on this species by W. E. Banko, *The Trumpeter Swan*, US Fish and Wildlife Service, North American Fauna 63 (1960). Terry McEneaney analyzed long-term changes in trumpeter swan populations in *Yellowstone National Park: Field Observations, Analyses, and Interpretation of a 77-Year Yellowstone Trumpeter Swan Data Set*, Yellowstone Wildlife Publication No. 1 (Gardiner, MT: Yellowstone Library and Museum Association, 2008).

See also the species account of the trumpeter swan in *The Birds of North America* (see "Supplemental References" below). Summaries of the social and sexual behavior of trumpeter swans, ruddy ducks, and other waterfowl mentioned in this chapter can be found online through the University of Nebraska's DigitalCommons website in my *Waterfowl of North America*, 2nd ed. (2010, http://digitalcommons.unl.edu/biosciwaterfowlna/1), and in my *Handbook of Waterfowl Behavior* (http://digitalcommons.unl.edu/bioscihandwaterfowl/7).

Details of the breeding biology of the Wilson's (previously "common") snipe can be found in L. M. Tuck's *The Snipes*, Canadian Wildlife Service Monograph Series No. 5 (1972), and in my *Plovers, Sandpipers, and Snipes of the World* (Lincoln: University of Nebraska Press, 1981). Information on the white-crowned sparrow was based on O. L. Austin Jr., ed., *Life Histories of North American Cardinals, Grosbeaks, Buntings, Towhees, Finches, Sparrows, and Allies*, US. National Museum Bulletin 237 (1968). See also the species accounts of the common snipe and white-crowned sparrow in *The Birds of North America* (see "Supplemental References" below).

A nontechnical survey of the wetlands of Yellowstone Park and their remarkable value to plants and wildlife is C. R. Elliott and M. M. Hektner's *Wetland Resources of Yellowstone National Park* (Gardiner, MT: Yellowstone National Park, 2000).

The Oxbow Bend

Nearly all the information on the breeding behavior of the bald eagle was based on F. H. Herrick's *The American Eagle* (New York: D. Appleton-Century, 1934). There is also an ecological study in Yellowstone Park by J. E. Swenson et al., "The Ecology of Bald Eagles in the Greater Yellowstone Ecosystem," *Wildlife Monographs* 95 (1996): 1–46. Most of the information on osprey nesting was based on R. Green's "Breeding Behaviour of Ospreys *Pandion haliaetus* in Scotland," *Ibis* 118 (1976): 475–90. See also accounts of these species in my *Hawks, Eagles, and Falcons of North America: Biology and Natural History* (Washington, DC: Smithsonian Institution Press, 1990) and in *The Birds of North America* (see "Supplemental References" below).

Three references on great blue herons were especially useful: H. M. Pratt's "Breeding Biology of Great Blue Herons and Common Egrets in Central California," *Condor* 72 (1970): 407–16; W. P. Cottrille and B. D. Cottrille's "Great Blue Heron: Behavior at the

Nest," *University of Michigan Museum of Zoology Miscellaneous Publications* 102 (1958); and D. M. Mock's "Pair-Formation Displays of the Great Blue Heron," *Wilson Bulletin* 88 (1976): 185–230. See also the species account of the great blue heron in *The Birds of North America* (see "Supplemental References" below).

The Aspen Island

The ecology of aspens in Jackson Hole is described by A. A. Beetle, "Range Survey in Teton County, Wyoming, Part IV: Quaking Aspen," *Agricultural Experiment Station Publication* SM 27 (1974), and in G. Gruell and L. Loope, "Relationships among Aspen, Fire, and Ungulate Browsing in Jackson Hole, Wyoming" (Washington, DC: US Forest Service and National Park Service, 1974).

Much of the information on common ravens is based on J. L. Dorn's "The Common Raven in Jackson Hole, Wyoming" (master's thesis, University of Wyoming, Laramie, 1972). The account of ravens stealing eggs and young from herons is based on my own observations, as is the earlier description of a raven attack on a trumpeter swan nest. See also the species account of the common raven in *The Birds of North America* (see "Supplemental References" below).

The account of elk calving and calf behavior was based on two studies by M. Altmann: "Social Behavior of Elk, *Cervus canadensis nelsoni*, in the Jackson Hole Area of Wyoming," *Behaviour* 4 (1952): 116–43, and "Patterns of Herd Behavior in Free-Ranging Elk of Wyoming, *Cervus canadensis nelsoni*," *Zoologica* 41 (1956): 65–71. For more on regional elk movements and populations, see J. Craighead, G. Atwell, and R. W. O'Gara's "Elk Migration in and near Yellowstone National Park," *Wildlife Monographs* 29 (1972): 1–45; M. S. Boyce's *The Jackson Elk Herd: Intensive Wildlife Management in North America* (Cambridge: Cambridge University Press, 1989); and D. B. Houston's *Northern Yellowstone Elk: Ecology and Management* (New York: Macmillan, 1982).

The account of behavior and biology of the prairie falcon was partly based on H. H. Enderson's "A Study of the Prairie Falcon in the Central Rocky Mountain Region," *Auk* 81 (1964): 332–52, supplemented by my own observations. See also the prairie falcon account in my *Hawks, Eagles, and Falcons of North America: Biology and Natural History* (Washington, DC: Smithsonian Institution Press, 1990) and the *Birds of North America* species account (see "Supplemental References" below).

For Uinta ground squirrel biology, see D. Balph and A. W. Stokes's "On the Ethology of a Population of Uinta Ground Squirrels," *American Midland Naturalist* 69 (1963): 106–26, and T. W. Clark and C. Russell's "Agonistic Behavior in Uinta Ground Squirrels," *Northwest Science* 51 (1977): 36–42.

The Spruce Forest

The biology of the ruffed grouse is summarized in my *Grouse and Quails of North America* (Lincoln: University of Nebraska Press, 1972, and the University of Nebraska's DigitalCommons version: http://digitalcommons.unl.edu/bioscigrouse/1). The northern goshawk's biology is summarized in my *Hawks, Eagles, and Falcons of North America:*

Biology and Natural History (Washington, DC: Smithsonian Institution Press, 1990). See also the *Birds of North America* monograph series for species accounts of the ruffed grouse and northern goshawk (see "Supplemental References" below).

Information on the pine marten family was derived from J. D. Remington's "Food Habits, Growth, and Behavior of Two Captive Pine Martens," *Journal of Mammalogy* 33 (1952): 66–70, and M. H. Markley and C. F. Bassett's "Habits of Captive Marten," *American Midland Naturalist* 28 (1942): 604–16. One of the few studies of pine martens in the region is Adolph Murie's "Some Food Habits of the Marten," *Journal of Mammalogy* 42 (1961): 16–21. A more general study on martens in the Rocky Mountains is W. H. Marshall's "The Biology and Management of the Pine Marten in Idaho" (PhD diss., University of Michigan, Ann Arbor, 1942). A comprehensive book on the biology of pine martens was edited by S. Buskirk, A. Harestad, M. Rapheal, and R. Powell: *Martens, Sables, and Fishers: Biology and Conservation* (New York: Cornell University Press, 1994).

The description of beaver activities was mostly based on L. Trevis's "Summer Behavior of a Family of Beavers in New York State," *Journal of Mammalogy* 31 (1950): 40–65. Most of my information on beavers in Jackson Hole came from T. C. Collins's "Population Characteristics and Habitat Relations of Beavers, *Castor canadensis,* in Northwest Wyoming" (PhD diss., University of Wyoming, Laramie, 1976). W. Ruderstorf's "The Coactions of Beaver and Moose on a Joint Food Supply in the Buffalo River Meadows and Surrounding Area in Jackson Hole, Wyoming" (master's thesis, Utah State University, Logan, 1952) provides additional local information.

The information on the calliope hummingbird was mostly based on my own observations, supplemented by published descriptions of nest characteristics and nest-building behavior. See also my monograph *The Hummingbirds of North America* (Washington, DC: Smithsonian Institution Press, 1997) and the *Birds of North America* monograph series (see "Supplemental References" below) for detailed accounts of the calliope hummingbird.

The Cirque

The two primary references for the dipper were H. W. Hann's "Nesting Behavior of the American Dipper in Colorado," *Condor* 52 (1950): 49–62, and G. J. Bakus's "Observations on the Life History of the Dipper in Montana," *Auk* 76 (1959): 190–207. See also the *Birds of North America* species account of the American dipper (see "Supplemental References" below).

The description of pika behavior was mostly derived from H. E. Broadbook's "Ecology and Distribution of the Pikas of Washington and Alaska," *American Midland Naturalist* 73 (1965): 299–335. Two related studies are H. R. Krear's "An Ecological and Ethological Study of the Pika (*Ochotona princeps* Bangs) in the Front Range of Colorado," (PhD diss., University of Colorado, Boulder, 1965), and J. H. Sevaraid's "The Natural History of the Pika (mammalian genus *Ochotona*)," (PhD diss., University of California, Berkeley, 1955). See also D. F. Barash's "Territorial and Foraging Behavior of Pika (*Ochotona princeps*) in Montana," *American Midland Naturalist* 89 (1973): 202–7. A popular article is "The Art of Making Hay," *National Wildlife* 35, no. 3 (1997): 31–35, by A. Smith.

The account of the mountain sheep was based on information in V. Geist's *Mountain Sheep* (Chicago: University of Chicago Press, 1971). Of related interest are R. F. Honess and N. M. Frost's "A Wyoming Bighorn Sheep Study," *Wyoming Fish and Game Department Bulletin* 1 (1942); A. Wolfe's "Summer Ecology of Bighorn Sheep in Yellowstone National Park" (master's thesis, Colorado State University, Fort Collins, 1968); and R. Valdez and P. R. Krausman's *Mountain Sheep of North America* (Tucson: University of Arizona Press, 1999).

The account of black rosy-finch nesting was derived from N. R. French's "Life History of the Black Rosy Finch." *Auk* 76 (1959): 159–80. See also the *Birds of North America* species account of the black rosy-finch (see "Supplemental References" below).

A Yellowstone Autumn

The account of elk social behavior was based on the papers by M. Altmann mentioned above, and T. T. Struhsaker's "Behavior of Elk (*Cervus canadensis*) during the Rut," *Zeitschrift fur Tierpsychologie* 4 (1967): 80–114. Bison and elk populations in Yellowstone's northern range as well as population management efforts there through hunting and culling have been discussed in M. A. Franke's *To Save the Wild Bison: Life on the Edge in Yellowstone* (Norman: University of Oklahoma Press, 2005). Yellowstone bison hunting is described in D. Peacock's "The Yellowstone Massacre," *Audubon* 93, no. 3 (1997): 40–49, 102–3, 106–7. For a comprehensive study of elk, see M. S. Boyce and L. D. Hayden-Wing's *North American Elk: Ecology, Behavior, and Management* (Laramie: University of Wyoming, 1979). Jackson Hole elk populations and the autumn elk hunt in Jackson Hole and around the National Elk Refuge are discussed in Dean Krakel's *Season of the Elk* (Oklahoma City: National Cowboy Hall of Fame and Western Heritage Center, 1976).

An illustrated account of a cougar rearing its young in the National Elk Refuge is provided in Tom Mangelsen and Cara Blessley's *Spirit of the Rockies: The Mountain Lions of Jackson Hole* (Omaha, NE: Images of Nature, 1999). For a comprehensive account of cougar biology, see H. P. Danz's *Cougar!* (Athens: Swallow Press/Ohio University Press, 1999).

The complex problems associated with maintaining viable populations of wolves, cougars, bears, and other large predators in a human-dominated environment such as the Yellowstone ecosystem are discussed in T. W. Clark, A. P. Curlee, S. C. Minta, and P. M. Kareiva's *Carnivores in Ecosystems: The Yellowstone Experience* (New Haven, CT: Yale University Press, 1999) and in T. W. Clark, M. B. Rutherford, and D. Casey's *Coexisting with Large Carnivores: Lessons from Greater Yellowstone* (Washington, DC: Island Press, 2005). For further information on large-mammal ecology in Yellowstone's northern ranges, see D. Despain, D. Houston, M. Meager, and P. Schullery's *Wildlife in Transition: Man and Nature in Yellowstone's Northern Range* (Boulder, CO: Roberts Rinehart, 1986).

Supplemental References

Geology and Regional Landscapes

Chronic, H. 1984. *Pages of Stone: Geology of Western Parks and Monuments*. Seattle: Mountaineer Press.

Dorn, R. D. 1986. *The Wyoming Landscape, 1805–1878*. Cheyenne, WY: Mountain West.

Howard, A. D. 1937. *History of the Grand Canyon of the Yellowstone.* vol. 6. Geological Society of America, Special Paper. Boulder, CO: Geological Society of America.

Knight, D. H. 1994. *Mountains and Plains: The Ecology of Wyoming Landscapes.* New Haven, CT: Yale University Press.

Lageson, D., and D. Spearing. 1991. *Roadside Geology of Wyoming.* Missoula, MT: Mountain Press.

Recent History and Regional Ecology

Hejl, S. J., R. L. Hutto, C. R. Preston, and D. M. Finch. 1995. "Effects of Silviculture Treatments in the Rocky Mountains." In *Ecology and Management of Neotropical Migratory Birds*, edited by T. E. Martin and D. M. Finch, 220–44. New York: Oxford University Press.

Jehl, J. R., Jr., and N. K. Johnson, eds. 1994. *A Century of Avifaunal Change in Western North America.* Studies in Avian Biology 15. Manhattan, KS: Cooper Orinthological Society.

Johnsgard, P. A. 1982. *Teton Wildlife: Observations by a Naturalist.* Boulder: Colorado Associated University Press.
  (This title is also available online through the University of Nebraska's DigitalCommons website: http://digitalcommons.unl.edu/biosciornithology/52/.)

Keiter, R. B., and M. S. Boyce, eds. 1991. *The Greater Yellowstone Ecosystem: Redefining America's Wilderness Heritage.* Princeton, NJ: Princeton University Press.

Mathews, D. 2003. *Rocky Mountain Natural History: Grand Teton to Jasper.* Portland, OR: Raven Editions.
  (A very informative and readable survey of the region's landscapes, animals, and plants.)

Pritchard, J. A. 1999. *Preserving Yellowstone's Natural Conditions.* Lincoln: University of Nebraska Press.

Ripple, W. J., and E. J. Larsen. 2000. "Historic Aspen Recruitment, Elk and Wolves in Northern Yellowstone National Park." *Biological Conservation* 95 (3): 361–70. http://dx.doi.org/10.1016/S0006-3207(00)00014-8.

Romme, W. H., and M. G. Turner. 1991. "Implications of Global Climatic Changes for Biogeographic Patterns in the Greater Yellowstone Ecosystem." *Conservation Biology* 5 (3): 373–86. http://dx.doi.org/10.1111/j.1523-1739.1991.tb00151.x.

Scharf, R., ed. 1966. *Yellowstone and Grand Teton National Parks.* New York: David McKay Co.

Scullery, P. 1997. *Searching for Yellowstone: Ecology and Wonder in the Last Wilderness.* Boston: Houghton Mifflin.

Fire Ecology and Regional Fire History

Houston, D. B. 1973. "Wildfires in Northern Yellowstone National Park." *Ecology* 54 (5): 1111–17. http://dx.doi.org/10.2307/1935577.

Kotliar, N. B., S. J. Heil, R. L. Hutto, V. A. Saab, C. P. Melcher, and M. E. McFadzen. 2002. "Effects of Fire and Post-Fire Salvage Logging on Avian Communities in Conifer-Dominated Forests of the Western United States." In *Effects of Habitat Fragmentation on Birds in Western Landscapes: Contrasts with Paradigms for the Eastern United States*, edited by T. George and D. S. Dobkin, 49–64. Studies in Avian Biology 25. Manhattan, KS: Cooper Orinthological Society.

Loope, L. L., and G. E. Gruell. 1973. "The Ecological Role of Fire in the Jackson Hole Area, Northwestern Wyoming." *Quaternary Research* 3 (3): 425–43. http://dx.doi.org/10.1016/0033-5894(73)90007-0.

Morrison, M. 1993. *Fire in Paradise: The Yellowstone Fires and the Politics of Environmentalism*. New York: HarperCollins.

Romme, W. H., M. G. Turner, L. L. Wallace, and J. Walker. 1995. "Aspen, Elk and Fire in Northern Yellowstone National Park." *Ecology* 76 (7): 2097–106. http://dx.doi.org/10.2307/1941684.

Saab, V. A., and H. Powell, eds. 2005. *Fire and Fire Ecology in North America*. Studies in Avian Biology 30. Manhattan, KS: Cooper Orinthological Society.

Smith, J. K., and W. C. Fischer. 1997. *Fire Ecology of Forest Habitat Types of Northern Idaho*. Report INT-GTR-363. Ogden, UT: USDA Forest Service.

Smucker, K. M., R. L. Hutto, and R. M. Steele. 2005. "Changes in Bird Abundance after Wildfire: Importance of Fire Severity and Time since Fire." *Ecological Applications* 15 (5): 1535–49. http://dx.doi.org/10.1890/04-1353.

Taylor, D. L., and W. J. Barmore Jr. 1980. "Post-Fire Succession of Avifauna in Coniferous Forests of Yellowstone and Grand Teton National Parks, Wyoming." In *Management of Western Forests and Grasslands for Nongame Birds*, edited by R. M. DeGraaf and N. Tilghman, 130–44. US Forest Service General Technical Report INT-86. Ogden, UT: USDA Forest Service, Rocky Mountain Forest and Range Experiment Station.

Wuerther, G., ed. 2006. *Wild Fire: A Century of Failed Forest Policy*. Sausalito, CA: Foundation for Deep Ecology and Island Press.

Rocky Mountain Vertebrates and Invertebrates

MAMMALS

American Society of Mammalogists. *Mammalian Species*.
(Individual species monographs; years of publication vary.)

Anderson, C. C. 1958. *The Elk of Jackson Hole*. Cheyenne: Wyoming Game and Parks Commission.

Armstrong, D. M. 1987. *Rocky Mountain Mammals*. Boulder: Colorado Associated University Press.
(Includes only those species occurring in Rocky Mountain National Park.)

Boyce, M. S., and L. D. Hayden-Wing, eds. 1979. *North American Elk: Ecology, Behavior, and Management*. Laramie: University of Wyoming.

Broderick, H. J. 1954. *Wild Animals of Yellowstone National Park*. Yellowstone National Park, WY: Yellowstone Library and Museum Association.

Clark, T. W., and M. R. Stromberg. 1987. *Mammals of Wyoming*. Public Education Series No. 10. Lawrence: University of Kansas Museum of Natural History.

Craighead, F. C., Jr. 1979. *Track of the Grizzly*. San Francisco: Sierra Club Books.

Dary, D. A. 1989. *The Buffalo Book: The Full Saga of the American Animal*. Chicago: Swallow Press and Ohio University Press.

Hayward, G. D., and P. H. Hayward. 1995. "Relative Abundance and Habitat Associations of Small Mammals in Chamberlain Basin, Central Idaho." *Northwest Science* 69:114–25.

Irby, L. R., and J. E. Knight, eds. 1998. *Bison Ecology and Management in North America*. Bozeman: Montana State University.

Johnsgard, P. A. 2005. *Prairie Dog Empire: A Saga of the Shortgrass Prairie*. Lincoln: University of Nebraska Press.

Long, C. A. 1965. *The Mammals of Wyoming*. University of Kansas Museum of Natural History Publication, vol. 14, no. 18: 493–754. Lawrence, KS: Museum of Natural History.

Lott, D. F. 2002. *American Buffalo: A Natural History*. Berkeley: University of California Press.

McEneaney, T. 2008. *Field Checklist of the Mammals of Yellowstone National Park*. Yellowstone Wildlife Publication No. 2. Gardiner, MT: Yellowstone Wildlife Guides.

Murie, O. 1951. *The Elk of North America*. New York: A. Knopf.

Negus, N. C., and J. S. Findley. 1959. "The Mammals of Jackson Hole, Wyoming." *Journal of Mammalogy* 40 (3): 371–81. http://dx.doi.org/10.2307/1376561.

Pease, C. M., and D. J. Mattson. 1999. "Demography of the Yellowstone Grizzly Bears." *Ecology* 80 (3): 957–75. http://dx.doi.org/10.1890/0012-9658(1999)080[0957:DOTYGB]2.0.CO;2.

Roe, F. G. 1970. *The North American Buffalo: A Critical Study of the Species in its Wild State*. 2nd ed. Toronto: University of Toronto Press.

Ruggiero, L. F., K. B. Aubry, S. W. Buskirk, L. J. Lyon, and W. J. Zielinski, eds. 1994. *American Marten, Fisher, Lynx, and Wolverine in the Western United States*. Denver: USDA Forest Service. (Summary of twentieth-century records.)

Schullery, P. 1992. *The Bears of Yellowstone*. Worland, WY: High Plains Publishing.

Steelquist, R. U. 1998. *Field Guide to the North American Bison*. Seattle: Sasquatch Books.

Streubel, D. P. 1995. *Small Mammals of the Yellowstone Ecosystem*. Boulder, CO: Roberts Rinehart.

Ulrich, T. J. 1990. *Mammals of the Northern Rockies*. Missoula, MT: Mountain Press. (Includes species occurring from Grand Teton to Watertown-Glacier national parks.)

Wambolt, C. 1998. "Sagebrush and Ungulate Relationships in Yellowstone's Northern Range." *Wildlife Society Bulletin* 26:429–37.

Wassink, J. L. 1993. *Mammals of the Central Rockies*. Missoula, MT: Mountain Press. (Covers Colorado, Wyoming, Montana, and Idaho.)

Wilson, D., and S. Ruff. 1999. *The Smithsonian Book of North American Mammals*. Washington, DC: Smithsonian Institution Press.

BIRDS

Single-species monographs on over 400 species of North American birds have been published under the auspices of the American Ornithologists' Union in the 716-part series *The Birds of North America*, edited by A. Poole and F. Gill (Philadelphia: The Birds of North America, Inc.); electronic versions, many updated, are now available online at http://bna.birds.cornell.edu/bna/). The following accounts are especially relevant to this book: *American Dipper*, No. 229 (H. E. Kingery, 1996, 28 pp.); *American Three-toed Woodpecker*, No. 588 (D. L. Leonard, 2001, 24 pp.); *Bald Eagle*, No. 506 (D. A. Buehler, 2000, 40 pp.); *Black Rosy-Finch*, No. 678 (R. E. Johnson, 2002, 28 pp.); *Black-backed Woodpecker*, No. 509 (R. D. Dixon and V. A. Saab, 2000, 20 pp.); *Black-billed Magpie*, No. 389 (C. H. Trost, 1999, 28 pp.); *Black Rosy-Finch*, No. 678 (R. E. Johnson, 2002, 28 pp.); *Calliope Hummingbird*, No. 135 (W. A. Calder and L. L. Calder, 1994, 16 pp.); *Clark's Nutcracker*, No. 331 (D. F. Tomback, 1998, 24 pp.); *Common Raven*, No. 476 (W. I. Boarman and B. Heinrich, 1999, 32 pp.); *Dusky ("Blue") Grouse*, No. 15 (F. C. Zwickel, 1992, 28 pp.); *Golden Eagle*, No. 684 (M. N. Kochert, K. Steenhof, C. L. McIntyre, and E. H. Craig, 2003, 44 pp.); *Gray Jay*, No. 40 (D. Strickland and H. Ouellet, 1993, 24 pp.); *Great Blue Heron*, No. 25 (R. W. Butler, 1992, 20 pp.); *Great Gray Owl*, No. 41 (E. L. Bull and J. R. Duncan, 1993. 16 pp.); *Hairy Woodpecker*, No. 702 (J. A. Jackson, H. R. Ouellet, and B. J. S. Jackson, 2003, 32 pp.); *Lewis's*

Woodpecker, No. 284 (B. W. Tobalske, 1997, 28 pp.); *Northern Goshawk*, No. 298 (J. R. Squires and R. T. Reynolds, 1997, 32 pp.); *Osprey*, No. 683 (A. F. Poole, R. O. Bierregaard, and M. S. Martell, 2003, 44 pp.); *Prairie Falcon*, No. 346 (K. Steenhof, 1998, 28 pp.); *Red-naped Sapsucker*, No. 663 (E. L. Walters, E. H. Miller, and P. E. Lowther. 2002, 32 pp.); *Ruffed Grouse*, No. 515 (D. Rusch, S. Destafano, M. Reynolds, and D. Lauten, 2000, 28 pp.); *Trumpeter Swan*, No. 105 (C. D. Mitchell, 1994, 24 pp.); *Williamson's Sapsucker*, No. 285 (R. C. Dobbs, T. E. Martin, and C. J. Conway, 1997, 20 pp.); *White-crowned Sparrow*, No. 183 (G. Chilton, M. C. Baker, C. D. Barrentine, and M. A. Cunningham, 1995, 28 pp.); *Wilson's ("Common") Snipe*, No. 417 (H. Mueller, 1999, 20 pp.).

Brodrick, H. J. 1952. *Birds of Yellowstone National Park*. Yellowstone Interpretive Series No. 2. Mammoth, WY National Park Service, Yellowstone Library and Museum Association.

Dobkin, D. S. 1994. *Conservation and Management of Neotropical Migrant Landbirds in the Northern Rockies and Great Plains*. Moscow: University of Idaho Press.

Dorn, J. L. 1978. *Wyoming Ornithology: A History and Bibliography with Species and Wyoming Area Indexes*. Washington, DC: US Bureau of Land Management; Lander: Wyoming Game & Fish Department.

Dorn, J. L., and R. D. Dorn. 1990. *Wyoming Birds*. Cheyenne, WY: Mountain West.

Faulkner, D. C. 2010. *Birds of Wyoming*. Greenwood Village, CO: Ben Roberts & Co.
(Includes species accounts, range maps, and about 600 references on Wyoming birds through 2009.)

Follet, D. 1986. *Birds of Yellowstone and Grand Teton National Parks*. Boulder, CO: Roberts Rinehart and Yellowstone Library and Museum Association. http://dx.doi.org/10.5962/bhl.title.54845

Johnsgard, P. A. 1997. *Hummingbirds of North America*. 2nd ed. Washington, DC: Smithsonian Institution Press.

Johnsgard, P. A. 2009. *Birds of the Rocky Mountains, with Particular Reference to the National Parks in the Northern Rocky Mountain Region*. 2nd ed. Lincoln: University of Nebraska DigitalCommons. http://digitalcommons.unl.edu/biosci/birdsrockymtns/1, with updated supplement: http://digital commons.unl.edu/bioscibirdsrockymtns/3. First published 1986 by Colorado Associated University Press.

Johnsgard, P. A. 2011. *Sandhill and Whooping Cranes: Ancient Voices over America's Wetlands*. Lincoln: University of Nebraska Press.

McEneaney, T. 1988. *Birds of Yellowstone*. Boulder, CO: Roberts Rinehart.
(Includes habitat affiliations, route descriptions, and a park checklist of 279 species; out of print.)

McEneaney, T. 1993. *The Birder's Guide to Montana*. Helena, MT: Falcon Press.
(Describes forty-five birding sites or local areas, including northern Yellowstone Park.)

McEneaney, T. 2007a. *2006 Yellowstone Bird Report*. YCR-2007-01. Yellowstone National Park, WY: Yellowstone Center for Research.
(See also McEneaney's website [ravenidiot.com] for annual *Yellowstone Bird Report* summaries from 1999 to 2006, which contain population trend data for many of the larger or rarer species.)

McEneaney, T. 2007b. *Yellowstone National Park Checklist of Birds*. Mammoth, WY: Yellowstone National Park and Yellowstone Association.
(A twelve-page foldout, with a checklist of 323 species and general abundance and breeding status information.)

McEneaney, T. 2008. *Field Checklist of the Birds of Yellowstone National Park. Yellowstone Wildlife Publication #3*. Gardiner, MT: Yellowstone Wildlife.

Rashid, S. 2010. *Small Mountain Owls*. Atglen, PA: Schiffler.
(Describes four species of Rocky Mountain owls.)

Raynes, B. 1984. *Birds of Grand Teton National Park and the Surrounding Area*. Moose, WY: Grand Teton Natural History Association.
(Includes a regional checklist of 293 species.)

Raynes, B. 2000. *A Pocket Guide to Birds of Jackson Hole: Their Occurrence, Arrival and Departure Dates, and Preferred Habitats of Birds of the Jackson Hole, Wyoming, Area*. Moose, WY: Homestead Publishing.
(Includes a regional checklist of 301 species, a monthly abundance calendar, and habitat information.)

Raynes, B., and G. Raynes. 2008. *Birds of Jackson Hole*. Jackson, WY: Grand Teton Association, Wyoming Game and Fish Department and U.S. Fish & Wildlife Service.
(A seasonal regional checklist of 340 species covering the southern half of the Greater Yellowstone Ecoregion.)

Sauer, J. R., J. E. Hines, and J. Fallon. 2008. *The North American Breeding Bird Survey, Results and Analysis, 1966–2007. Version 5.15*. Laurel, MD: Patuxent Wildlife Research Center.
(See Patuxent website: http://www.mbr-pwrc.usgs.gov/bbs/bbs.html.)

Wyoming Game and Fish Department. 2008. *Wyoming Bird Checklist*. Lander: Wyoming Game and Fish Department.

Zardus, M. J. 1967. *Birds of Yellowstone and Grand Teton Park*. Salt Lake City, UT: Wheelwright Press.

OTHER VERTEBRATES

Baxter, G., and J. R. Simon. 1970. *Wyoming Fishes*. Cheyenne: Wyoming Game & Fish Department.

Koch, E. D., and C. R. Peterson. 1995. *Amphibians and Reptiles of Yellowstone and Grand Teton National Parks*. Salt Lake City: University of Utah Press.

Luce, R., R. Oakleaf, A. Cerovski, L. Hunter, and J. Friday, eds. 1997. *Atlas of Birds, Mammals, Reptiles, and Amphibians in Wyoming*. Lander: Wyoming Game & Fish Department.
(See also 2004 update on the Wyoming Game & Fish Department website: http://state.wyo.us /downloads/pdf/nongame/WYBirdMammHerpAtlas.04/pdf.)

Stebbins, R. C. 1995. *A Field Guide to Western Reptiles and Amphibians*. Boston: Houghton Mifflin.

Turner, F. B. 1955. *Amphibians and Reptiles of Yellowstone National Park*. Yellowstone National Park, WY: Yellowstone Library and Museum Association.

Varley, J. D., and P. Schullery. 1998. *Yellowstone Fishes*. Mechanicsburg, PA: Stackpole.

INVERTEBRATES

Brown, F. M., D. Eff, and B. Rotger. 1957. *Colorado Butterflies*. Denver: Denver Museum of Natural History.

Brock, J. P., and K. Kaufman. 2003. *Butterflies of North America*. Boston: Houghton Mifflin.

Ferris, C. D., and F. M. Brown. 1981. *Butterflies of the Rocky Mountain States*. Norman: University of Oklahoma Press.

Kondratieff, B. C., coord. 2000. *Dragonflies and Damselflies (Odonata) of the United States*. Jamestown, ND: Northern Prairie Research Center. http://www.npwrc.usgs.gov/resource/distr/insects/dfly /wy/toc.htm.

Opler, P. A., and A. B. Wright. 1999. *A Field Guide to Western Butterflies*. Boston: Houghton Mifflin.
(Describes 590 butterfly species.)

Opler, P. A., K. Lotts, and T. Naberhaus, coords. 2010. *Butterflies and Moths of North America*. Mountain
Prairie Information Node. http://www.butterfliesandmoths.org/species/Papilio-rutulus.

Paulson, D. 2009. *Dragonflies and Damselflies of the West*. Princeton, NJ: Princeton University Press.

Simon, J. R. 1939. *Yellowstone Fishes*. Yellowstone National Park, WY: Yellowstone Library and Museum
Association.

Rocky Mountain Plants, Plant Ecology, and Conservation

Cary, M. 1917. *Life Zone Investigations in Wyoming*. USDA Bureau of Biological Survey, North American
Fauna No. 40.
(The first ecological analysis of the biological communities of Wyoming.)

Clark, T. W., and R. D. Dorn, eds. 1981. *Rare and Endangered Vascular Plants and Vertebrates of
Wyoming*. 2nd ed. Jackson, WY: Published by the authors.

Craighead, J. J., F. C. Craighead Jr., and R. J. Davis. 1963. *A Field Guide to Rocky Mountain Wildflowers*.
Boston: Houghton Mifflin.
(Includes more than 200 color photos, 118 line drawings, and descriptions of 590 species
occurring from Arizona and New Mexico to southern Canada.)

DeGraaf, R. M., and N. G. Tilghman, eds. 1980. *Workshop Proceedings: Management of Western Forests and
Grasslands for Nongame Birds*. General Technical Report INT-86. Ogden, UT: USDA Forest Service.

Despain, D. G. 1990. *Yellowstone Vegetation: Consequences of Environment and History in a Natural
Setting*. Boulder, CO: Roberts Rinehart.

Fertig, W. 1992. "A Floristic Survey of the West Slope of the Wind River Range, Wyoming." Master's thesis,
University of Wyoming, Laramie.

Guennel, G. K. 1995. *Guide to Colorado Wildflowers*. 2 vols. Englewood, CO: Westcliffe Publishers.
(Volume 1 includes color paintings and photos of over 300 species of trees, shrubs, forbs, and
grasses found on the plains and foothills. Volume 2 covers more than 300 montane species.
Organized by flower color.)

Kershaw, L., A. MacKinnon, and J. Polar. 1998. *Plants of the Rocky Mountains*. Edmonton, AB: Lone
Pine Publishing.
(Identification guide to over 1,300 plant species occurring from Mexico to southern Canada.)

McDougall, W. B., and H. A. Baggley. 1956. *Plants of Yellowstone National Park*. Rev. ed. Yellowstone
National Park, WY: Yellowstone Library and Museum Association.
(Keys, line drawings, and both color and black-and-white photos of Yellowstone's flora.)

Phister, R. D., B. L. Kovalchik, S. F. Arno, and R. C. Presby. 1977. *Forest Habitat Types of Montana*.
General Technical Report INT-34. Ogden, UT: USDA Forest Service.

Phillips, H. W. 1999. *Central Rocky Mountain Wildflowers: Including Yellowstone and Rocky Mountain
National Parks*. Helena, MT: Falcon Press.
(Identification guide to 260 species of Greater Yellowstone plants, with color photos and
organized by flower color.)

Porter, C. L. 1962. "Vegetation Zones of Wyoming." *University of Wyoming Publications* 27 (2): 6–12.

Reed, R. M. 1969. "A Study of Vegetation of the Wind River Mountains, Wyoming." PhD diss.,
Washington State University, Pullman.

Shaw, R. J. 2001. *Plants of Yellowstone and Grand Teton National Parks*. Camano Island, WA: Wheelwright Press.
> (Photographic guide to 213 species of regional trees, shrubs, and wildflowers.)

Vizgirdas, R. S. 2007. *A Guide to Plants of Grand Teton and Yellowstone National Parks*. Salt Lake City: University of Utah Press.
> (Comprehensive identification guide to the plants of the Greater Yellowstone region.)

Whitlock, C. 1993. "Postglacial Vegetation and Climate in Grand Teton and Southern Yellowstone National Parks." *Ecological Monographs* 63 (2): 173–98. http://dx.doi.org/10.2307/2937179.

Tourism and Birding Information

Burt, N. 2002. *Wyoming*. New York: Compass American Guides.

Jones, J. O. 1990. *Where the Birds Are: A Guide to All 50 States and Canada*. New York: William Morrow.
> (Includes site information and bird lists for four Wyoming refuges.)

McEneaney, T. 1993. *The Birder's Guide to Montana*. Helena, MT: Falcon Press.
> (Includes birding sites in northern Yellowstone National Park.)

Pettingill, O. S. 1981. *A Guide to Bird Finding West of the Mississippi*. 2nd ed. New York: Oxford University Press.
> (Describes eleven Wyoming locations.)

Raynes, B., and D. Wile. 1994. *Finding the Birds of Jackson Hole*. Jackson, WY: Darwin Wile.

Scott, O. K. 1993. *A Birder's Guide to Wyoming*. Colorado Springs: American Birding Association.
> (Describes nineteen birding locations or areas, with suggestions for finding most species; includes an annotated checklist of 389 Wyoming birds.)

Wauer, R. 1993. *Visitor's Guide to the Birds of the Rocky Mountain Parks, U.S. and Canada*. Santa Fe, NM: John Muir.

Wilkinson, T. 2008. *Watching Yellowstone and Grand Teton Wildlife*. Helena, MT: Riverbend Publishing.
> (Suggests locations for finding forty-five regional species of mammals and birds.)

Wyoming Game and Fish Department. 1996. *Wyoming Wildlife Viewing Guide*. Lander: Wyoming Game and Fish Department.
> (Describes over fifty viewing locations.)

General Information Addresses

Bridger-Teton National Forest, P.O. Box 1888, Jackson, WY 83001. Phone 307/733-2752 or 307/739-5500.

Custer National Forest, P.O. 2556, Billings, MT 59103. Phone 406/657-6361.

Gallatin National Forest, Federal Building, P.O. Box 130, Bozeman, MT 59715. Phone 406/587-5271.

Grand Teton National Park, P.O. Drawer 170, Moose, WY 63012-0170. Phone 303/339-3300. www.nps.gov/grte

Grand Teton Natural History Association, P.O. Box 170, Moose, WY 83012. Phone 307/739-3606. www.grandtetonpark.org

Greater Yellowstone Coalition, P.O. Box 1874, Bozeman, MT 59771 Phone 408/586-1593. www.greateryellowstone.org

National Elk Refuge, P.O. Box C, Jackson, WY 83001. Phone 307/733-9212.

National Parks Conservation Association, 777 6th Street NW, Washington, DC 2001-3723. Phone 1-800-NATPARK. www.npc.org

Shoshone National Forest. W. Yellowstone Highway, P.O. Box 2140, Cody, WY 82414. Phone 307/527-6241.

Wyoming Game & Fish Department, 260 Buena Vista Dr., Lander, WY 82520-9902. Phone 307/777-4600.

Yellowstone Association. P.O. Box 117, Yellowstone National Park, WY 82190. Phone 307/344-2293. www.YellowstoneAssociation.org

Yellowstone National Park. P.O. Box 168, Yellowstone National Park, WY 82190. Phone 307/344-7381. www.nps.gov/yell

Index